BLOOM

Olympiad ACE

A Comprehensive Practice Book

for School Olympiads & Talent Search Exams

MATHS

Class 10

by

Sagar Verma

Olympiad ACE

BLOOM

Bloom Cap Edu Ventures Pvt. Ltd.

Administrative & Production Office

'Ramchhaya' 4577/15, Agarwal Road, Darya Ganj, New Delhi -110002
Tele: 011- 47630600, 43518550

PRICE: ₹125.00

PO No. : TXT-59-T063325-02-25

Published by Arihant Publications (I) Ltd.

For further information about the books log on to
www.bloomcap.org

Follow us on

Preface

"Future belongs to those Who prepares for it today"

School Olympiads are National & International level competitions conducted by different Government, Non-Government & Educational Organisations with the purpose of making the children ready to face competitive exams. The challenging Questions asked in Olympiads motivate them to learn more & more and bring out the best result with improved academic performance. The Awards & Scholarship offered in Olympiads motivate children to aspire & strive for doing better and emerge out to be the best.

Maths Olympiads

Mathematics is an integral part of all competitive exams be it Aptitude or Commerce or Science. Maths Olympiads are meant to develop Mathematical aptitude in school students. They provide students with an opportunity to master their concepts and comprehend tricky questions effortlessly. Challenging Questions of Maths Olympiads encourage students to develop a logical approach to solve Mathematical Problems.

'Bloom Mathematics Olympiad Study Book Class 10' is a perfect resource to Study & Practice for Olympiad Exams and other National & State Level Talent Search Exams & Other Competitions.

Some Special Features of Bloom Maths Olympiad Study Books are;

- Chapterwise Exercises having different types of Objective Questions at par with the Olympiad Level.
- Detailed Explanation for each question.
- Olympiad Pattern Practice Sets at the end.

This book is prepared by Expert Panel with the utmost care, still if you have any suggestions regarding its improvement, then feel free to contact us at support@bloomcap.org. We will try to inculcate your suggestions in the further editions.

Contents

01.	Real Numbers	1-4
02.	Polynomials	5-7
03.	Pair of Linear Equations in Two Variables	8-10
04.	Quadratic Equations	11-13
05.	Arithmetic Progressions	14-16
06.	Similarity of Triangles	17-21
07.	Coordinate Geometry	22-24
08.	Trigonometry	25-27
09.	Applications of Trigonometry	28-30
10.	Circles	31-35
11.	Areas Related to Circle	36-40
12.	Surface Area and Volume	41-43
13.	Statistics	44-46
14.	Probability	47-49
•	Practice Set 1	50-55
•	Practice Set 2	56-62
•	Hints & Solutions	63-108

Chapter 01

Real Numbers

1 Mark Questions

1. There are 44 boys and 32 girls in a class. These students are arranged in row for a prayer in such a way that each row consists of only either boys or girls, and every row contains an equal number of students. From the following 4 options, choose the minimum number of rows in which all the students can be arranged.

(a) 4 (b) 12
(c) 12 (d) 19

2. Which of the following is the correct HCF of 108 and 288?

(a) 108 (b) 12 (c) 288 (d) 36

3. The maximum number of students among whom 1001 pens and 910 pencils can be distributed in such a way that each student gets the same number of pens and same number of pencils is

(a) 91 (b) 910
(c) 1001 (d) 1911

4. Three numbers which are coprime to each other are such that the product of first two numbers is 42 and the product of last two numbers is 78. Then, the sum of all the three numbers is

(a) 25 (b) 32
(c) 26 (d) 13

5. Let N be the greatest number that will divide 1305, 4665 and 6905, leaving the same remainder in each case. Then, sum of the digits of N is

(a) 4 (b) 5
(c) 6 (d) 8

6. **Assertion** (A) The ratio (in the simplest form) of two coprime numbers a and b is $a:b$.

Reason (R) The HCF of coprime numbers is 1.

Which of the following is true?

(a) (A) is true and (R) is the correct explanation of (A)
(b) (A) is false and (R) is the correct explanation of (A)
(c) (A) is true and (R) is false
(d) Both (A) and (R) are false

7. The factor tree shows the prime factorization of 1314.

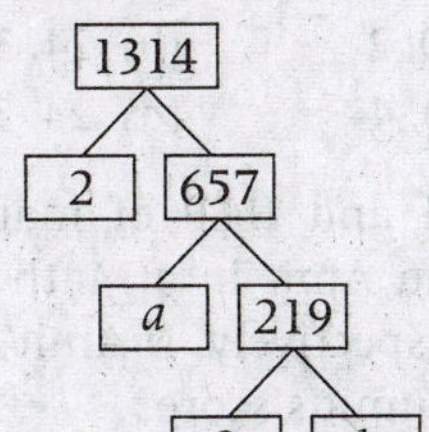

Find the respective values of 'a' and 'b'.

(a) 3, 37 (b) 3, 73
(c) 73, 3 (d) 9, 73

8. The least number of five digits which is exactly divisible by 12, 15 and 18, is

(a) 10010 (b) 10015
(c) 10020 (d) 10080

9. Ashok has two vessels which contain 720 mL and 405 mL of milk respectively. Milk in each vessel is poured into glasses of equal capacity to their brim. Find the minimum number of glasses which can be filled with milk.

(a) 45 (b) 35
(c) 25 (d) 30

10. Arrange the following in ascending order $\frac{17}{18}, \frac{43}{45}, \frac{59}{60}$ and $\frac{31}{36}$.

(a) $\frac{17}{18} < \frac{59}{60} < \frac{43}{45} < \frac{31}{36}$

(b) $\frac{31}{36} < \frac{17}{18} < \frac{43}{45} < \frac{59}{60}$

(c) $\frac{43}{45} < \frac{59}{60} < \frac{31}{36} < \frac{17}{18}$

(d) $\frac{59}{60} < \frac{43}{45} < \frac{31}{36} < \frac{17}{18}$

11.

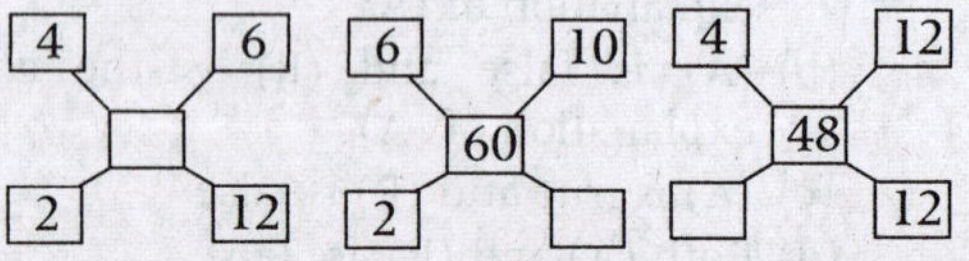

(i) (ii) (iii)

Choose the correct sequence of numbers to match the above pattern.

(a) 48, 30, 2 (b) 24, 30, 2
(c) 24, 10, 4 (d) 24, 30, 4

12. The LCM and HCF of marks scored by Sumit and Amit in a Math test are 5040 and 12 respectively. If Amit's score is 144, what is Sumit's score?

(a) 288 (b) 132
(c) 564 (d) 420

13. $1.43\overline{28}$ is

(a) an integer
(b) a rational number
(c) an irrational number
(d) a natural number

14. Pick the odd one out.

(a) $\sqrt{9}$
(b) π
(c) 2.13113111311113...
(d) $\sqrt{2}$

15. Find the value of $\sqrt{6+\sqrt{6+\sqrt{6+\ldots}}}$.

(a) 0 (b) 3
(c) -2 (d) None of these

16. Out of the following irrationals, which has sum and product both rationals?

(a) $\sqrt{3}+5$ and $\sqrt{3}-5$
(b) $\sqrt{3}+\sqrt{5}$ and $\sqrt{3}-\sqrt{5}$
(c) $5+\sqrt{3}$ and $5-\sqrt{3}$
(d) All of the above

17. If $a=\sqrt{11}+\sqrt{3}$, $b=\sqrt{12}+\sqrt{2}$ and $c=\sqrt{6}+\sqrt{4}$, then which of the following holds true?

(a) $c>a>b$
(b) $a>b>c$
(c) $a>c>b$
(d) $b>a>c$

18. Choose the correct value of $\frac{1}{\sqrt{9}+\sqrt{10}}+\frac{1}{\sqrt{10}+\sqrt{11}}+\frac{1}{\sqrt{11}+\sqrt{12}}+\ldots\ldots$ up to 91 terms from the following options.

(a) 7 (b) 8
(c) 6 (d) 9

19. If $a=\sqrt[8]{6}-\sqrt[8]{5}$, $b=\sqrt[8]{6}+\sqrt[8]{5}$, $c=\sqrt[6]{6}+\sqrt[6]{5}$, $d=\sqrt[4]{6}+\sqrt[4]{5}$ and $e=\sqrt{6}+\sqrt{5}$, then which of the following is a rational number ?

(a) $abcde$ (b) $abde$
(c) ab (d) cd

20. Which of the following is an incorrect statement?

(a) If $\sqrt{a}+\sqrt{b}$ is an irrational number, then $\sqrt{ab}$ is also an irrational number.

(b) The reciprocal of an irrational number is always an irrational number.

(c) There are infinitely many rational numbers between any two irrational numbers.

(d) $7 \times 13 + 13$ is a prime number.

21. Match the following:

	List I	List II
A.	LCM of two coprime numbers whose product is 117, is	i. $a = \frac{1}{b}$
B.	If LCM $(a, b) \times$ HCF $(a, b) = 1$, then	ii. 36
C.	LCM of $\frac{2}{3}, \frac{3}{5}, \frac{4}{7}$ and $\frac{9}{13}$ is	iii. 117

Codes

	A	B	C
(a)	i	ii	iii
(b)	ii	iii	i
(c)	iii	i	ii
(d)	i	iii	ii

22. Match the following.

	List I	List II
A.	HCF of the smallest composite number and smallest prime number	i. 2
B.	HCF of 32 and 54 is	ii. 6
C.	HCF of 336 and 54	iii. 5
D.	HCF of 475 and 495	iv. 4

Codes

	A	B	C	D
(a)	i	ii	iii	iv
(b)	iv	ii	i	iii
(c)	iv	i	ii	iii
(d)	iii	iv	i	ii

2 Marks Questions

23. The HCF of the polynomials $(x^2 - 4x + 4)(x + 3)$ and $(x^2 + 2x - 3)(x - 2)$ is

(a) $x + 3$

(b) $x - 2$

(c) $(x + 3)(x - 2)$

(d) $(x + 3)(x - 2)^2$

24. The area of a rectangular park is 2028 with highest possible common factor in its length and breadth be 13. Which of the following pairs of dimensions are possible?

(i) (13, 156) (ii) (13, 169)

(iii) (39, 52) (iv) (26, 78)

(a) (i) and (ii)

(b) (i) and (iii)

(c) (ii) and (iv)

(d) (ii) and (iii)

25. If $x = 28 + (1 \times 2 \times 3 \times 4 \times \ldots\ldots \times 16 \times 28)$ and $y = 17 + (1 \times 2 \times 3 \times \ldots \times 17)$, then which of the following is/are true?

A. x is a composite number

B. y is a prime number

C. $x - y$ is a prime number

D. $x + y$ is a composite number

(a) Both (A) and (D)

(b) Both (B) and (C)

(C) Both (B) and (D)

(D) Both (A) and (B)

26. A five-digit number is a multiple of 11 and 91. If the second digit from the left is 8, then the third digit from the left of the number is

(a) 0 (b) 9

(c) 4 (d) 8

27. A, B and C start at the same time in the same direction to run around a circular stadium. A completes a round in 252 s, B in 308 s and C in 198 s, all starting at the same point. After what time will they meet again at the starting point?

(a) 26 min 18 s (b) 42 min 36 s
(c) 45 min (d) 46 min 12 s

28. Two friends Aisha and Succhi have 40 and 61 numbers of same type of toys respectively, which they have to distribute among two groups of children, such that each one gets equal number of toys.

After distributing in such a manner, Aisha and Succhi are left with 5 toys each. Then, the total number of children who got the toys and the toys received by each child, is

(a) 7, 9
(b) 13, 7
(c) 7, 13
(d) Can't be determined

29. A charitable trust donates 28 different books of Maths, 16 different books of Science and 12 different books of Social Science to poor students. Each student is given maximum number of books of only one subject of their interest and each student got equal number of books.

(A) Find the number of books each student got.
(B) Find the total number of students who got books.

	A	B		A	B
(a)	4	14	(b)	3	10
(c)	4	10	(d)	3	15

30. A circular field has a circumference of 360 km. Two cyclists Sumeet and John start together and can cycle at speeds of 12 km/h and 15 km/h respectively round the circular field. They will meet again at the starting point after.

(a) 40 h (b) 30 h
(c) 180 h (d) 120 h

Chapter

02

Polynomials

1 Mark Questions

1. The value of k, in polynomial $f(x) = x^2 - 4x + k$ such that $f(2) = 0$, is

(a) 0 (b) 2
(c) 4 (d) None of these

2. Find the quadratic polynomial whose zeroes are $\frac{2}{3}$ and $-\frac{1}{4}$.

(a) $\frac{1}{12}(4x^2 - 5x - 2)$ (b) $\frac{1}{12}(12x^2 - 5x - 2)$
(c) $\frac{1}{12}(12x^2 - 2x + 5)$ (d) $\frac{1}{12}(12x^2 + 5x - 2)$

3. Choose the zeroes of the polynomial whose graph is given.

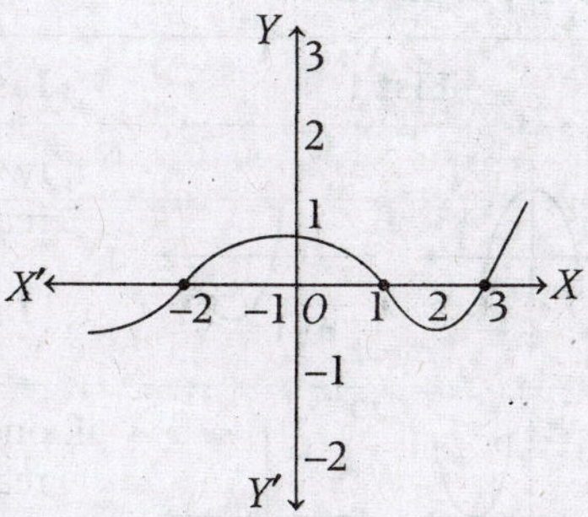

(a) 1, − 1, 2 (b) − 2, 1, 3
(c) − 2, 0, 3 (d) − 2, 2, 3

4. The pair of zeroes of the polynomial $2x^2 + 14x + 20$ is

(a) 2 and 5 (b) − 2 and − 5
(c) 2 and − 5 (d) −2 and 5

5. If $(x + 1)$ is a factor of $f(x) = a_0x^n + a_1x^{n-1} + a_2x^{n-2} + \ldots + a_n = 0$, then

(a) $a_0 + a_1 + a_2 + \ldots + a_n = 0$
(b) $a_0 + a_2 + a_4 + \ldots + a_n = 0$
(c) $a_1 + a_3 + a_5 + \ldots + a_n = 0$
(d) $a_0 + a_2 + a_4 + \ldots + a_n = a_1 + a_3 + a_5 + \ldots + a_n$

6. The value of k for which (−4) is a zero of the polynomial $x^2 - x - (2k + 2)$, is

(a) 3 (b) 9 (c) 6 (d) 1

7. If the zeroes of the quadratic polynomial $x^2 + (a + 1)x + b$ are 2 and − 3, then

(a) $a = -7$ and $b = -1$
(b) $a = 5$ and $b = -1$
(c) $a = 2$ and $b = -6$
(d) $a = 0$ and $b = -6$

8. If the zeroes of polynomial $x^2 - 8x + k = 0$ are the HCF of (6, 12), then find the value of k.

(a) 6 (b) 12
(c) 24 (d) None of these

9. If l, m, n are the zeroes of polynomial $x^3 - px^2 + dx - r$, then what is the value of $\frac{1}{lm} + \frac{1}{mn} + \frac{1}{nl}$?

(a) $\frac{p}{r}$ (b) $\frac{r}{p}$ (c) $-\frac{p}{r}$ (d) $\frac{-r}{p}$

10. For what value of 'm', one zero of the polynomial $(m^2+9)x^2+13x+6m$ is reciprocal of the other?

(a) 9 (b) – 3
(c) 6 (d) 3

11.

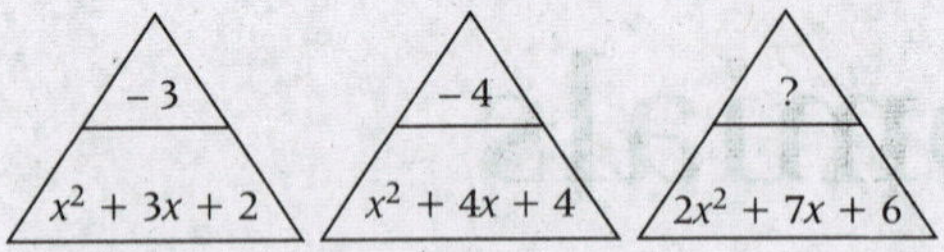

The missing term is

(a) –7 (b) –6
(c) –7/2 (d) 7

12. If α and β are the zeroes of $x^2-8x+\gamma$, such that $\alpha-\beta=2$, then γ is

(a) 8 (b) 60 (c) 22 (d) 15

13. If the sum of the square of the zeroes of the polynomial $p(x)=x^2+7x+k$ is 25, then k is equal to

(a) 12 (b) 49
(c) –24 (d) –12

14. The zeroes of the equation $lx^2+hx+n=0$ are in the ratio $p:q$. Then,

(a) $\sqrt{\frac{p}{q}}+\sqrt{\frac{q}{p}}+\sqrt{\frac{n}{l}}=0$

(b) $\sqrt{\frac{p}{q}}-\sqrt{\frac{q}{p}}+\sqrt{\frac{n}{l}}=0$

(c) $\sqrt{\frac{p}{q}}-\sqrt{\frac{q}{p}}-\sqrt{\frac{n}{l}}=0$

(d) $\sqrt{\frac{p}{q}}=\sqrt{\frac{q}{q}}+\sqrt{\frac{n}{l}}=1$

15. Find the quadratic polynomial one of whose zeroes is $\frac{\sqrt{3}}{4}$ and the product of zeroes is $-\frac{1}{2}$.

(a) $4\sqrt{3}x^2+5x+2\sqrt{3}$ (b) $x^2+\frac{5}{4\sqrt{3}}x-\frac{1}{2}$

(c) $4\sqrt{3}x^2-5x+2\sqrt{3}$ (d) $2x^2+\frac{5}{4\sqrt{3}}x-\frac{1}{2}$

16. Find the values of P and Q, if $(x+2)$ and $(x+1)$ are the factors of $x^3+3x^2-2Px+Q$.

(a) $P=-1$ and $Q=0$ (b) $P=2$ and $Q=1$
(c) $P=1$ and $Q=2$ (d) $P=0$ and $Q=1$

17. If α and β are the zeroes of the polynomial $f(x)=x^2-3x+2$, then a quadratic polynomial whose zeroes are $\frac{2\alpha}{\beta}$ and $\frac{2\beta}{\alpha}$, is

(a) x^2-4x+4 (b) x^2-2x+1
(c) x^2-5x+4 (d) Can't be determined

18. What is the cubic polynomial in which the sum of zeroes, sum of the products of its zeroes taken at a time and product of its zeroes as 2, – 7, – 14 respectively?

(a) $k(x^3-2x^2-7x+14)$
(b) $k(x^3-2x^2+8x-14)$
(c) $k(x^3+2x^2-7x-4)$
(d) $k(x^3-x^2-x-14)$

19. If $a^2x+2ax^2-b^3$ is divisible by $(x+a)$, then

(a) $a=b$ (b) $a^2+ab+b^3=0$
(c) $a=b=0$ (d) None of these

20. Match the number of zeroes with the given polynomial.

	List I	List II
A.	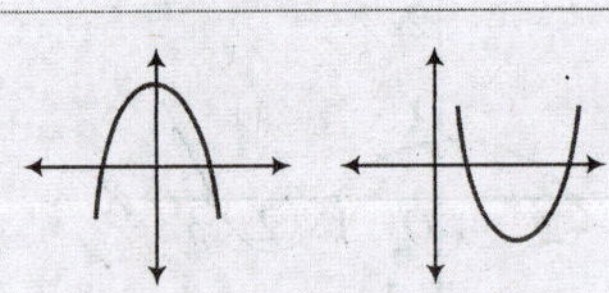	i. two zeroes, real
B.	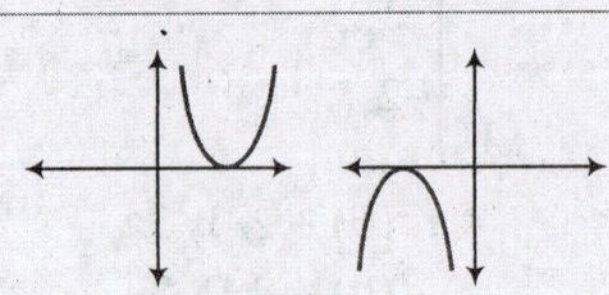	ii. one zero, real
C.	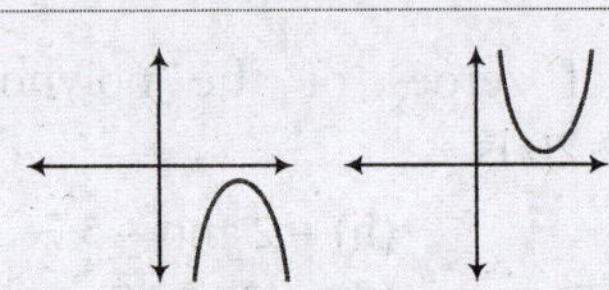	iii. no real zero

Codes

	A	B	C		A	B	C
(a)	i	iii	ii	(b)	i	ii	iii
(c)	ii	iii	i	(d)	iii	ii	i

21. If $P(x)=\frac{1+5x}{1-5x}$ and $Q(x)=\frac{1-5x}{1+5x}$, then $\frac{P(x)}{Q(x)}$ will be

(a) 1 (b) $\frac{1-25x^2}{1+25x^2}$

(c) $\frac{(1+5x)^2}{(1-5x)^2}$ (d) $\frac{1+25x^2}{1-25x^2}$

22. If $f(x)=x^2+6x+a$, $g(x)=x^2+4x+b$, $h(x)=x^2+14x+c$ and the LCM of $f(x)$, $g(x)$ and $h(x)$ is $(x+8)(x-2)(x-6)$, then find $a+b+c$ (where a, b and c are constants)

(a) 20 (b) 16 (c) 32 (d) 10

23. Which one should be added among the following options to $\frac{1}{x-2}+\frac{1}{x+2}$ to get $\frac{4x^3}{x^4-16}$?

(a) $\frac{2x^2}{x^2+4}$ (b) $\frac{2x}{x^2+4}$

(c) $\frac{2x^2}{x^2-4}$ (d) $\frac{2}{x^2+4}$

24. A rectangular garden of length $(2x^3+5x^2-7)$ m has the perimeter $(4x^3-2x^2+4)$ m. Find the breadth of the garden.

(a) $(6x^2-9)$ m (b) $(-6x^2+9)$ m

(c) $(2x^3-7x^2+11)$ m (d) $(6x^3+7x^2+9)$ m

2 Marks Questions

25. If $(x-3)(x+2)$ is the HCF of the polynomials $P(x)=(x^2-2x-3)(2x^2+ax-2)$ and $Q(x)=(x^2+x-2)(3x^2+bx-3)$, then a and b are equals to

(a) 3 and – 8 (b) 8 and – 3

(c) 2 and – 8 (d) – 8 and 2

26. If α and β are the zeroes of $p(x)=4x^2+10x+k$ such that $\alpha^2+\beta^2+\alpha\beta=\frac{21}{4}$, then k is equal to

(a) 12 (b) 4

(c) 2 (d) – 12

27. If one zero of the polynomial $2x^2-5x-(2k+1)$ is twice the other, then find both the zeroes of the polynomial and the value of k.

(a) $\frac{5}{3},\frac{5}{6}; k=\frac{-9}{17}$ (b) $\frac{3}{5},\frac{6}{5}; k=\frac{-17}{9}$

(c) $\frac{5}{6},\frac{5}{3}; k=\frac{-17}{9}$ (d) $\frac{5}{6},\frac{5}{3}; k=\frac{-68}{36}$

28. If α and β are the zeroes of the quadratic polynomial $2S^2-8S+4$, then the value of $\frac{\alpha}{\beta}+\frac{\beta}{\alpha}+2\left(\frac{1}{\alpha}+\frac{1}{\beta}\right)+3\alpha\beta$ is

(a) 8 (b) 4

(c) 16 (d) 12

29. State 'T' for true and 'F' for false.

I. If the square of sum of the zeroes of a quadratic polynomial is 4 times the product of them, then the zeroes are equal in magnitude.

II. A quadratic polynomial, the sum of whose zeroes is 0 and one zero is 4, then the linear term of the polynomial doesn't exist.

III. If the sum of the zeroes of a cubic polynomial is 5 and the sum of the product of two zeroes is 8, then the sum of the square of the zeroes will be 10.

Codes

	I	II	III		I	II	III
(a)	T	F	T	(b)	F	T	F
(c)	T	F	F	(d)	T	T	F

Chapter 03

Pair of Linear Equations in Two Variables

1 Mark Questions

1. Identify the pair of linear equations in two variables.

(a) $3x = 7$ (b) $7x - 2 = 0$

(c) $2x + 3y = 2$ (d) $4x^2 - 9y^2 = 0$

2. In a test of 50 questions, each correct answer fetches two marks and each wrong answer fetches $-\frac{1}{2}$ marks. A candidate attempted all the questions and scored 40 marks. How many questions did he attempt correctly?

(a) 24 (b) 26

(c) 22 (d) 20

3. The semi-perimeter of a triangle exceeds each of its side by 5, 3 and 2 respectively. What is the perimeter of the triangle?

(a) 12 (b) 10

(c) 15 (d) 20

4. Mallesh has some cows and some hens in his shed. The total numnber of legs is 92 and total number of head is 29. Find the number of cows in his shed?

(a) 12 (b) 14

(c) 17 (d) 19

5. Sridevi purchased cakes of two varieties of soap, lux and dove spending a total ₹360 if each lux cost ₹30 and each dove costs ₹40, then in how many different combinations could she have purchased the cakes?

(a) 3 (b) 4 (c) 5 (d) 2

6. A teacher wanted to distribute 900 chocolates among the students of a class. Each boy receives 12 chocolates and each girls received 6 chocolates. If each girl has been given 10 chocolates, then each boy would have received 5 chocolates. Find the number of students of the class.

(a) 80 (b) 90

(c) 100 (d) 110

7. The average weight of the students of a class is 60 kg. If eight new students of average weight 64 kg join the class, the average weight of the entire class becomes 62 kg. How many students were there in the class initially?

(a) 12 (b) 10

(c) 8 (d) 14

8. If $x + 2y = -1$ and $2x - 3y = 12$, then x and y are

(a) -2 and 3 (b) 3 and -2
(c) 2 and -3 (d) -3 and -2

9. The ratio of monthly income of Mr. X and Mr. Y is 3 : 4 and the ratio of their monthly expenditures is 5 : 7. If the ratio of their montly savings is 3 : 2 and Mr. X saves ₹ 500 more than Mr. Y per month, then find the monthly income of Mr. Y.

(a) ₹ 35000
(b) ₹ 32000
(c) ₹ 26000
(d) ₹ 22000

10. The area of a rectangle increases by 76 square units, if the length and breadth are each increased by 2 units. However, if the length is increased by 3 units and breadth is decreased by 3 units, the area gets reduced by 21 square units. Find the sum of the length and breadth of the rectangle.

(a) 40 units (b) 42 units
(c) 4 units (d) 36 units

11. A fraction becomes $\frac{4}{5}$ when 1 is added to each of the numerator and denominator. However, if we subtract 5 from each of them, it becomes $\frac{1}{2}$. Then, the numerator of fraction is

(a) 6 (b) 7 (c) 8 (d) 9

12. A lady has 50 paise and 40 paise coins in her purse. If in all she has 50 coins totalling ₹ 22, then number of coins of each type, she has

(a) 50 paise coins = 20 and 40 paise coins = 30
(b) 50 paise coins = 10 and 40 paise coins = 40
(c) 50 paise coins = 40 and 40 paise coins = 10
(d) 50 paise coins = 15 and 40 paise coins = 25

13. Find the values of x and y, such that $x + y = a + b$ and $ax - by = a^2 - b^2$ have a solution.

(a) $x = b$ and $y = a$ (b) $x = a^2$ and $y = b^2$
(c) $x = a$ and $y = b$ (d) $x = b^2$ and $y = a^2$

14. If the total depreciation of machinery and equipment in one year is ₹ 8000 and the ratio of the amount of depreciation of machinery and equipment is 1 : 3, then the rate of depreciation of equipment is

(a) 10% (b) 20%
(c) 30% (d) None of these

15. Determine the values of angles A, B, C and D and mark the correct option.

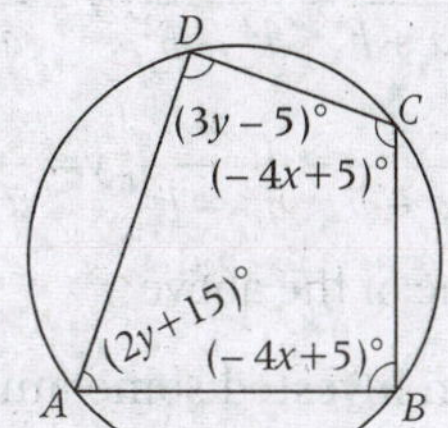

(a) 55°, 125°, 125°, 55°
(b) 45°, 135°, 125°, 55°
(c) 45°, 55°, 125°, 55°
(d) 55°, 55°, 135°, 45°

16. Solve $3x + 7y = 32$ and $7x + 3y = 48$

(a) $x = 2, y = 6$ (b) $x = 3, y = 1$
(c) $x = 6, y = 2$ (d) $x = 1, y = 3$

17. A two-digit number is such that, it exceeds the sum of the number formed by reversing the digits and sum of the digits by 4. Also, the original number exceeds the reversed number by 18. Find the product of the digits.

(a) 48
(b) 36
(c) 42
(d) 56

18. **Assertion** (A) 2 yr ago, father was 5 times as old as his son. 2 yr later, father's age will be 8 yr more than 3 times the age of his son. Then, present age of father is 42 yr.

Reason (R) The linear equations used are $x - 3y - 10 = 0$ and $x - 7y + 30 = 0$.

Which of the following is true?

(a) Both (A) and (R) are true and (R) is the correct explanation of (R)
(b) Both (A) and (R) are true but (R) is not the correct explanation of (A)
(c) (A) is true and (R) is false
(d) Both (A) and (R) are false

2 Marks Questions

19. Determine the values of x and y, if $ax + by - c = 0$ and $bx + ay - (1 + c) = 0$.

(a) $x = \frac{c}{a+b} - \frac{b}{a^2 - b^2}, y = \frac{c}{a+b} + \frac{a}{a^2 - b^2}$

(b) $x = \frac{c}{a+b} + \frac{a}{a^2 - b^2}, y = \frac{c}{a+b} - \frac{b}{a^2 - b^2}$

(c) $x = \frac{c}{a-b} - \frac{b}{a^2 - b^2}, y = \frac{c}{a-b} + \frac{a}{a^2 - b^2}$

(d) None of the above

20. A person invested some amount at the rate of 12% simple interest and some other amount at the rate of 10% simple interest. He received yearly interest of ₹ 130. But if he had interchanged the amounts invested, then he would have received ₹ 4 more as interest. Total amount received for original rates is

(a) ₹ 1330
(b) ₹ 560
(c) ₹ 770
(d) ₹ 1200

21. Mr Linda invested different amount at 8% and 9%, all at simple interest. Altogether, she invested ₹ 40000 and earns ₹ 7000 after two years. How much does she have earned, if she had interchanged the invested amount?

(a) ₹ 7600 (b) ₹ 6600
(c) ₹ 5600 (d) ₹ 4600

22. For which of the following system of equations, $x = 6$, $y = -4$ is the solution?

(a) $\frac{1}{2x} - \frac{1}{y} = -1$ and $\frac{1}{x} + \frac{1}{2y} = 8$

(b) $\frac{2}{x} + \frac{2}{3y} = \frac{1}{6}$ and $\frac{3}{x} + \frac{2}{y} = 0$

(c) Both (a) and (b)
(d) None of the above

23. If $\left(\frac{1+b}{b}\right)x + \left(\frac{1+a}{a}\right)y = b - a$ and $\frac{x}{b} - \frac{4y}{a} = 5$, $a \neq 0$, $b \neq 0$, then x and y are

(a) $-a$ and b (b) b and a
(c) b and $-a$ (d) a and $-b$

24. If an ordered pair satisfying the equations $2x - 3y = 18$ and $4x - y = 16$ also satisfy the equation $5x - py - 23 = 0$, then find the value of p.

(a) 1 (b) 2
(c) –1 (d) –2

25. A mother said to her son, the sum of our present ages is twice my age 12 yr ago and 9 yr hence, the sum of our ages will be thrice my age 14 yr ago. What is her son's present age? (in yr)

(a) 8
(b) 12
(c) 15
(d) 10

Chapter 04

Quadratic Equations

1 Mark Questions

1. If $ax^m + bx^n + c = 0$ is a quadratic equation, then

(a) $m = 1, n = 1$ (b) $m = 2, n = 1$
(c) $m = 1, n = 2$ (d) Both (b) and (c)

2. Rakhi's mother is 26 yr elder than her. The product of their ages 3 yr from now will be 360. What will be the required equation?

(a) $x^2 + 42x - 373 = 0$
(b) $x^2 + 32x - 373 = 0$
(c) $x^2 + 42x - 273 = 0$
(d) $x^2 + 32x - 273 = 0$

3. If $\frac{x+3}{x+2} = \frac{3x-7}{2x-3}$, then x is

(a) -1 (b) 5
(c) Both (a) and (b) (d) None of these

4. What are the roots of
$17a^2 - 20a + 10 = 10a^2 + 2a + 7$?

(a) $\frac{1}{7}, 3$ (b) $3, \frac{-1}{7}$
(c) $\frac{-1}{7}, -3$ (d) $-3, -\frac{1}{7}$

5. $x^2 - 120x + 2000 = 0$ $\longrightarrow$ $(x + \alpha)^2 = c^2$

Then, α and c are

(a) -60 and 40 (b) 60 and -40
(c) -60 and -40 (d) 60 and 40

6. The roots of a quadratic equation are 7 and -3, then what is the equation?

(a) $x^2 + 10x - 21 = 0$ (b) $x^2 - 4x - 21 = 0$
(c) $x^2 - 4x - 21 = 0$ (d) $x^2 - 7x + 21 = 0$

7. Which of the following is the quadratic equation one of whose root is $3 + 2\sqrt{3}$?

(a) $x^2 + 6x - 3 = 0$ (b) $x^2 - 6x - 3 = 0$
(c) $x^2 + 6x + 3 = 0$ (d) $x^2 - 6x + 3 = 0$

8. For what value of k does the equation $(k-2)x^2 + (k-2)x + 2 = 0$ has equal roots?

(a) $k = 2$ (b) $k = 10$
(c) Both (a) and (b) (d) None of these

9. For what respective values of 'm' and 'n' are $x = \frac{-2}{5}$ and $x = \frac{5}{3}$ roots of $mx^2 + nx - 10 = 0$?

(a) 15, -19 (b) -19, 15
(c) 19, -15 (d) -15, 19

10. Complete the following, for having real and equal roots.

(i) $x^2 + ax - 4 = 0$; $a = \pm 4$

(ii) $9x^2 + 3kx + 4 = 0$; $k = ?$

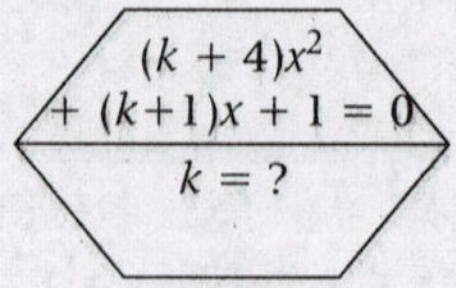

(iii)

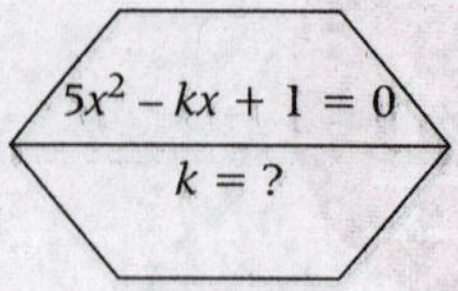

(iv)

(a) 4, 5 and $\sqrt{20}$
(b) -4, -3 and $-\sqrt{20}$
(c) Both (a) and (b)
(d) None of the above

11. Match the following.
The nature of roots for the given equations in List I to List II.

List I	List II
A. $2x^2 + x - 1 = 0$	i. Not real
B. $4x^2 - 4x + 1 = 0$	ii. Real and distinct
C. $2x^2 + 5x + 5 = 0$	iii. Real and equal

Codes

	A	B	C		A	B	C
(a)	i	ii	iii	(b)	ii	iii	i
(c)	ii	i	iii	(d)	i	iii	ii

12. If $(a^2 + b^2)x^2 + 2(ac + bd)\,x + c^2 + d^2 = 0$ has no real roots, then
(a) $ad = bc$ (b) $ab = cd$
(c) $ac = bd$ (d) $ad \neq bc$

13. Choose the correct statement to correct the following (if required), for $2x^2 + bx + 8 = 0$ to have non-real roots $-8 < b < 4$.
(a) $-8 < b < 8$ (b) $-4 < b < 8$
(c) $0 < b < 8$ (d) $8 < b < 0$

14. If the difference of the root $x^2 - px + q = 0$ is unity, then
(a) $p^2 - 4q = 1$
(b) $p^2 + 4q = 1$
(c) $p^2 + 4q^2 = (1 + 2q)^2$
(d) $4p^2 + q^2 = (1 + 2p)^2$

15. Sum of the areas of two squares is 468 m^2. If the difference of their perimeters is 24 m, then which of the following is correct?
(a) $x^2 + 6x - 216 = 0$
(b) $x^2 + 6x - 468 = 0$
(c) $x^2 + 7x - 216 = 0$
(d) $x^2 + 7x - 468 = 0$

16. If a two-digit number is four times the sum and three times the product of its digit, then the number is
(a) 24 (b) 20
(c) 28 (d) 30

17. An n-sided polygon has $\frac{1}{2}n(n-3)$ diagonals. How many sides does a figure have, if it has 90 diagonals?
(a) 12 (b) 18
(c) 15 (d) 10

18. The age of a man is the square of his son's age. A year ago, the man's age was eight times the age of his son. What is the present age of the man?
(a) 47 yr (b) 49 yr
(c) 36 yr (d) 48 yr

19. If a person gives gift to every other person in the party and the number of gifts distributed is 1980, then the number of persons and the gifts distributed by each will be
(a) 45 and 46
(b) 45 and 44
(c) 44 and 43
(d) Can't be determined

20. An aeroplane left 30 min later than its scheduled time and in order to reach its destination 1500 km away in time, it had to increase its speed by 250 km/h from its average speed. What is the average speed?
(a) 1000 km/h (b) 1200 km/h
(c) 750 km/h (d) 800 km/h

21. The sum of square of two consecutive positive even numbers is 340.
Find them.
(a) 12, 14
(b) 12, 10
(c) 10, 8
(d) 14, 16

22. The length and breadth of a rectangle are $(3k+1)$ cm and $(2k-1)$ cm, respectively.
Find the perimeter of the rectangle if its area is 144 cm^2.
(a) 50 cm (b) 10 cm
(c) 32 cm (d) 25 cm

2 Marks Questions

23. If the hypotenuse of a right angled triangle is 1 m less than twice the shortest side. If the third side is 1 m more than the shortest side, then the area of triangle (in m^2) is
(a) 4 (b) 3
(c) 5 (d) 6

24. A takes 6 days less than the time taken by B to finish a piece of work. If both A and B together can finish it in 4 days, then time taken by B to finish the work, is
(a) 24 days (b) 12 days
(c) 8 days (d) None of these

25. If -2 is a root of the quadratic equation $x^2+px-2=0$ and the quadratic $x^2+px+k=0$ has equal roots, then k is
(a) 1 (b) 3/4
(c) 1/2 (d) None of these

26. Three consecutive natural numbers are such that the square of the middle number exceeds the difference of the squares of the other two by 60. Then, the sum of the numbers will be
(a) 40 (b) 35
(c) 30 (d) None of these

27. A school bus transported an excursion party to a picnic spot 150 km away. While returning, it was raining and the bus had to reduce its speed by 5 km/h and took 1 h longer to reach, then the time taken to return will be
(a) 5 h (b) 6 h
(c) 7 h (d) 4 h

28. If roots of the equation $x^2+2cx+ab=0$ are real and unequal, then the equation $x^2-2(a+b)x+a^2+b^2+2c^2=0$ has
(a) real root (b) not real root
(c) equal roots (d) real and equal

29. If car A travels x km for every litre of petrol, while car B travels $(x+5)$ km for every litre of petrol, then find the total quantity of petrol used by both the cars.
I. If A and B covered a distance of 400 km each.
II. If car A uses 4 L of petrol more than car B in covering 400 km of distance.

Which of the following is true?
(a) Statement I alone is sufficient to answer the question but statement II is not
(b) Only statement II is sufficient to answer
(c) Both the statements are required to answer the question
(d) None of the statement is sufficient

30. An online trading site spectacular in the run of competition plans to increase its profit by the same percentage every year. In order to increase its sales, the company is required to increase its discount schemes by a percentage which is half of the percentage increase in its profit. The profit for at the end of 2 yr is ₹ 70 lakh, which is four times the profit earned two years before.
Find the percentage increase, if the output is known to be four times after two years.
(a) 400% (b) 300%
(c) 200% (d) 100%

Chapter

05

Arithmetic Progressions

1 Mark Questions

1. For the AP $\frac{-3}{2}, \frac{-1}{2}, \frac{1}{2}, \frac{3}{2}, \ldots$, the first term and common difference are

(a) $a = \frac{-3}{2}$ and $d = 1$

(b) $a = \frac{-3}{2}$ and $d = -1$

(c) $a = \frac{3}{2}$ and $d = 1$

(d) $a = \frac{3}{2}$ and $d = -1$

2. If $(a-b)^2$, (a^2+b^2) are the first two terms of an AP, then which of the following will be the next term?

(a) $2ab$ (b) $(a+b)^2$ (c) $-2ab$ (d) $-(a+b)^2$

3. If the numbers a, b, c, d and e form an AP, then the value of $a - 4b + 6c - 4d + e$ is

(a) 1 (b) 2

(c) 0 (d) None of these

4. Which of the following options correctly fills the question mark?

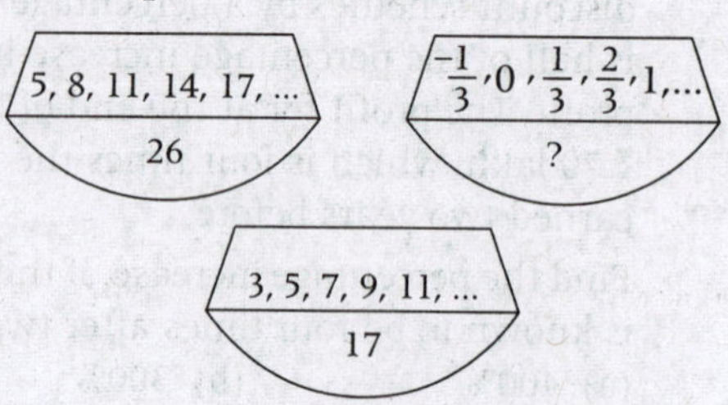

(a) 4/3 (b) − 4/3 (c) 2 (d) −2

5. The sum of the three numbers in arithmetic progression is 12. The sum of their cubes is 288. What are the numbers?

(a) 2, 4, 6 (b) 4, 6, 8

(c) 6, 8, 10 (d) None of these

6. If apples are piled in the shape of a pyramid with 1 apple in the first layer (from the top), 4 apples in the second layer, 7 apples in the third layer and 10 apples in the fourth layer, then how many apples will be there on the 10th layer?

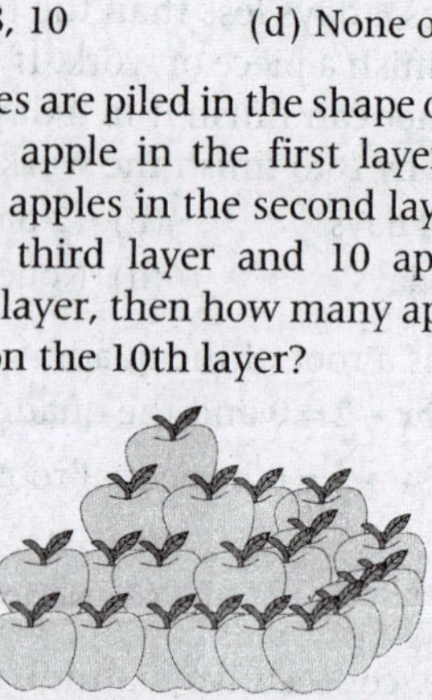

(a) 15 (b) 20 (c) 25 (d) 28

7. If $\frac{p^{n+1} + q^{n+1}}{p^n + q^n}$ is the AM of p and q. Then, n will be

(a) 1 (b) 0

(c) −1 (d) None of these

8. A piece of wire is used to make circles of the following pattern.

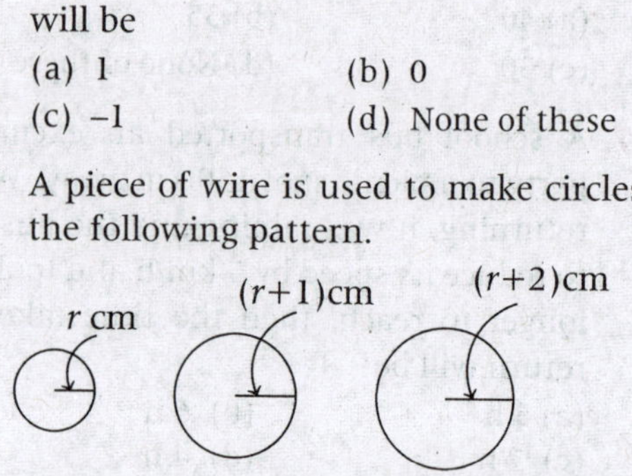

The radius of the first circle is 'r' cm and it is increased by 1 cm successively. Find the length of the wire that is required to make 5 such circles.

(a) $(10\pi + r)$ cm (b) 2π cm
(c) $10\pi(r+2)$ cm (d) $2\pi(r+2)$ cm

9. The nth term of the AP $\frac{1}{1\cdot 2}, \frac{1}{2\cdot 3}, \frac{1}{3\cdot 4}$ will be

(a) $\frac{1}{n(n+2)}$ (b) $\frac{1}{n(n+1)}$
(c) $\frac{1}{n\cdot 2n}$ (d) None of these

10. The first, second and last terms of an AP are respectively 3, 7 and 47. How many terms are there in the given AP?

(a) 10 (b) 12
(c) 14 (d) 16

11. If the tth term of an AP is s and sth term of the same AP is t, then a_n is

(a) $t+s+n$ (b) $t+s-n$
(c) $t-s+n$ (d) $t-s-n$

12. Sides of a pentagon are in AP. If the perimeter of the pentagon is 100, then sum of its largest and smallest sides is

(a) 40 (b) 32
(c) 50 (d) None of these

13. If two AP's have same common difference i.e. $d_a = d_b$. The first term of one of these is 3 and that of the other is 8. Then, $a_2 - b_2$ is

(a) -5
(b) -4
(c) -3
(d) Can't be determined

14. In a flower bed, there are 25 rose plants in the first row, 22 rose plants in the second row, 19 rose plants in the third row and so on. If there are 7 plants in the last row. How many rows are there in the flower bed?

(a) 8 (b) 7
(c) 9 (d) 10

15. If 8 times the 8th term of an AP is equal to 15 times the 15th term of that AP, then 23rd term of the same AP is

(a) 144 (b) 1
(c) 0 (d) None of these

16. John invested a sum of ₹ 1000 with an increasing rate of interest on simple interest basis, the rate of interest being 10% for the first year, 11.5% for the second year, 13% for the third year. The amount received at the end of 11th year, would be

(a) ₹ 2500 (b) ₹ 2750
(c) ₹ 3750 (d) ₹ 3500

17. A ball is thrown vertically upward reaching a height of 3.2 m in 1 s, 3.4 m in 2 s, 3.6 m in 3 s and so on.

Seconds	1	2	3	4	...
Metres	3.2	3.4	3.6	3.8	...

The time taken to reach the height of 6 m will be

(a) 10 s (b) 12 s
(c) 15 s (d) 18 s

18. A group of 48 workers can complete a piece of work in 11 days. But 48 workers worked on first day, 44 workers worked on second day, 40 workers worked on third day and so on. Unfortunately, on the 10th day, all the work got ruined. Then, find the time taken by the workers left on 10th day to complete the entire work.

(a) 40 days (b) 41 days
(c) Can't be determined (d) None of these

19. How many number of terms 1, 7, 13, 19, ... would sum upto 1160?

(a) 10 (b) 20
(c) 30 (d) 40

20. If the ratio of the sum of mth and nth terms of an AP is 1 : 1, then which of the following is true?

(a) $2a-d=0$ (b) $2a=d+2$
(c) $2a+d=0$ (d) None of these

21. If in an arithmetic progression the sum of m terms in n and the sum of n terms is m then what is the sum of $(m+n)$ terms?

(a) $m+n$ (b) $2m$
(c) $-(m+n)$ (d) $2n$

22. The sum of n terms of two AP's are in the ratio $5n+9:9n+6$, then the ratio of their 18th term is

(a) $\frac{179}{321}$ (b) $\frac{184}{321}$
(c) $\frac{175}{321}$ (d) None of these

23. The sum of n terms of the three arithmetic progression are S_1, S_2, S_3.
The first term of each arithmetic progression is unity. The common differences are 1, 2, 3 respectively, then which of the following options is correct?

(a) $S_1 + S_3 = 2S_2$
(b) $S_1 - S_3 = S_2$
(c) $S_1 + S_2 = S_3$
(d) $S_1 + S_3 = S_2$

2 Marks Questions

24. If the mth term of an AP is twice the nth term and nth term of the same AP is thrice the pth term, then

(a) $2m-5n+3p=0$ (b) $2m+3n+3p=0$
(c) $3m-2n+p=0$ (d) $3m+2n+p=0$

25. A sum of ₹ 2000 is invested at 4% simple interest per year. If the total interest at the end of each year forms an AP, then the interest at the end of 30 yr will be

(a) ₹ 1200 (b) ₹ 2400
(c) ₹ 4800 (d) No AP is formed

26. If S_n denotes the sum of first n terms of an AP, then $(S_{2n}-S_n):S_{3n}$ is

(a) $1/n$ (b) $1/3n$
(c) $1/3$ (d) None of these

27. If $p \neq q$ and the sequences p, a, b, q and p, m, n, q each are in AP, then $\frac{b-a}{n-m}$ is

(a) $\frac{2}{3}$ (b) $\frac{3}{2}$
(c) 1 (d) $\frac{3}{4}$

28. In a flag race, a pole is placed at the starting point, which is 10 m from the first flag and the other flags are placed 6 m apart in a straight line. There are n flags in the line.
Each competitor starts from the pole, picks up the nearest flag, comes back with it, place it on the pole, runs back to pick up the next flag and continues the same way until all the flags are on the pole. The total distance covered is

(a) 740 m (b) 760 m
(c) 820 m (d) 860 m

29. The sum of the series
$45^2-43^2+44^2-42^2+43^2-41^2+42^2-40^2+\ldots$ 15 terms is

(a) 1900 (b) 1290
(c) 1650 (d) 2220

30. The digits of a positive integer whose three digits are in AP and their sum is 21. The number obtained by reversing the digits is 396 less than the original number. Find the number.

(a) 795 (b) 579
(c) 975 (d) None of these

31. The number of integers existing from 1 to 1000 such that they leave a remainder 4 when divided by 7 and a remainder 9 when divided by 11, are

(a) 11 (b) 14
(c) 12 (d) 13

Chapter 06

Similarity of Triangles

1 Mark Questions

1. If $\Delta ABC \sim \Delta PQR$, then PR is

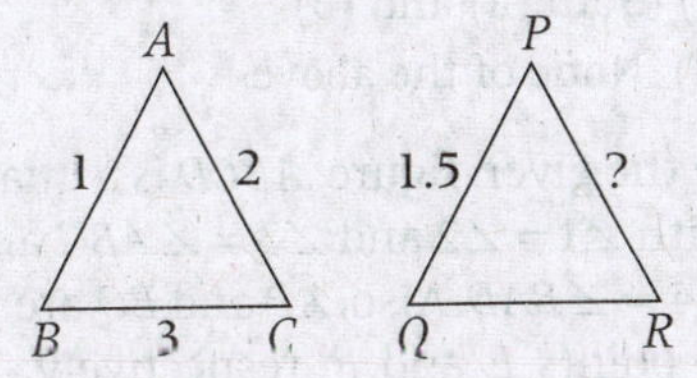

(a) 4 cm (b) 4.5 cm
(c) 3 cm (d) 3.5 cm

2. E is the mid-point of AB and D is the mid-point of AC. If $BC = z - 33$ and $DE = z - 37$, then BC is equal to

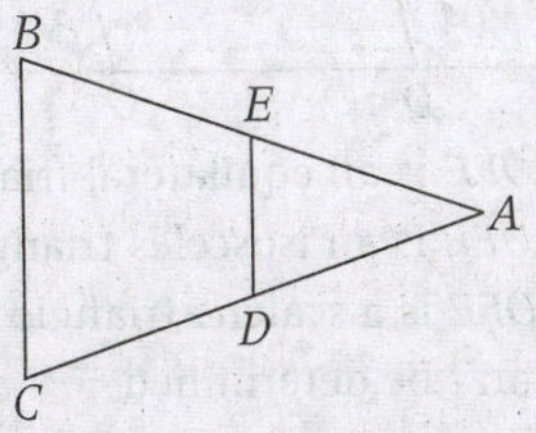

(a) 41 (b) 40
(c) 8.5 (d) 8

3. In the given figure, if $ED \| AB$, then which of the following is correct?

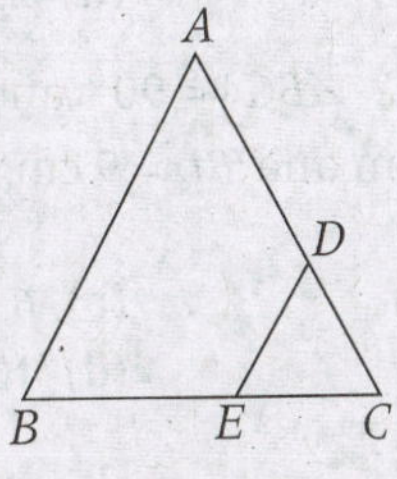

(a) $\dfrac{CD}{AD} + 1 \neq \dfrac{CE}{EB} + 1$

(b) $\dfrac{CD}{AD} \neq \dfrac{CE}{EB}$

(c) $\dfrac{AD}{CD} + 1 = \dfrac{EB}{CE} + 1$

(d) None of the above

4. If $\Delta ABC \sim \Delta DFE$, $\angle A = 30°$, $\angle C = 50°$, $AB = 5$ cm, $AC = 8$ cm and $DF = 7.5$ cm. Which of the following is true?

(a) $DE = 12$ cm, $\angle F = 50°$
(b) $DE = 12$ cm, $\angle F = 100°$
(c) $EF = 12$ cm, $\angle D = 100°$
(d) $EF = 12$ cm, $\angle D = 30°$

5. If $LM \| AB$, $AL = 2x + 4$, $AC = 4x$, $BM = x + 2$ and $BC = 2x + 3$, then x is $(x > 0)$

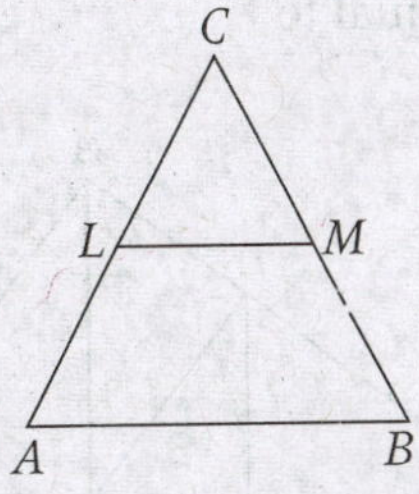

(a) 2 (b) $\dfrac{4}{5}$
(c) $\dfrac{5}{4}$ (d) 5

6. If $\Delta ADE \sim \Delta ACB$, $\angle DEC = 105°$ and $\angle ECB = 65°$, then $\angle DAE$ is

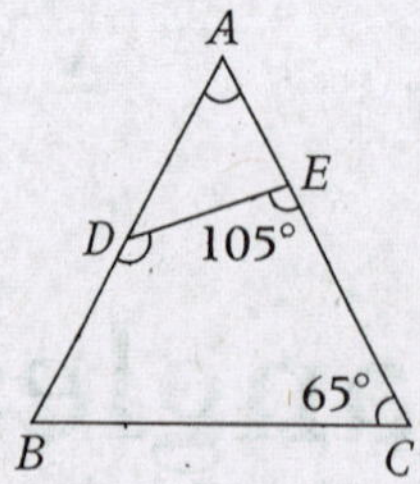

(a) 65°
(b) 75°
(c) 40°
(d) Can't be determined

7. If $PQRS$ is a parallelogram, with point A on QR, then $\frac{AP}{AB}$ is equal to

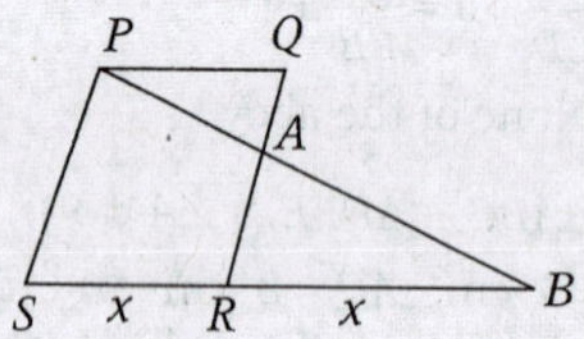

(a) 1
(b) 2
(c) $\frac{1}{2}$
(d) Can't be determined

8. In the given figure, $DE \parallel AC$ and $DC \parallel AP$, such that $BC = 4$ cm and $BP = 6$ cm, then $\frac{BE}{EC}$ is equal to

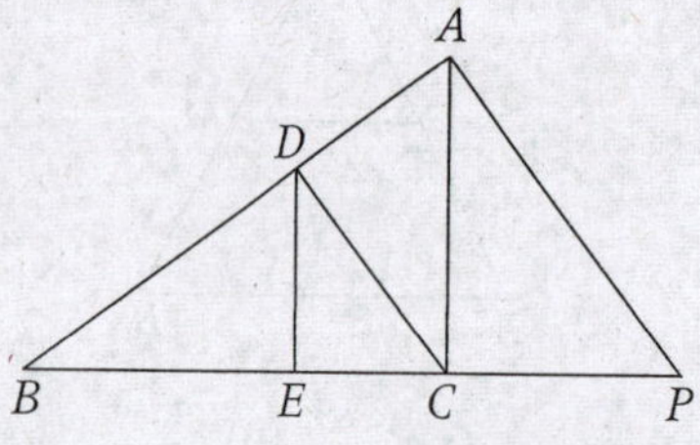

(a) 1 : 1 (b) 1 : 2
(c) 2 : 1 (d) 1 : 3

9. In ΔABC with $AB = BC = CA$ and having P, Q and R as mid-points.

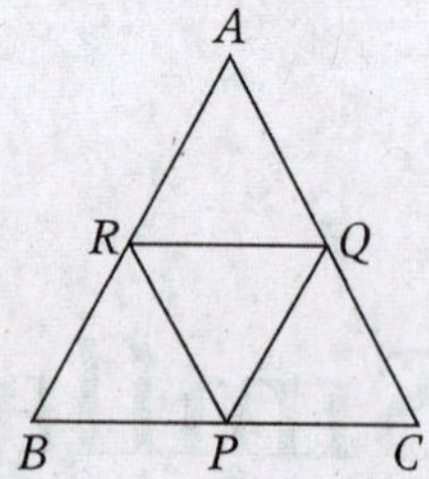

State which of the following is true?
(a) ΔPQR is an equilateral triangle
(b) $PQ + QR + RP = \frac{1}{2}(AB + BC + CA)$
(c) Both (a) and (b)
(d) None of the above

10. In the given figure, $ABCD$ is a quadrilateral with $\angle 1 = \angle 2$ and $\angle 3 = \angle ABC$ and $\angle 4 = \angle BAD$. Also, AP and BQ are produced to points E and F, respectively. Then, we can say that

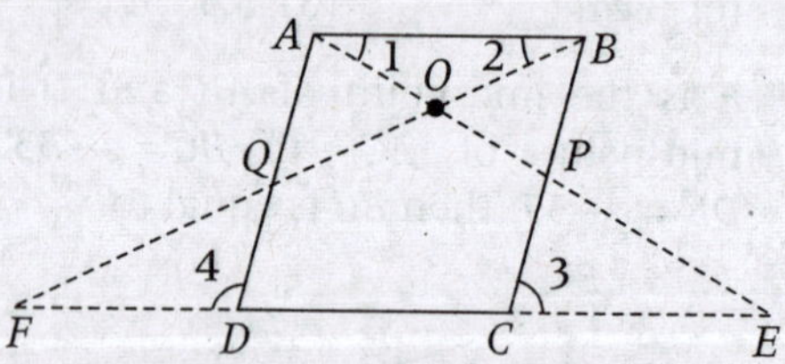

(a) ΔOFE is an equilateral triangle
(b) ΔOFE is an isosceles triangle
(c) ΔOFE is a scalene triangle
(d) Can't be determined

11. A person is standing 50 ft away from a street light which is 60 ft tall. How tall is he, if his shadow is 10 ft long?
(a) 10 ft (b) 20 ft
(c) 30 ft (d) 25 ft

12. In ΔABC, $\angle BCA = 90°$ and $CD \perp AB$, with $AD = 4$ cm and $BD = 9$ cm. Then, the value of DC is
(a) 8 cm (b) 6 cm
(c) 4 cm (d) 10 cm

13. In the given figure, $PD \parallel BC$ and $\frac{AD}{DC} = \frac{CE}{BE}$.

Identify the correct statement.

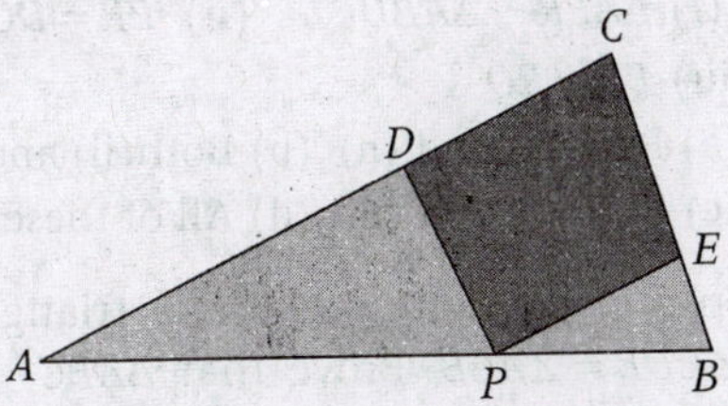

(a) $AD = DC$ (b) $PE \parallel AC$
(c) $PB = CE$ (d) $PD \perp AC$

14. If AD is external bisector of $\angle A$ which meets BC at D and $CE \parallel DA$. Then, which of the following is true?

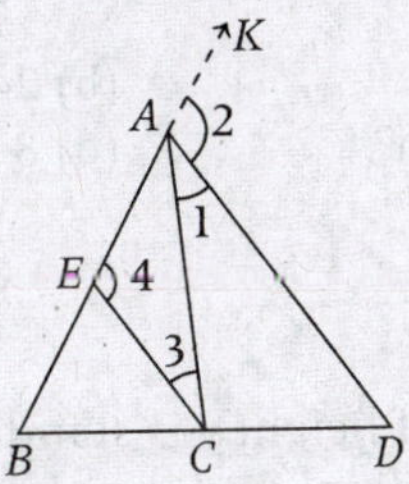

(a) $\frac{BD}{CD} = \frac{AB}{AC}$

(b) $\frac{BD}{CE} = \frac{AB}{AD}$

(c) Both (a) and (b)

(d) None of the above

15. If $\Delta ABC \sim \Delta PQR$, $AB = 6.5$ cm, $PQ = 10.4$ cm and perimeter of $\Delta ABC = 60$ cm, find the perimeter of ΔPQR

(a) 37.5 (b) 60 cm
(c) 96 cm (d) 105.625

16. It is given that $\Delta ABC \sim \Delta EDF$ such that $AB = 5$ cm, $AC = 7$ cm, $DF = 15$ cm and $DE = 12$ cm. Find the lengths of the remaining side of the triangles.

(a) $EF = 2.91$ cm, $BC = 4$ cm
(b) $EF = 16.8$ cm, $BC = 6.25$ cm
(c) $EF = 8.57$ cm, $BC = 36$ cm
(d) $EF = 6.25$ cm, $BC = 16.8$ cm

17. In the given figure (not to scale) $AM : MC = 3:4, BP : PM = 3:2$ and $BN = 12$ cm, then find AM

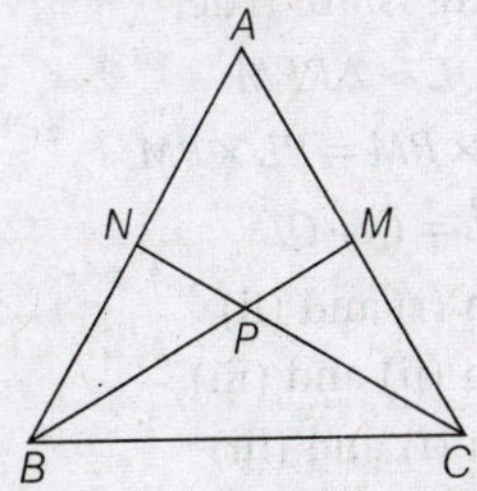

(a) 10 cm (b) 12 cm
(c) 14 cm (d) 16 cm

18. In the given figure, $DE \parallel AC$. Find the value of x.

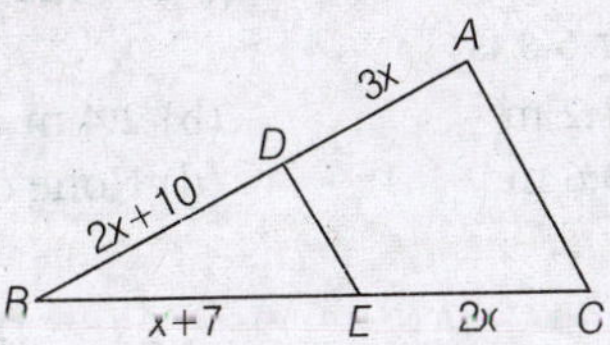

(a) 1 (b) 2 (c) 3 (d) 4

19. In ΔPQR, if $ST \parallel QR$, $\frac{PS}{SQ} = \frac{3}{5}$ and $PR = 28$ cm, then find PT.

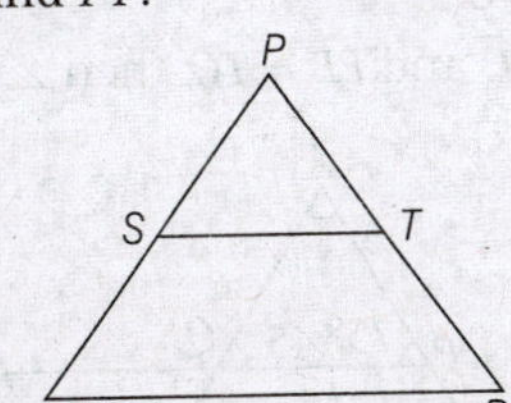

(a) 9 (b) 9.5 (c) 10 (d) 10.5

20. In the given figure, $\angle ABC = 90°$ and $BD \perp AC$. If $BD = 8$ cm and $AD = 4$ cm, then find the value of CD.

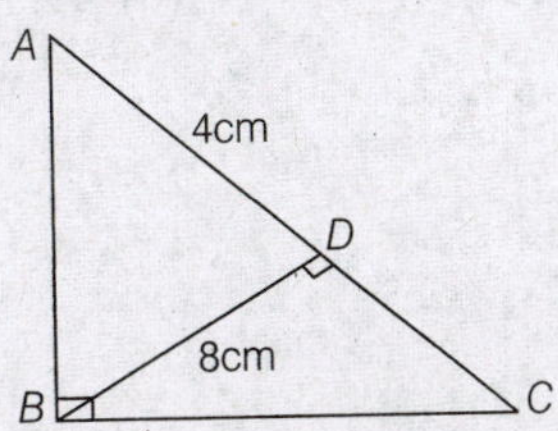

(a) 2 cm (b) 4 cm (c) 16 cm (d) 8 cm

21. In a ΔPQR, L and M are two points on base QR such that $\angle LPQ = \angle QRP$ and $\angle RPM = \angle RQP$. Then, which of the following is/are true.

(i) $\Delta PQL \sim \Delta RPM$

(ii) $QL \times RM = PL \times PM$

(iv) $PQ^2 = QR \cdot QL$

(a) Both (i) and (ii)
(b) Both (ii) and (iii)
(c) Both (i) and (iii)
(d) All of the above

22. A boy of height 90 cm is walking away from the base of lamp-post at a speed of 1.2 m/s. If the lamp is 3.6 m above the ground, then the length of his shadow after 6 s is

(a) 1.2 m (b) 2.4 m
(c) 3.6 m (d) None of these

23. In a ΔABC, P and Q are points on AB and AC respectively and $PQ \| BC$. Also, AD is the median. Then,

(i) $\Delta APR \sim \Delta ABD$ (ii) $PR = DC$
(iii) $PR = RQ$

(a) Both (i) and (ii) (b) Both(ii) and (iii)
(c) Both (i) and (iii) (d) All of these

24. In a given figure, ABC is a triangle with $\angle EDB = \angle ACB$. Prove that $\Delta ABC \sim \Delta EBD$. If $BE = 6$ cm, $EC = 4$ cm, $BD = 5$ cm, then calculate the length of AB.

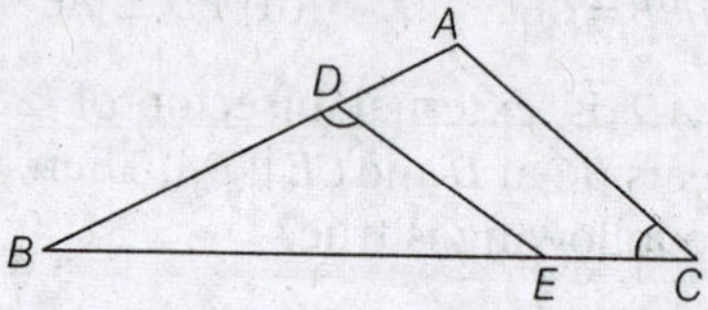

(a) 6 cm (b) 24 cm
(c) 12 cm (d) 8 cm

2 Marks Questions

25. In ΔABC, with points P and Q on sides AB and AC, respectively such that $\frac{AP}{PB} = \frac{AQ}{QC}$. If, PQ is extended to T such that $PT = BC$ and $PB = TC$, then $\angle x$ is equal to

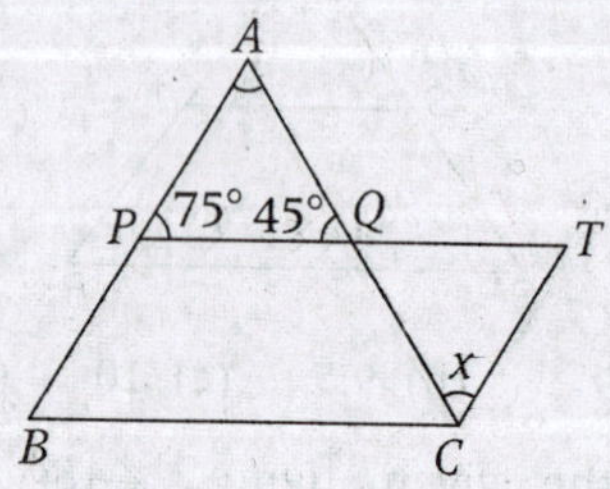

(a) 60° (b) 120°
(c) 75° (d) 45

26. A man of height y is standing between two buildings with heights x and z respectively. Then, which of the following statements is true about the relation of the heights?

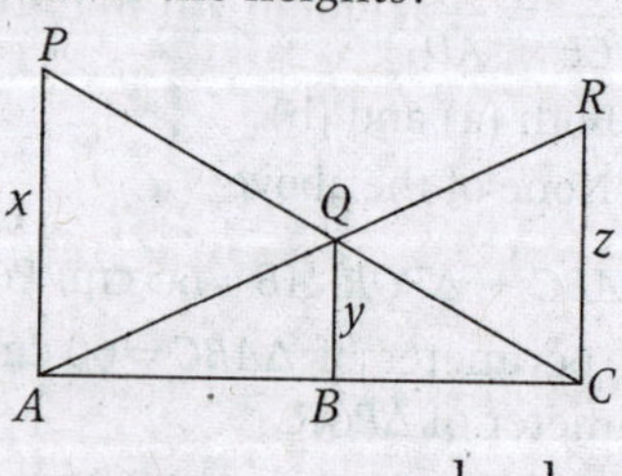

(a) $x = y = z$ (b) $\frac{1}{x} = \frac{1}{y} = \frac{1}{z}$

(c) $\frac{1}{x} + \frac{1}{y} = \frac{1}{z}$ (d) $\frac{1}{x} + \frac{1}{z} = \frac{1}{y}$

27. In a given figure, if $PQRS$ is a parallelogram and $AB||PS$, then

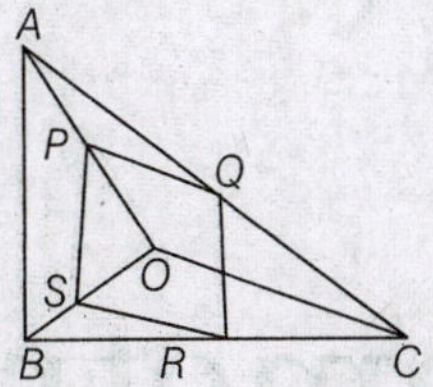

(a) $OC||SR$ (b) $OB||QR$
(c) $OA||SR$ (d) None of these

28. O is the point of intersection of the diagonals AC and BD of a trapezium $ABCD$ with $AB||DC$. Through O, a line segment PQ is drawn parallel to AB meeting AD in P and BC in Q, then OP is equal to

(a) $OP = OQ$ (b) $OP = 2OQ$
(c) $OQ = 2OP$ (d) $OP = \frac{1}{3}OQ$

29. Radhika wants to visit her friend who recently moves to a new house. The road map between Radhika's home and her friend's as well as the distance known to Radhika are as shown in the given figure below. To reach the friend's house, the shortest distance which Radhika has to travel, is

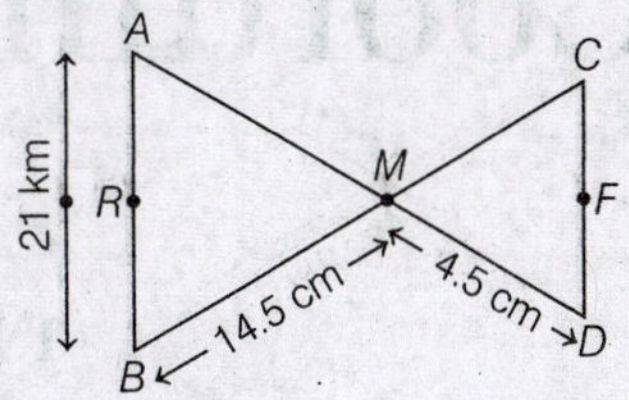

(a) 30.95 km
(b) 32.5 km
(c) 28.5 km
(d) 35.35 km

Chapter

07

Coordinate Geometry

1 Mark Questions

1. If a reflection in the line $y = -x$ occurs, then (x, y) changes to

(a) $(x, -y)$ (b) (y, x)

(c) $(-x, y)$ (d) $(-y, -x)$

2. Under the translation $T_{(2, 3)}$, the point $(5, 2)$ becomes

(a) $(5, 7)$ (b) $(3, 2)$

(c) $(2, 3)$ (d) $(7, 5)$

3. The reflection of the point $P(4, 6)$ reflected in the line $x = 6$ and then again reflected in the line $y = 4$ will be

(a) $(8, 6)$ (b) $(4, 2)$

(c) $(8, 2)$ (d) None of the above

4. If $P(a - b, a + b)$ and $Q(a + b, a - b)$, then PQ is equal to

(a) $a^2 + b^2$ (b) $8ab$

(c) 0 (d) None of these

5. Point $\left(\frac{11}{2}, \frac{7}{2}\right)$ is at a distance of

(a) $\frac{170}{4}$ units from the origin

(b) $\frac{\sqrt{170}}{4}$ units from the origin

(c) $\frac{170}{2}$ units from the origin

(d) $\frac{\sqrt{170}}{2}$ units from the origin

6. The point on X-axis equidistant from points $A(2, 4)$ and $B(-4, 8)$ is

(a) $(-5, 0)$ (b) $(5, 0)$

(c) $(0, 0)$ (d) None of these

7. The figure formed by the points $A(a, a)$, $B(-a, -a)$ and $C(-\sqrt{3}a, \sqrt{3}a)$ will be

(a) an isosceles triangle

(b) an equilateral triangle

(c) a scalene triangle

(d) None of the above

8. A man starts walking from the origin towards East, covering a distance of 4 km, then he turned left and started walking covering a distance of 3 km. Find the distance of the final position of man from the starting position.

(a) 7 km (b) 25 km

(c) 49 km (d) 5 km

9. If the distance of the point $P(x, y)$ from $A(7, 1)$ and $B(-1, 7)$ lying on the line AB is equal, then which of the following is true?

(a) $3x = 2y$ (b) $3x = 4y$

(c) $2x = 3y$ (d) $4x = 3y$

10. What is the circumradius of the triangle whose vertices are $(2, -2)$, $(8, 6)$ and $(8, -2)$?

(a) 25 (b) 5

(c) $\sqrt{5}$ (d) None of these

Directions (Q. Nos. 11 and 12) *Study the graph given below carefully and answer the following questions.*

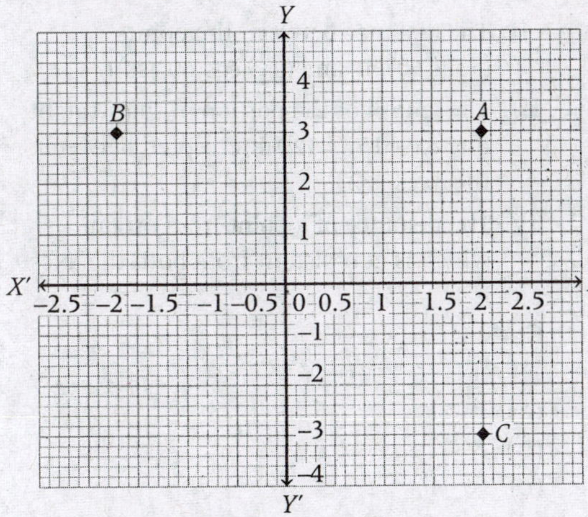

11. Find the distance between the marked point and write its sides in ascending order.

(a) $AB < AC < BC$
(b) $AC < AB < BC$
(c) $BC < AC < AB$
(d) None of the above

12. Find the perimeter of the triangle.

(a) 24 units (b) 16 units
(c) 14 units (d) None of these

13. The centre of a circle is $(4a-2, 6a+2)$ and is passing through the point $(-6,-2)$. If the diameter of the circle is 40, then a is equal to

(a) 2 (b) -2
(c) 4 (d) -4

14. The shape of the figure formed will be,

I. If lengths of two of its sides are 5 units and $5\sqrt{2}$ units.

II. If the coordinates of the points are $A(-3,0)$, $B(1,-3)$ and C (x, y), with $BC = 5\sqrt{2}$.

(a) Statement I alone is sufficient to answer
(b) Statement II alone is sufficient to answer
(c) Both statements are required to answer
(d) Data is insufficient

15. If a point $P(8,4)$ divides the joining of points $A(5,-2)$ and $B(9,6)$ in a ratio. Then,

(a) $AP = 3PB$ (b) $3AP = PB$
(c) $AP = 2PB$ (d) $2AP = PB$

16. A path is to be constructed between two corners of the park, A and B. If a water pipe is being laid in the following manner inside the park, then the ratio in which the pipe divides the path between A and B will be

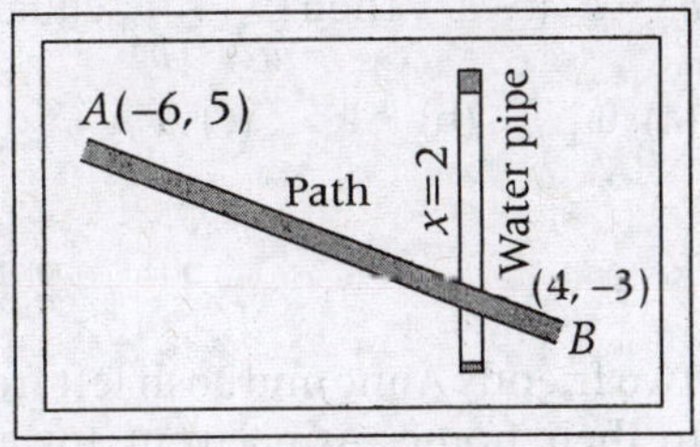

(a) 2 : 1 (b) 1 : 2
(c) 1 : 4 (d) 4 : 1

17. The coordinates of the point M are $(-6,4)$. The coordinates of the point N which lies on the line joining M and origin such that $MN = ON$, is

(a) (2, 3) (b) (−2, 3)
(c) (3, 2) (d) (−3, 2)

18. The line segement joining $A(2,3)$ and $B(-3,5)$ is extended through each end by a length equal to its original length. Find the coordinates of new ends.

(a) $Q(-8,7)$, $P(7,1)$
(b) $Q(-4,13)$, $P(1,11)$
(c) $P(-8,7)$, $Q(7,1)$
(d) $P(-4,13)$, $Q(1,11)$

19. In a square of $ABCD$, the vertices of the diagonals are $A(9, -9)$ and $C(1, -3)$. Find the area of square $ABCD$.

(a) 40 sq units (b) 50 sq units
(c) 55 sq units (d) 60 sq units

20. $ABCD$ is a quadrilateral formed by the points $A(-1, -1), B(-1, 4), C(5, 4)$ and $D(5, -1)$. P, Q, R and S are the mid-points of AB, BC, CD and DA, respectively. Then, the quadrilateral $PQRS$ is a

(a) square (b) rectangle
(c) rhombus (d) parallelogram

21. A point (x, y) moves, so that the sum of its distances from $(ae, 0)$ and $(-ae, 0)$ is $2a$. If $b^2 = a^2(1-e^2)$, then $\frac{x^2}{a^2} + \frac{y^2}{b^2}$ equal to

(a) 0 (b) -1 (c) 1 (d) 2

22. State 'T' for true and 'F' for false.

I. Coordinates of the point which divides the join of $(-1, 7)$ and $(4, -3)$ in the ratio $2:3$ is $(1, 3)$.

II. The distance between the points $(5\sin 60°, 0)$ and $(0, 5\cos 60°)$ is 1.

III. The length of the portion of the straight line $8x + 15y = 120$ intercepted between the axes is 23.

IV. The distance of a point from origin, which is equidistant from both the axes is 1.

Codes

	I	II	III	IV
(a)	T	F	F	F
(b)	T	T	F	F
(c)	F	F	T	T
(d)	T	T	F	F

2 Marks Questions

23. Two friends Anne and Josh left from office to their home. Anne went towards East covering a distance of 8 km and reached home whereas Josh went towards North and covered a distance of 6 km to reach his place. Evaluating the figure so formed by the position of their office and homes, the shortest distance between the homes of Anne and Josh will be

(a) 14 km (b) 7 km
(c) 10 km (d) Can't be determined

24. The centre and radius of the circumcircle of the triangle whose vertices are $(-2, 3), (2, -1)$ and $(4, 0)$ are

(a) $(3, 5) : 5\sqrt{2}$

(b) $(0, 0); \frac{5\sqrt{2}}{2}$

(c) $\left(\frac{1}{2}, \frac{3}{2}\right); \frac{\sqrt{2}}{2}$

(d) $\left(\frac{3}{2}, \frac{5}{2}\right); \frac{5\sqrt{2}}{2}$

25. Lengths of the medians of the triangle having vertices $(1, -1), (0, 4)$ and $(-5, 3)$ are respectively

(a) $\frac{\sqrt{130}}{2}, \sqrt{13}, \frac{\sqrt{130}}{2}$ (b) 12, 13, 12

(c) $\sqrt{140}, \sqrt{14}, \frac{\sqrt{130}}{2}$ (d) $\frac{\sqrt{130}}{2}, \sqrt{13}, \sqrt{140}$

26. If G is the centroid of ΔABC and P be any other point in the plane, then $GA^2 + GB^2 + GC^2 + 3GP^2$ is equal to

(a) $PA^2 + PC^2 - PB^2$ (b) $PB^2 + PC^2 - PA^2$
(c) $PA^2 + PB^2 - PC^2$ (d) $PA^2 + PB^2 + PC^2$

27. The line joining the points $A(2, 1)$ and $B(5, -8)$ is being divided by the points $P(x, y)$ and $Q(4, -5)$ such that $\frac{AP}{PB} = \frac{BQ}{QA}$, then the value of k for which the point P lies on the line $2x + y + k = 0$, is

(a) 4 (b) -4
(c) 2 (d) -2

Chapter 08

Trigonometry

1 Mark Questions

1. If $\sin\theta = m$ and $\cos\theta = n$, then what is $m^2 + n^2$ equal to?

(a) $1 + \tan^2\theta$ (b) $\tan^2\theta$

(c) $\cos^2\theta$ (d) $\sin^2\theta$

2. If $3\tan\theta = 5$, then $\dfrac{3\sin\theta - 5\cos\theta}{3\sin\theta + 5\cos\theta}$ is equal to

(a) $\dfrac{3}{5}$ (b) $\dfrac{5}{3}$

(c) 1 (d) 0

3. For an acute angle θ, $\sin\theta + \cos\theta$ gives the greatest value when θ is

(a) 30° (b) 45°

(c) 60° (d) 90°

4. If $\operatorname{cosec}\theta = \dfrac{13}{12}$, find the value of $\dfrac{2\sin\theta - 3\cos\theta}{4\sin\theta - 9\cos\theta}$.

(a) 0 (b) 1

(c) 3 (d) 2

5. Given $\sin\theta + \dfrac{1}{\sin\theta} = 4$, what is the value of $\sin^2\theta + \dfrac{1}{\sin^2\theta}$?

(a) 20 (b) 16

(c) 14 (d) 4

6. In ΔABC, if $\angle B = 90°$, $AB = 5$ cm and $AC = 10$ cm, then

(a) $\angle B = 50°$ (b) $\angle A = 30°$

(c) $\angle C = 30°$ (d) $\angle C = 60°$

7. If $\dfrac{x}{a}\cos\theta + \dfrac{y}{b}\sin\theta = 1$ and $\dfrac{x}{a}\sin\theta - \dfrac{y}{b}\cos\theta = 1$, then what is the value of $\dfrac{x^2}{a^2} + \dfrac{y^2}{b^2}$?

(a) 0 (b) 1

(c) 2 (d) None of these

8. If $\dfrac{1+\sin\alpha}{1-\sin\alpha} = \dfrac{m^2}{n^2}$, then $\sin\alpha$ is

(a) $\dfrac{m^2+n^2}{m^2-n^2}$ (b) $\dfrac{m^2-n^2}{m^2+n^2}$

(c) $\dfrac{m^2+n^2}{n^2-m^2}$ (d) $\dfrac{n^2-m^2}{m^2+n^2}$

9. A triangle with sides 12 units and 5 units inscribed in a circle with BC as diameter, then $\sin^2\theta + \cos^2\theta - 1$ will be

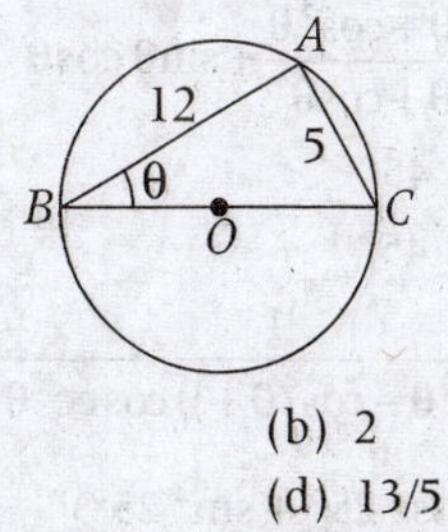

(a) 1 (b) 2

(c) 0 (d) 13/5

10. If $x\cos\theta - y\sin\theta = z$, then choose which one of the following expressions is equivalent to $x\sin\theta + y\cos\theta$?

(a) $\pm\sqrt{x^2+y^2+z^2}$ (b) $x+y-z$

(c) $\pm\sqrt{x^2+y^2-z^2}$ (d) $x+y+z$

11. The value of

$$\frac{\cot^2 30^\circ + 8\sin^2 45^\circ + \frac{3}{2}\sec^2 30^\circ + 2\cos^2 90^\circ}{2\sec 60^\circ + 3\,\text{cosec}\,30^\circ - \frac{7}{3}\tan^2 60^\circ}$$

is

(a) 3 (b) 4

(c) 5 (d) None of these

12. Evaluate

$$[4(\sin^2 30^\circ + \cos^4 60^\circ) - 3(\cos^2 45^\circ - \sin^2 90^\circ)] \times \frac{2\cos^2 60^\circ + 3\sec^2 30^\circ - 2\tan^2 45^\circ}{\sin^2 30^\circ + \cos^2 45^\circ}$$

(a) $\frac{55}{6}$ (b) 0

(c) 1 (d) $\frac{32}{3}$

13. Evaluate $\frac{\cot\theta + \text{cosec}\,\theta - 1}{\cot\theta - \text{cosec}\,\theta + 1}$

(a) $\text{cosec}\,\theta + \cot\theta$

(b) $\frac{1+\cos\theta}{\sin\theta}$

(c) Both (a) and (b)

(d) None of the above

14. Pick the odd one out.

(a) $\frac{\sin^3\theta + \cos^3\theta}{\sin\theta + \cos\theta} + \sin\theta\cos\theta$

(b) $\frac{\cos^2 45^\circ}{\tan^2 45^\circ}$

(c) $\frac{1}{(\sin^4\theta - \cos^4\theta + 1)\,\text{cosec}^2\theta}$

(d) $\frac{1}{2}(\cos^2 25^\circ + \sin^2 25^\circ)$

15. If $\tan\theta = -1$, then the value of $\frac{\sec\theta + \text{cosec}\,\theta}{\cos\theta - \sin\theta}$ is

(a) 0 (b) 1

(c) $-\sqrt{2}$ (d) $\sqrt{2}$

16. Choose the correctly marked pair.

(a) $\frac{\sin^2\theta - \cos^2\theta}{\cos\theta\tan\theta + \sin\theta\cot\theta} \rightarrow \sin\theta + \cos\theta$

(b) $\frac{\sin^2\theta - \cos^2\theta}{\cos\theta\tan\theta - \sin\theta\cot\theta} \rightarrow \sin\theta - \cos\theta$

(c) Both (a) and (b)

(d) None of the above

17. $(\text{cosec}\,A - \sin A)(\sec A - \cos A)(\tan A + \cot A)$ is equal to

(a) -1 (b) 2

(c) 0 (d) 1

18. $\frac{\sin\theta + \cos\theta}{\sin\theta - \cos\theta} + \frac{\sin\theta - \cos\theta}{\sin\theta + \cos\theta}$ is equal to

(a) $\frac{2}{1 - 2\cos^2\theta}$ (b) $\frac{2}{2\sin^2\theta - 1}$

(c) Both (a) and (b) (d) None of these

19. If $\text{cosec}\,\theta - \sin\theta = m$ and $\sec\theta - \cos\theta = n$, then the value of $(m^2 n)^{2/3} + (mn^2)^{2/3}$ is

(a) 0 (b) $\sin\theta$

(c) 1 (d) $\cos\theta$

20. If $P_n = \cos^n x + \sin^n x$, then find $2P_6 - 3P_4 + 1$.

(a) 0 (b) 1

(c) 2 (d) 3

21. If $\text{cosec}\,\theta - \sin\theta = x^3$ and $\sec\theta - \cos\theta = y^3$ then the value of $x^2y^2(x^2+y^2)$ is

(a) 0 (b) 1

(c) 2 (d) 3

22. If $\tan(\theta_1 + \theta_2) = \sqrt{3}$ and $\sec(\theta_1 - \theta_2) = \frac{2}{\sqrt{3}}$, then $\sin 2\theta_1 + \tan 3\theta_2$ is equal to

(a) $\sqrt{3}$ (b) 2

(c) 3 (d) 1

Chapter 09

Applications of Trigonometry

1 Mark Questions

1. The angle of depression will be

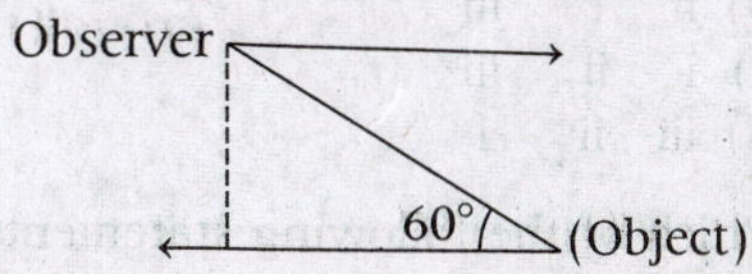

(a) 60°
(b) 30°
(c) None of these
(d) Can't be determined

2. If the shadow of a tree is given in the figure, then θ is

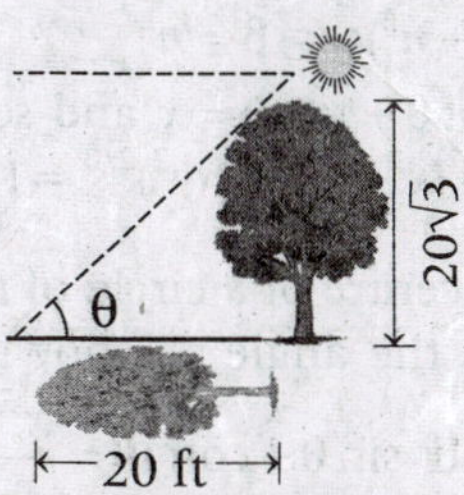

(a) 30° (b) 45°
(c) 60° (d) 90°

3. A ladder of length 16 units is resting against a wall of height 8 units. The angle made by the leg of the ladder with the ground is
(a) 60° (b) 30°
(c) 45° (d) 90°

4. A ladder of length 13 units resting on the wall of height 12 units, slips down to the height of 5 units. The distance between the new position of the leg of ladder from its old position will be
(a) 5 units (b) 7 units
(c) 10 units (d) 13 units

5. The height of a kite from the ground is $100\sqrt{3}$ m. If the angle of elevation from a point on the ground is 45°, what is the length of the string of the kite?
(a) $100\sqrt{3}$ m (b) $100\sqrt{2}$ m
(c) $100\sqrt{6}$ m (d) 100 m

6. An eagle flying at an altitude of 1200 m flies vertically above another eagle at the same time, when the angles of elevation of the two birds are 60° and 45° respectively. How high above the second eagle is the first eagle flying?
(a) 507.20 m (b) 500 m
(c) 570.81 m (d) 300 m

7. A straight tree breaks due to storm and the broken part bends so that the top of the tree touches the ground making an angle of 30° with the ground. The distance from the foot of the tree to the point, where the top touches the ground

23. If $\sin^2 A + \cos^2 A = 1$, then choose the correct option.

I. $\dfrac{\cos A}{1-\sin A} + \dfrac{\sin A}{1-\cos A} + 1$

II. $\dfrac{(1+\cot A+\tan A)(\sin A-\cos A)}{\sec^3 A - \text{cosec}^3 A}$

	I	II
(a)	$\dfrac{\sin A\cos A}{(1-\sin A)(1-\cos A)}$	$\sin^2 A\cos^2 A$
(b)	$\dfrac{\sin^2 A\cos^2 A}{(1-\sin A)(1-\cos A)}$	$\sin A\cos A$
(c)	$\dfrac{\sin A}{1-\sin^2 A}$	$\sin^2 A\cos^2 A$
(d)	$\dfrac{\cos A}{1-\cos^2 A}$	$\sin A\cos^2 A$

2 Marks Questions

24. Given a set of statements. For each correct statement add 1 and for each incorrect statement subtract 1.

(i) If A and B are acute angles and $\sin A = \dfrac{1}{2}$, $\tan B = \sqrt{3}$, then $\cot(A+B)$ is not defined.

(ii) If $2\sin A = 1$, then $3A$ is a right angle.

(iii) If $1-\cos^2\theta = \dfrac{3}{4}$, then $\sin\theta$ is $\dfrac{1}{4}$.

(iv) For $\sin\theta = \dfrac{a}{b}$, $\cos\theta$ is $\dfrac{\sqrt{b^2-a^2}}{b}$.

Then, the total value will be

(a) 4 (b) −4
(c) 3 (d) 0

25. Match the following:

List I	List II
A. For $\sec A = \dfrac{17}{8}$, $\dfrac{3-4\sin^2 A}{4\cos^2 A-3}$ is equal to	i. $\dfrac{3}{7}$
B. For $\tan\theta = \dfrac{20}{21}$, $\dfrac{1-\sin\theta+\cos\theta}{1+\sin\theta+\cos\theta}$ is equal to	ii. $\dfrac{33}{611}$
C. If $\sin\theta = \dfrac{12}{13}$, then $\dfrac{\sin^2\theta-\cos^2\theta}{2\sin\theta\cos\theta} \times \dfrac{1}{\tan^2\theta}$	iii. $\dfrac{595}{3456}$

Codes

	A	B	C
(a)	ii	iii	i
(b)	ii	i	iii
(c)	i	ii	iii
(d)	iii	ii	i

26. Which of the following statements is not correct?

(a) If $\text{cosec}\,\theta - \sin\theta = l$ and $\sec\theta - \cos\theta = m$, then $l^2m^2(l^2+m^2+3) = 1$

(b) If $x\sin^3\theta + y\cos^3\theta = \sin\theta\cos\theta$ and $x\sin\theta = y\cos\theta$, then $x^2+y^2 = 0$

(c) If $\dfrac{\cos\alpha}{\cos\beta} = m$ and $\dfrac{\cos\alpha}{\sin\beta} = n$, then $(m^2+n^2)\cos^2\beta = n^2$

(d) If $\cot\theta + \tan\theta = x$ and $\sec\theta - \cos\theta = y$, then $(x^2y)^{2/3} - (xy^2)^{2/3} = 1$

27. C is the centre of a circle of radius 3 units, and θ is the angle as shown in the given figure. If $\sin\theta + \cos^2\theta = \dfrac{x^2+1}{x^2}$, find the value of x.

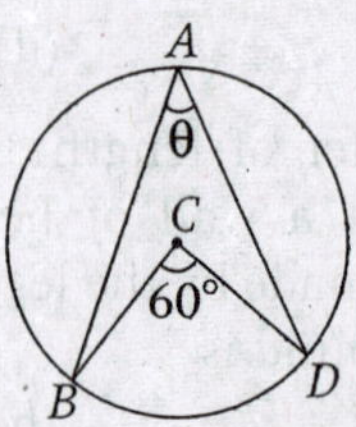

(a) 2 (b) 4
(c) 6 (d) 8

is 10 m. The height of the tree before breaking is ....

(a) $10\sqrt{3}$ m (b) $\frac{10\sqrt{3}}{3}$ m

(c) $10(\sqrt{3}+1)$ m (d) $10(\sqrt{3}-1)$ m

8. The angle of elevation of an object from a point 500 m above a lake is observed to be 30° and the angle of depression of its reflection in the lake is 45°. Find the height of the object above the lake.

(a) $\frac{500}{\sqrt{3}}(1+\sqrt{3})$ m

(b) $500(2+\sqrt{3})$ m

(c) $500(3+\sqrt{3})$ m

(d) $500(4+\sqrt{3})$ m

9. The distance between two vertical poles is 60 m. The height of one of the poles is double the height of the other. The angles of elevation of the tops of the poles from the middle point of the line segment joining their feet are complementary to each other. Find the heights of the poles.

(a) 21.21 m, 42.42 m

(b) 36.63 m, 67.76 m

(c) 42.24 m, 10.01 m

(d) 16.16 m 22.22 m

10. If the angles of elevation of a tower from two points at a distance a and b (where, $b > a$) from its foot and lying on the same side are 60° and 30°, then height of the tower is

(a) $\sqrt{a-b}$ (b) $\sqrt{b-a}$

(c) $\sqrt{ab}$ (d) $\sqrt{a/b}$

11. The angles of elevation of the top of a building from the ground floor and first floor of another building are 60° and 45° respectively. If the first floor is 40 m above the ground floor, what is the height of the building?

(a) 54.64 m (b) 94.64 m

(c) 40 m (d) 109.3 m

12. A person standing on the bank of a river observes that the angle of elevation of the top of a tower on the opposite bank is 30°. He moves 40 m towards the bank and finds the angle of elevation to be 60°. What is the width of the river?

(a) 24 m (b) 20 m

(c) 26 m (d) 15 m

13. If the angle of elevation of an aeroplane from a point on the ground is 60°. After 15 s, the angle of elevation changes to 30°. If the aeroplane is flying at a constant height of $1500\sqrt{3}$ m, then speed of aeroplane is

(a) 200 m/s

(b) 210 m/s

(c) 150 m/s

(d) 250 m/s

14. A round balloon of radius r subtends an angle α at the eye of the observer while the angle of elevation of its centre is β. The height of the centre of the balloon is

(a) $r\sin\beta\operatorname{cosec}\alpha/2$

(b) $r\sin\beta/2\cos\alpha/2$

(c) $r\sin\beta/2\cos\alpha$

(d) $r\sin\beta\cos\alpha$

2 Marks Questions

15. The shadow of a person X, when the angle of elevation of the sun is α (alpha), is equal in length to the shadow of person Y, when angle of elevation of the sun is $\left(\frac{\alpha}{2}\right)$. Which one of the following is correct?

(a) X is shorter than Y.
(b) X is twice as tall as Y.
(c) X is taller than Y but is not twice as tall as Y.
(d) Both X and Y are of equal of height.

16. From a window A, 10 m above the ground, the angle of elevation of the top C of a tower is x, where $\tan x = \frac{5}{2}$, and the angle of depression of the foot D of the tower is y, where $\tan y = \frac{1}{4}$. What is the height CD of the tower to the nearest metre?

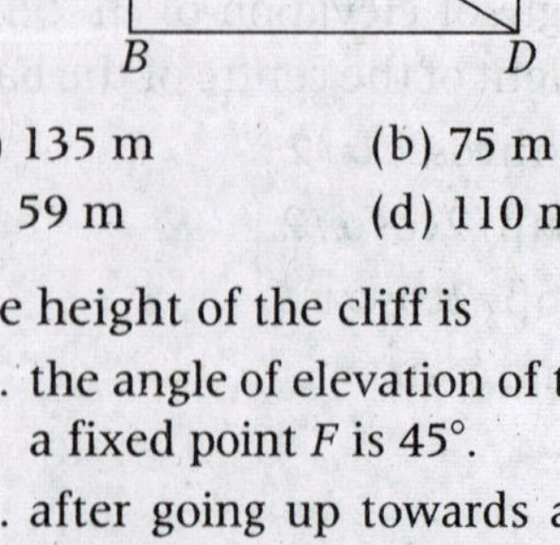

(a) 135 m (b) 75 m
(c) 59 m (d) 110 m

17. The height of the cliff is

I. the angle of elevation of the cliff from a fixed point F is 45°.

II. after going up towards a distance of 1000 m at an inclination of 30°, the angle of elevation is 60°.

(a) Only Statement I is required
(b) Only Statement II is required
(c) Both Statement I and II are required
(d) Neither of the statement is sufficient

18. Two stations due south of a leaning tower, which leans towards the north, are at distances a and b from its foot. If x and y are the angles of elevations of the top of the tower from these stations then its inclination θ to the horizontal is given by $\cot\theta$ is

(a) $\frac{b\cot x + a\cot y}{b-a}$ (b) $\frac{b\cot x - a\cot y}{b-a}$

(c) $\frac{a\cot x - b\cot y}{b+a}$ (d) None of these

19. A man is standing on a building of height h metre. The angle of elevation of the top and angle of depression of the bottom of another taller building from the first one is α and β, respectively, then match the following.

	List I	List II
A.	Distance between the height of smallest building and the bottom of the taller building is	i. $h\cot\beta$
B.	Difference of heights of the two buildings is	ii. $h(1+\tan\alpha\cot\beta)$
C.	Height of the taller building is	iii. $h/\sin\beta$
D.	Distance between the two buildings is	iv. $h\tan\alpha\cot\beta$

Codes

	A	B	C	D		A	B	C	D
(a)	iii	iv	ii	i	(b)	i	iii	ii	iv
(c)	ii	i	iii	iv	(d)	iv	ii	i	iii

Chapter 10

Circles

1 Mark Questions

1. In the given figure, the length of tangent will be

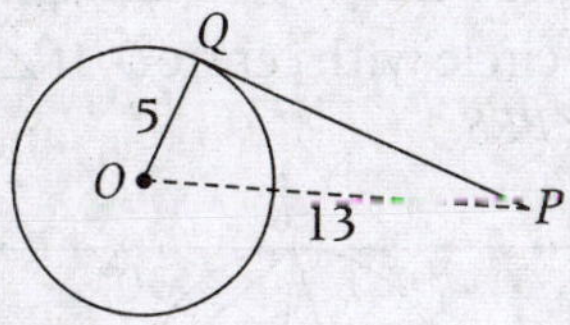

(a) 12 cm
(b) 18 cm
(c) 24 cm
(d) Can't be determined

2. In the below figure, the measure of $\angle a$ will be

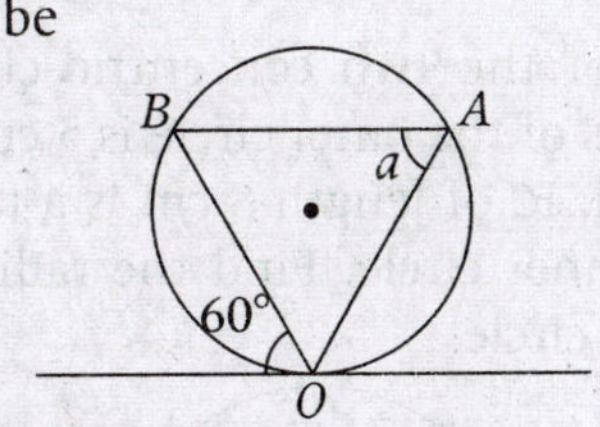

(a) 30°
(b) 90°
(c) 60°
(d) Can't be determined

3. In an equilateral triangular park *ABC*, a circular fountain is to be constructed such that circumference of fountain touches the mid-point of the sides of the park as shown in figure. Then, the diameter of the fountain will be

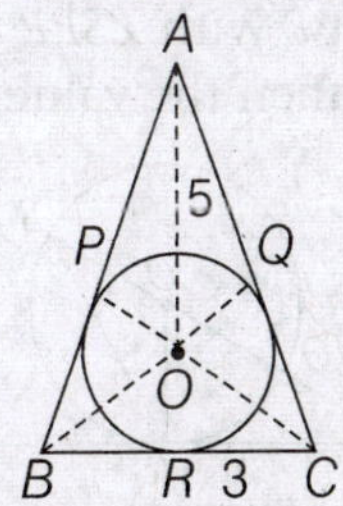

(a) 4 units
(b) 8 units
(c) 6 units
(d) Can't be determined

4. *P* and *Q* are the centres of two circles whose radii are 5 cm and 11 cm, respectively. If the direct common tangent to the circles meets *PQ* in *M*. Then, *M* divides *PQ* in the ratio

(a) 5 : 11 internally
(b) 11 : 5 internally
(c) 5 : 11 externally
(d) 11 : 5 externally

5. In the given figure, $ABCD$ is a cyclic quadrilateral, OB is the radius, PB is the tangent at point B and $\angle OBC = 30°$. Then, the value of x is

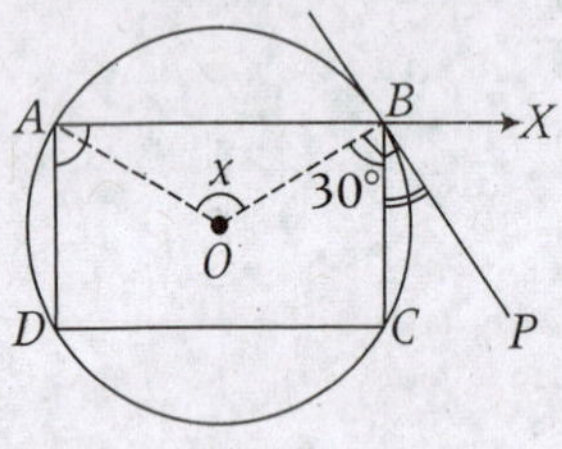

(a) 60° (b) 30°
(c) 120° (d) 90°

6. In the given figure, PT is a tangent of a circle, with centre O, at point R. If diameter SQ is produced, it meets with PT at point P with $\angle SPR = x$ and $\angle QSR = y$, then the value of $\angle x + 2\angle y$ is

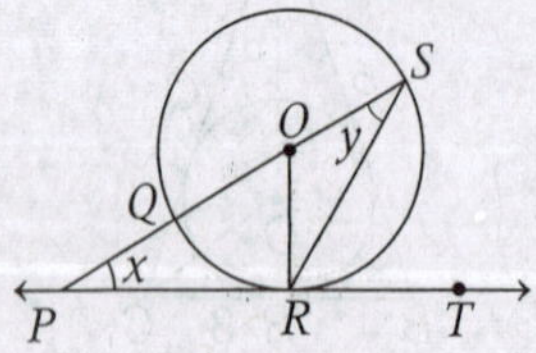

(a) 45° (b) 60°
(c) 90° (d) 150°

7. The radii of two concentric circles are 13 cm and 8 cm. AB is a diameter of the bigger circle. BD is a tangent to the smaller circle touching it at D. Find the length AD in figure.

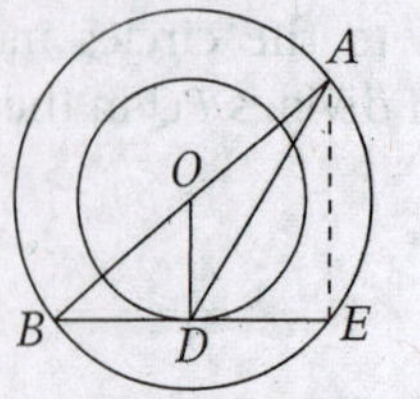

(a) 15 cm (b) 16 cm
(c) $\sqrt{361}$ cm (d) $\sqrt{289}$

8. In the given figure, O is the centre of the circle. PQ is a tangent to the circle at A. If $\angle PAB = 58°$, find $\angle ABQ$ and $\angle AQB$.

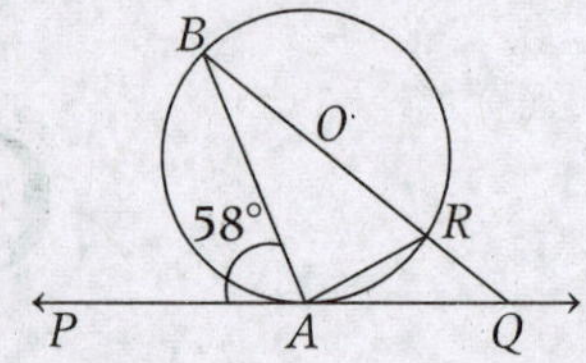

(a) 56°, 26°
(b) 32°, 26°
(c) 41, 29°
(d) 52, 28

9. In figure below, PQ is tangent at point R of the circle with centre O. If $\angle TRQ = 30°$, find $\angle PRS$.

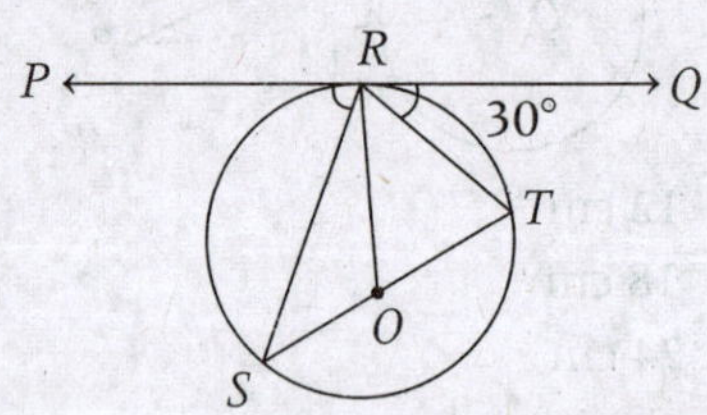

(a) 60° (b) 45°
(c) 75° (d) 90°

10. Out of the two concentric circles, the radius of the outer circle is 5 cm and the chord AC of length 8 cm is a tangent to the inner circle. Find the radius of the inner circle.

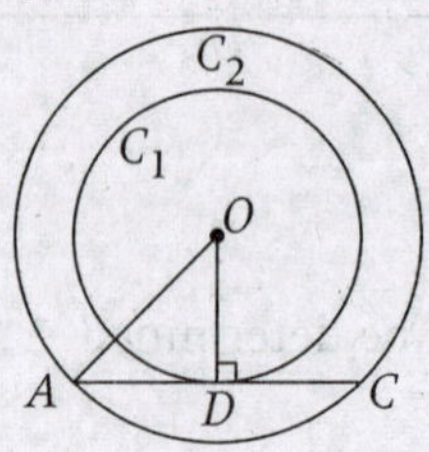

(a) 3 (b) 2.5
(c) 2 (d) 3.5

11. A circle of radius r is inscribed in a triangle of area 'Δ'. If the semi-perimeter of the triangle is s, then the correct relation is

(a) $2r = \frac{\Delta}{s}$ (b) $r = \frac{\Delta}{s}$

(c) $r = \frac{s}{\Delta}$ (d) $2s = \Delta r$

12. In the given figure, PQ is a chord of length 8 cm of a circle with centre O and radius 5 cm. If the tangents to the circle at the points P and Q intersect at T, then the length of PT is

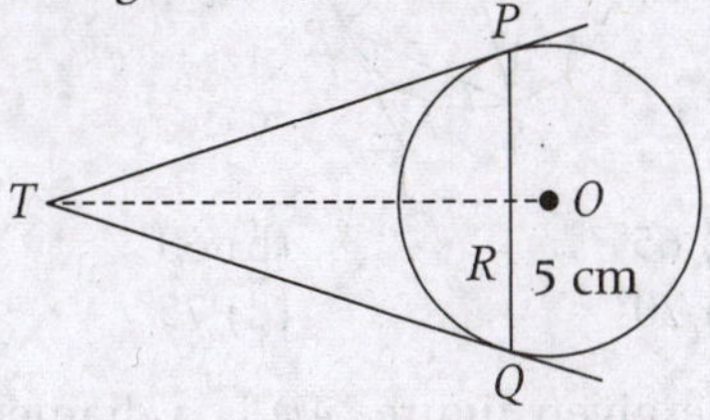

(a) 20 cm (b) $\frac{20}{3}$ cm

(c) 40 cm (d) $\frac{40}{3}$ cm

13. In an art class, Suneha sketched a design using geometrical shapes with the help of colours in the following way:

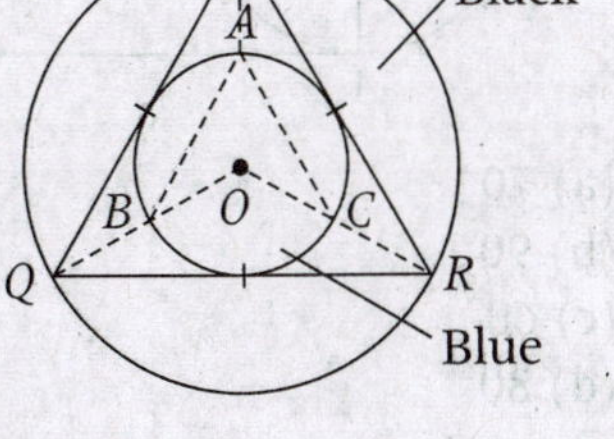

Here, circles in black and blue are the circumcircle and incircle (of the equilateral ΔPQR) respectively. Then, $\angle BAC$ is equal to

(a) 120° (b) 60°
(c) 30° (d) 90°

14. In the given figure, O is the centre of the circle with PA and PB as tangents. If measure of $\angle ADB = 60°$, then which of the following is true?

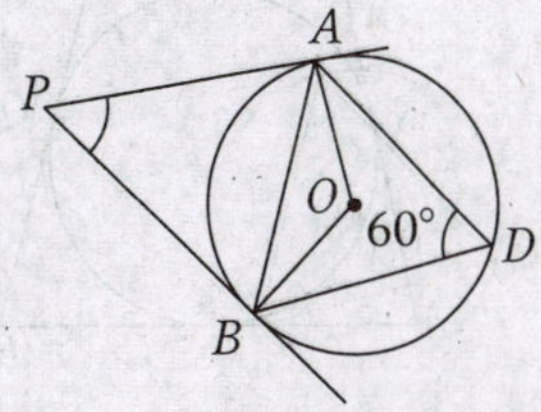

(a) ΔPAB is an isosceles triangle
(b) ΔPAB is an equilateral triangle
(c) ΔPAB is scalene triangle
(d) None of the above

15. In the given figure, two circles with centres A and B touch each other externally at k. The length of PQ is

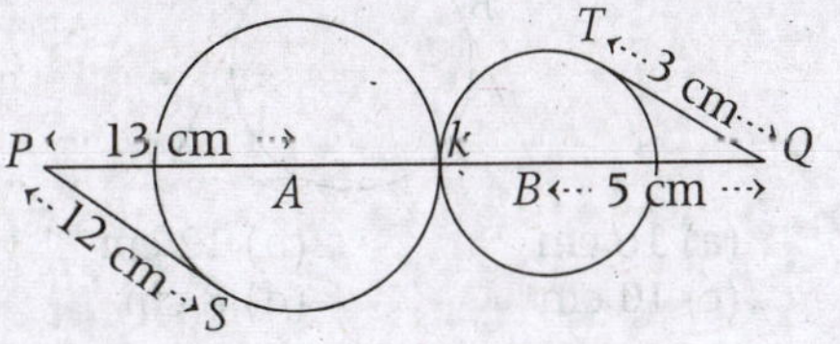

(a) 18 cm (b) 20 cm
(c) 27 cm (d) 24 cm

16. In the figure, ABC is a right triangle right-angled at B such that $BC = 6$ cm and $AB = 8$ cm. Find the radius of its in circle.

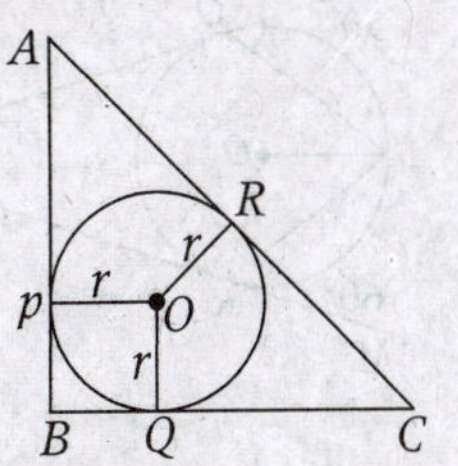

(a) 1 cm
(b) 2 cm
(c) 2.5 cm
(d) 1.5 cm

17. In the figure, a circle touches all the four sides of a quadrilateral $ABCD$ with $AB = 6$ cm $BC = 7$ cm, and $CD = 4$ cm. Find AD.

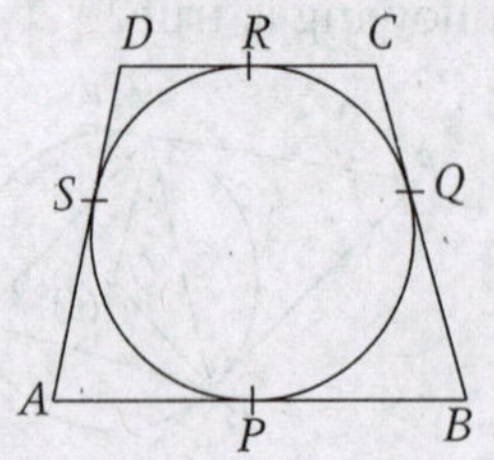

(a) 2.5 cm (b) 5 cm
(c) 4 cm (d) 3 cm

18. If AB, AC, PQ are the tangents in the figure, and $AB = 5$ cm, find the perimeter of ΔAPQ.

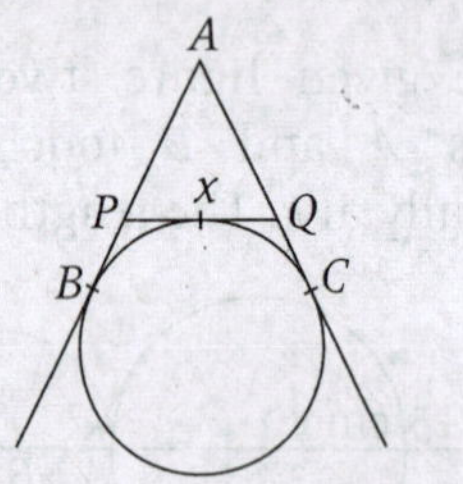

(a) 16 cm (b) 12 cm
(c) 10 cm (d) 8 cm

19. In figure PQL and PRM are tangents to the circle with centre O at the points Q and R respectively and S is a point on the circle such that $\angle SQL = 50°$ and $\angle SRM = 60°$. Then, calculate $\angle QSR$.

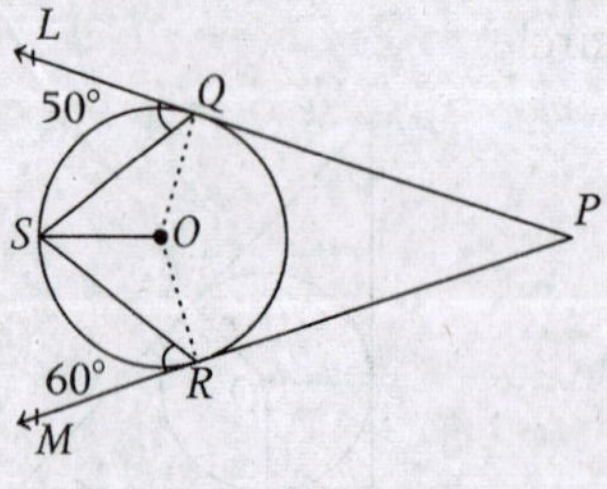

(a) 110° (b) 70°
(c) 45° (d) 80°

20. In given figure, O is centre of the circumcircle of ΔABC. Tangents at A and B intersect at D. Given, $\angle PQR = 70°$ and $\angle POS = 120°$. Calculate SPR.

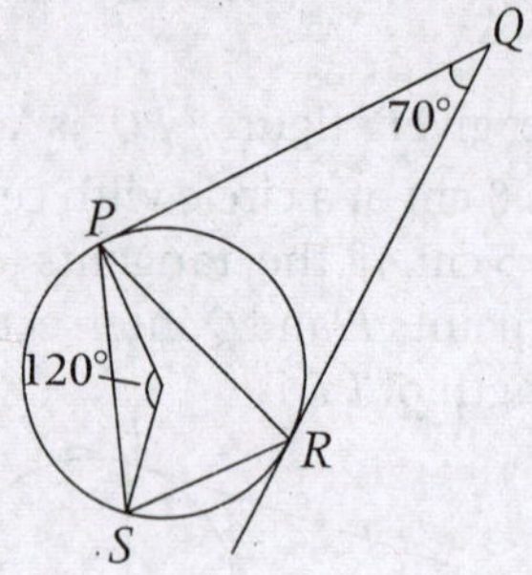

(a) 65° (b) 60°
(c) 70° (d) 75°

21. The given figure, AD is a diameter of a circle with centre O and AB is a tangent at A. C is a point on the circle such that DC produced intersects the tangent at B and $\angle ABD = 50°$. Find $\angle COA$.

(a) 70°
(b) 90°
(c) 60°
(d) 80°

2 Marks Questions

22. A is a point at a distance 13 cm from the centre O of a circle of radius 5 cm. AP and AQ are the tangents to the circle at P and Q. It a tangent BC is drawn at a point R lying on the minor arc PQ to intersect AP at B and AQ at C, find the perimeter of the ΔABC.

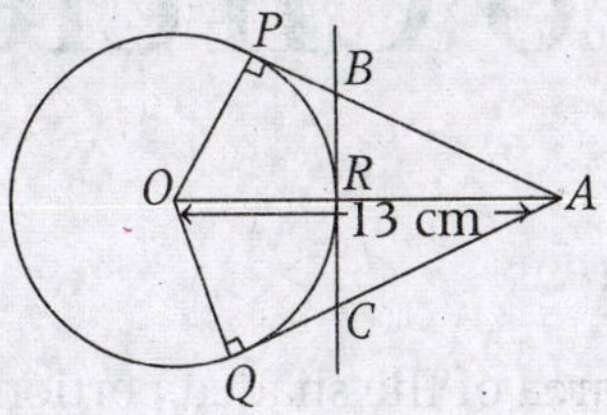

(a) 20 cm
(b) 24 cm
(c) 21 cm
(d) 18 cm

23. In the given figure, a circle with centre O is given. Diameter DE is produced to A and chord DC is produced to B, to form a ΔABD, right angled at B.

If $\angle EDC = \theta$, then match the following correctly.

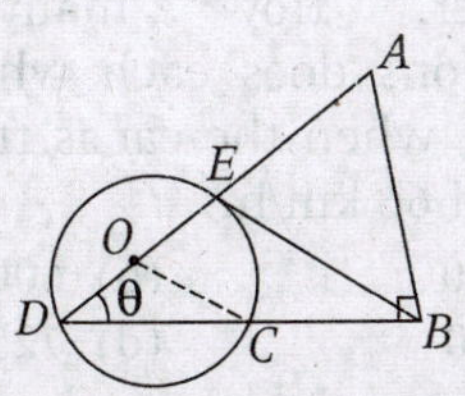

	List I		List II
A.	$\angle DAB$	i.	θ
B.	$\angle CEB$	ii.	$90° - \theta$
C.	$\angle DOC$	iii.	$2\angle DEC$

Codes

	A	B	C		A	B	C
(a)	ii	i	iii	(b)	i	ii	iii
(c)	iii	i	ii	(d)	ii	iii	i

24. In the given figure, two concentric circles with centre O such that AP is tangent to bigger circle and AB is tangent to smaller circle. If $\angle APB = \angle ABP = 30°$, $OA = 3$ cm and $OP = 5$ cm. Then, radius of the smaller circle is

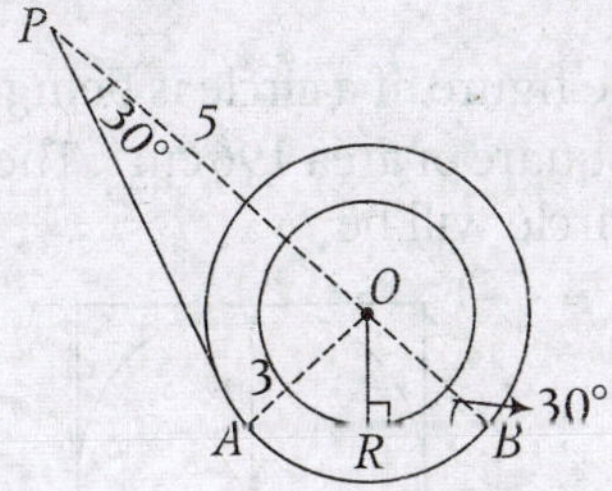

(a) 5 cm
(b) $\sqrt{5}$ cm
(c) 6 cm
(d) $\sqrt{6}$ cm

25. Consider the following statements

I. Two circles with centres A and B, radii 3 cm and 4 cm respectively intersect at two points C and D.

II. AC and BC are tangents to the two circles. Then, length of chord CD will be 4.8 cm.

Choose the correct option.

(a) Statement I alone is sufficient to answer.
(b) Statement II alone is sufficient to answer.
(c) Both statements are required to answer.
(d) Neither of the statement is sufficient.

Chapter

11

Areas Related to Circle

1 Mark Questions

1. In the figure, if a circle is being inscribed in a square of area 196 cm^2. Then, area of the circle will be

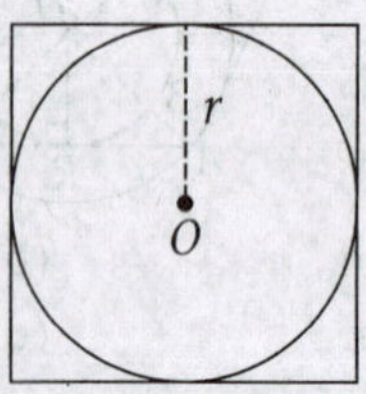

(a) 196 cm^2

(b) 144 cm^2

(c) 49 cm^2

(d) 154 cm^2

2. In the adjacent figure, a triangle is being inscribed in circle with one of its sides as the diameter and length of other side be 3 cm. If the area of the triangle is 6 cm^2, then area of the circle will be

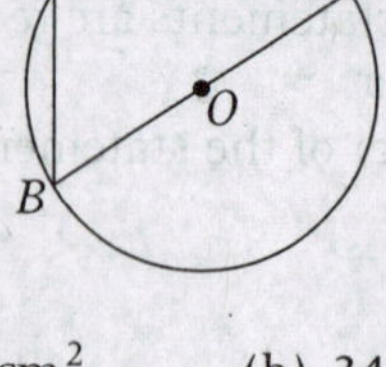

(a) $39\frac{2}{7} \text{ cm}^2$ (b) $34\frac{2}{7} \text{ cm}^2$

(c) $31\frac{4}{7} \text{ cm}^2$ (d) $19\frac{9}{14} \text{ cm}^2$

3. The area of the shaded portion, if radius of the larger circle is 6 cm and of the smaller circle 2 cm, is

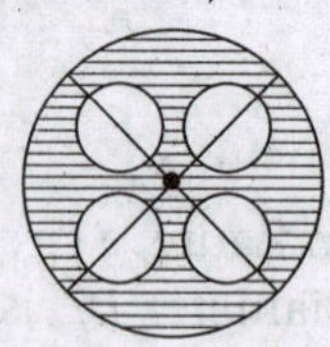

(a) 60.8 cm^2 (b) 61.8 cm^2

(c) 62.8 cm^2 (d) 63.8 cm^2

4. A car has wheels having 56 cm as diameter. How many complete revolutions does each wheel make in 10 min, when the car is travelling at a speed of 66 km/h?

(a) 6250 (b) 6000

(c) 6500 (d) 7250

5. Find the area of the shaded region in figure, where APD, AQB, BRC and CSD are semi-circles of diameter 14 cm , 3.5 cm, 7 cm and 3.5 cm respectively.

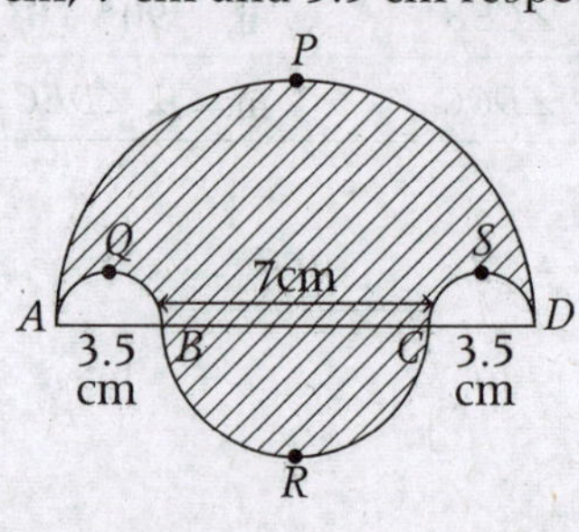

(a) 86.625 cm^2 (b) 79.762 cm^2
(c) 84.268 cm^2 (d) 68.765 cm^2

6. If a wire of length 44 cm is bent in the form of a circle and again bent in the form of a rectangle of length 12 cm, then area of the circle and the rectangle are in the ratio
(a) 7 : 6 (b) 77 : 60
(c) 70 : 60 (d) 70 : 66

7. In the figure given below $PQ = RS = 2QR = 2QX = 2RY$. In the middle, a circle with radius 2cm is drawn. In the rest figure all are the semicircular arcs. What is the perimeter of the whole figure?

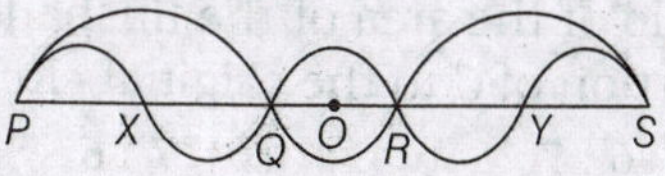

(a) 10π (b) 5π
(c) 20π (d) 40π

8. In figure, APB and AQO are semicircle, and $AO = OB$. If the perimeter of the figure is 40 cm, find the area of the shaded region.

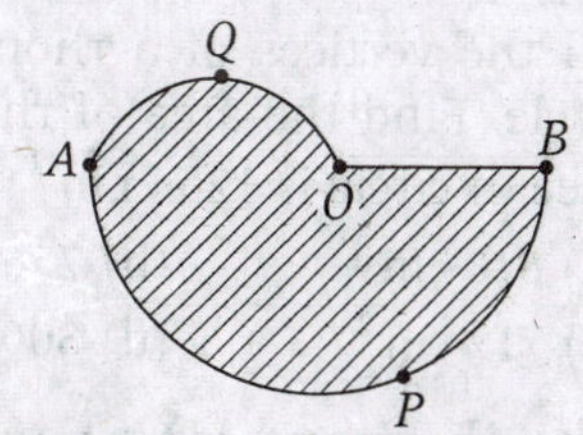

(a) 82.72 cm^2 (b) 93.54 cm^2
(c) 96.25 cm^2 (d) 112.36 cm^2

9. Area of sector of a circle with $\theta = 60°$ is equal to
(a) $\frac{1}{4}$ area of circle (b) $\frac{1}{6}$ area of circle
(c) $\frac{1}{8}$ area of circle (d) $\frac{1}{12}$ area of circle

10. The window shown in the shape of a semi-circle with radius 4 ft. The distance from S to T is 2 ft and the measure of AB is 45°. Area of glass in the region $ABCD$ is

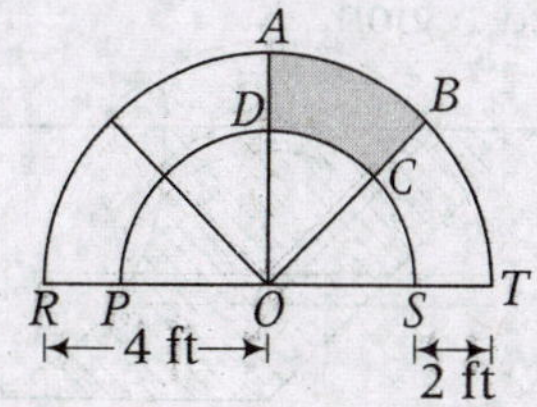

(a) 4.7 sq ft (b) 4.9 sq ft
(c) 4.5 sq ft (d) 5 sq ft

11. Two circles touch each other externally. The sum of their areas is 90π cm^2 and the distance between their centres 12 cm. Find the radii of the circles.
(a) $r_1 = 3$ cm, $r_2 = 6$ cm
(b) $r_1 = 6$ cm, $r_2 = 3$ cm
(c) $r_1 = 9$ cm, $r_2 = 3$ cm
(d) $r_1 = 3$ cm, $r_2 = 9$ cm

12. The diagram given alongside represents three circular garbage cans each of 2 m radius. The three cans are touching each other as shown. Find (in metres), the perimeter of the rope encompassing the three cans and hence the area of the circumscribing circle.

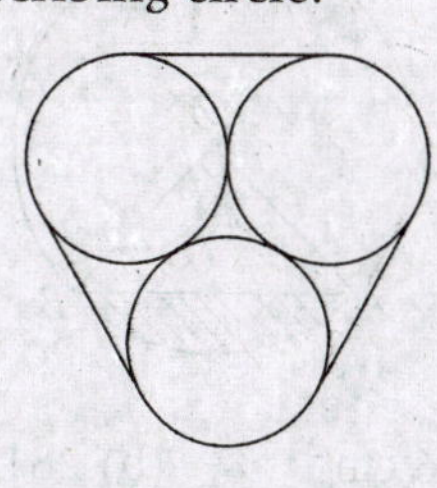

(a) 50.24 m^2, 24.56 cm
(b) 12.28 m, 12.56 m^2
(c) 24.56 m, 12.56 m^2
(d) 24.56 m, 24.56 m^2

13. In figure, $ABCD$ is a trapezium of area 24.5 sq cm. In it $AD \parallel BC$, $\angle DAB = 90°$, $AD = 10$ cm and $BC = 4$ cm. If ABE is a quadrant of a circle, find the area of the shaded region.

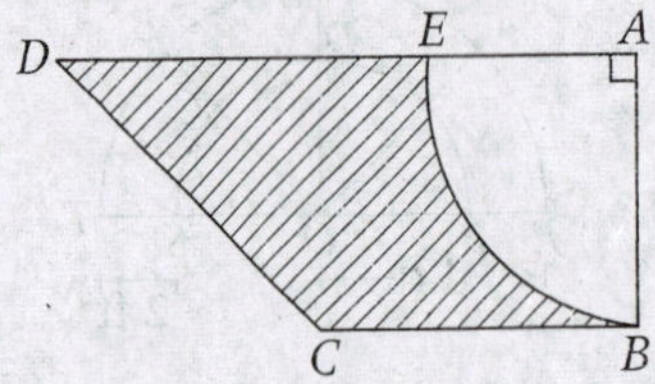

(a) 24.625 cm^2 (b) 19.75 cm^2
(c) 26.225 cm^2 (d) 14.875 cm^2

14. The long and short hand of a clock are 6 cm and 4 cm long respectively, find the sum of the distance travelled by their tips in 24 h.

(a) 954.56 cm (b) 982.62 cm
(c) 973.41 cm (d) 892.36 cm

15. In figure, AB is a chord of a circle, with centre O and radius 10 cm, that subtends a right angle at the centre of the circle. Find the area of the minor segment $AQBP$. Hence, find the area of major segment $ALBQA$.

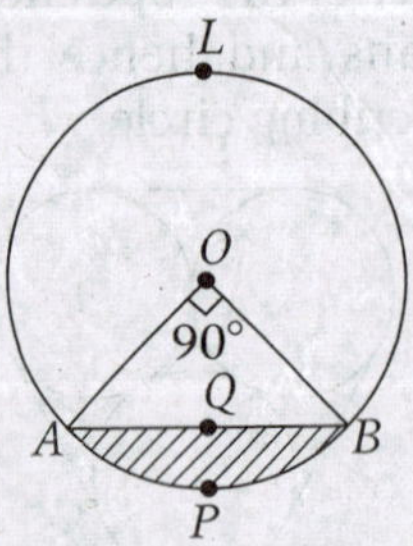

(a) 272.6 cm^2 (b) 281.2 cm^2
(c) 285.5 cm^2 (d) 277.6 cm^2

16. The radius of circle is so increased that, its circumference is increased by 10%. The area of the circle, then increased by

(a) 10.5% (b) 21%
(c) 10.25% (d) 5.25%

17. Four horses are tethered at 4 corners of a square field of side 70 m, with a rope of length 35 m so that they cannot reach one another. The area left ungrazed by the horses is

(a) 1050 m^2 (b) 3850 m^2
(c) 950 m^2 (d) 1075 m^2

18. Let C be *a* circle with centre O and PQ be the diameter of C. Suppose m_1 is the mid-point of the line segment OQ, m_2 is the mid-point of the line segment m_1Q and so on. Let $C_1, C_2, C_3, \ldots\ldots$ be the circles with diameters OM_1, M_1M_2, M_2M_3 .... respectively. Suppose the circles $C_1, C_2, C_3, \ldots$ are all shaded. The ratio of the area of the unshaded portion of C to the original circle C is

(a) 6 : 7 (b) 7 : 6
(c) 12 : 11 (d) 11 : 12

19. The hour hand of a clock is 6 cm long. Find the area (in cm^2) swept by it between 11 : 20 am and 11 : 55 am

(a) 2.75 (b) 5.5
(c) 11 (d) None of these

20. All the vertices of a rhombus lie on a circle. Find the area of rhombus, if the area of circle is 1256 cm^2

(a) 810 cm^2 (b) 756 cm^2
(c) 712 cm^2 (d) 800 cm^2

21. The short and long hands of a clock are 6 cm and 8 cm long, respectively. Find the sum of the distance traveled by their tips in 1 day.

$$\left[\text{Take } \pi = \frac{22}{7}\right]$$

(a) 1272.29 cm
(b) 1282.29 cm
(c) 1262.29 cm
(d) 1292.29 cm

22.

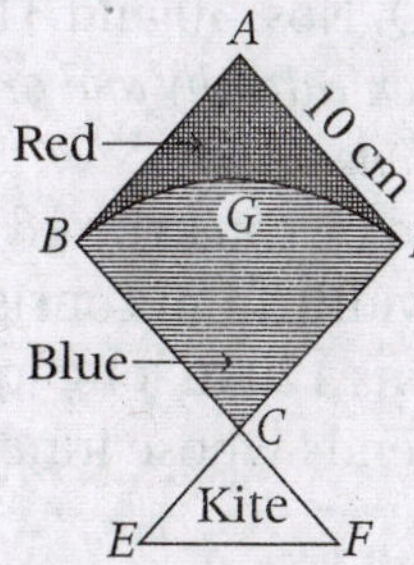

In the figure, if a kite has to be coloured with red and blue colours such that the region $ABGD$ is to be coloured red and $BGDC$ is to be coloured blue. Then, the ratio of the colour filled in the kite will be

(a) $\frac{43}{157}$

(b) $\frac{41}{157}$

(c) $\frac{43}{159}$

(d) None of the above

23. An equilateral triangle is incribed in a circle of circumference equal to perimeter of a square with side 11 cm. Find its sides.

(a) $7\sqrt{3}$ cm (b) $14\sqrt{3}$ cm

(c) 7 cm (d) 14 cm

24. The minute hand of a clock is 40 cm long. Find the area of the face of the clock described by the minute hand between 9 am and 19:35 am.

(a) 2933.3 cm^2 (b) 733.33 cm^2

(c) 183.3 cm^2 (d) 14.665 cm^2

25. If an arc substending an angle 105° at the centre of a circle A and another arc substending an angle of 45° at the centre of circle B, are of same length, then ratio of area of circle A to the area of circle B is

(a) 3 : 7 (b) 7 : 3

(c) 49 : 9 (d) 9 : 49

2 Marks Questions

26. If area of a sector of circle bounded by an arc of length 10π cm is equal to 40π cm^2, then its radius is

(a) 12 cm

(b) 16 cm

(c) 8 cm

(d) 24 cm

27. A chord of a circle of radius 15 cm substends an angle of 60° at the centre. Find the areas of the corresponding minor and major segments of the circle

[Take, $\pi = 3.14$ and $\sqrt{3} = 1.73$]

(a) 10.4375 cm^2, 696.0625 cm^2

(b) 10.4375 cm^2, 686.0625 cm^2

(c) 20.4375 cm^2, 696.0625 cm^2

(d) 20.4375 cm^2, 686.0625 cm^2

28. State 'T' for true and 'F' for false.

I. If the radius of a circle is $\frac{7}{\sqrt{\pi}}$ cm, then area of the circle is 49 cm^2.

II. If the ratio of the circumference of two circles is 3 : 5, then the ratio of their areas is 25 : 9.

III. If the area of a circle is A, radius r and circumference is C, then $\frac{C}{A} = \frac{r}{2}$.

IV. Perimeter of a square circumscribing a circle of radius $2a$ cm is $10a$ cm.

Codes

	I	II	III	IV
(a)	T	F	F	F
(b)	T	T	T	F
(c)	F	T	T	T
(d)	T	F	T	F

29. Match the following by choosing the correct area.

	List I		List II
A.	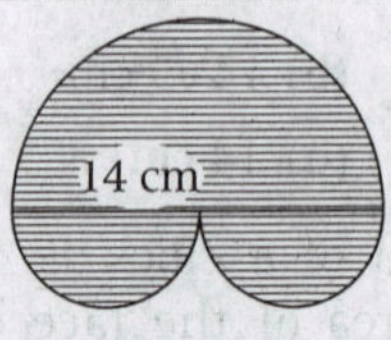	i.	500.5 cm^2
B.	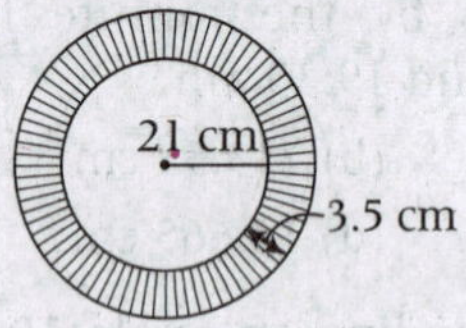	ii.	9.625 cm^2
C.	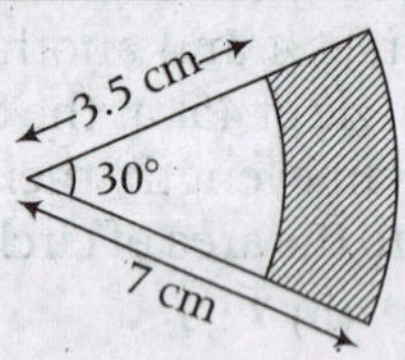	iii.	462 cm^2

Codes

	A	B	C
(a)	i	iii	ii
(b)	i	ii	iii
(c)	iii	ii	i
(d)	iii	i	ii

Directions (Q. Nos. 30 and 31) *Read the given information carefully and answer the following questions.*

If a pool has to be constructed with a boundary of width 14 m consisting of two straight sections 120 m long joining semi-circular ends whose inner radius is 35 m.

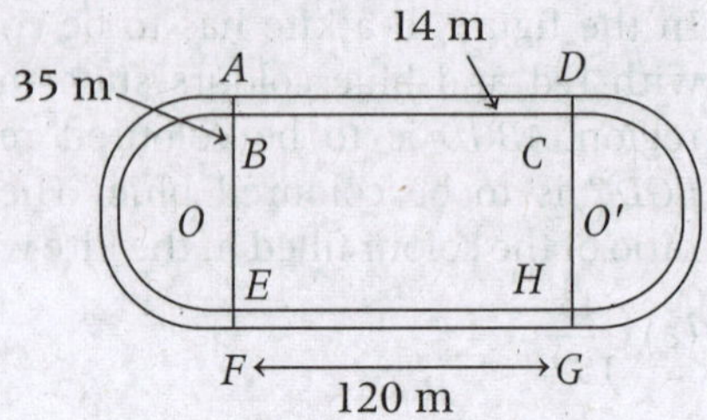

30. Then, the area of the boundary is

(a) 7056 m^2 (b) 7000 m^2

(c) 7500 m^2 (d) 7050 m^2

31. If the cost of flooring the boundary by tiles is ₹ 50 per sq m, then the cost incurred will be

(a) ₹ 352800 (b) ₹ 350000

(c) ₹ 375000 (d) ₹ 352500

Chapter 12

Surface Area and Volume

1 Mark Questions

1. Three cubes each of side 6 cm are joined end to end. The surface area of the resulting solid is
(a) 500 cm^2 (b) 504 cm^2
(c) 525 cm^2 (d) 550 cm^2

2. The diameter of a garden roller is 1.4 m, and 3 m long. How much area will it cover in 6 revolutions.
(a) 79.2 m^2 (b) 140 m^2
(c) 440 m^2 (d) 220 m^2

3. In metallic cylindrical pipe of length 14 cm 770 cc of metal is used and external radius 10 cm. Find the thickness of the pipe.
(a) 0.99 cm (b) 0.96 cm
(c) 0.92 cm (d) 0.95 cm

4. If the diameter of sphere is decreased by 25%, then by what percent the curved surface area will be decreased
(a) $\frac{139}{4}$% (b) $\frac{175}{4}$%
(c) 25% (d) 75%

5. What is the ratio of the volumes of a cube to that of a sphere which will exactly fit inside the cube?
(a) $2:\pi$ (b) $6:\pi$
(c) $4:\pi$ (d) $3:\pi$

6. A toy is the form of a cone mounted on a hemi-sphere of radius 3.5 cm. The total height of the toy is 15.5 cm. Find the total surface area. (use $\pi = \frac{22}{7}$)
(a) 214.5 cm^2 (b) 225.7 cm^2
(c) 220 cm^2 (d) 230 cm^2

7. Find the volume of greatest right circular cone, which can be cut from a cube of side 12 cm (in cm^3)
(a) 104 π (b) 144 π
(c) 134 π (d) 154 π

8. A solid is composed of a cylinder with hemi-spherical ends. If the whole length of the solid is 104 cm and the radius of each hemi-spherical end is 7 cm, then the cost of polishing its surface at the rate of ₹ 3 per dm^2 $\left[\text{take, } \pi = \frac{22}{7}\right]$ is
(a) ₹ 140.50 (b) ₹ 137.28
(c) ₹ 165.70 (d) ₹ 180

9. If a cone is cut into two parts by a horizontal plane passing through the mid-point of its axis, then the ratio of the volumes of the upper part and the cone is
(a) 1 : 2 (b) 1 : 4 (c) 1 : 6 (d) 1 : 8

10. A cubical block of side 7 cm is surmounted by a hemi-sphere such that its greatest diameter of the hemisphere exist. Find the surface area of the solid.

(a) 3390 cm^2 (b) 3340 cm^2

(c) 332.5 cm^2 (d) 3350 cm^2

11. How many spherical ball can be made out of a solid cube of lead whose edge is 44 cm, each ball being 2 cm in diameter?

(a) 23000 (b) 20300

(c) 20328 (d) 22000

12. A conical flask has 5 m of height has a curved surface area 94.2 m^2, then determine its volume.

(a) 100 m^3 (b) 108.67

(c) 113.67 (d) 104.67

13. A cone made of paper has height $3h$ and vertical angle 2α, it contains two other cones of height $2h$ and h and vertical angles 4α and 6α, respectively. Then, the ratio of the volumes of regions S and S_1 will be

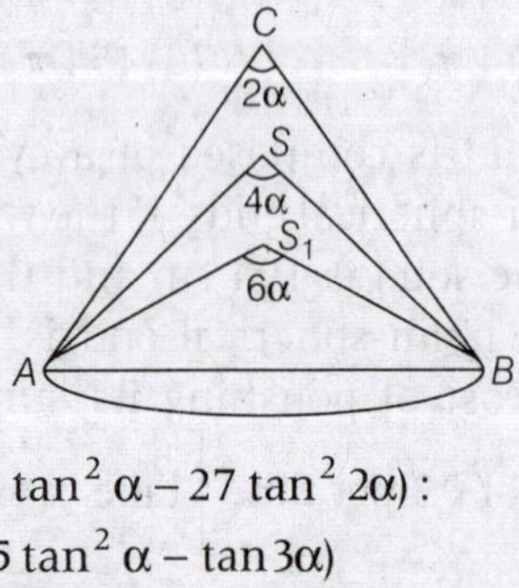

(a) $(8\tan^2\alpha - 27\tan^2 2\alpha)$: $(5\tan^2\alpha - \tan 3\alpha)$

(b) $(27\tan^2\alpha - 8\tan^2 2\alpha)$: $(8\tan^2 2\alpha - \tan^2 3\alpha)$

(c) $(25\tan^2\alpha - 7\tan^2 2\alpha)$: $(8\tan^2\alpha - \tan 3\alpha)$

(d) None of the above

14. A sphere of radius r units is immersed completely in water contained in a right circular cone of semi-vertical angle 30° and water is drained off from the cone till its surface touches the sphere. Then, the volume of water remaining in the cone will be

(a) $77\pi r^3$ (b) $\frac{5}{3}\pi r^3$ (c) $\frac{87}{3}\pi r^3$ (d) $\frac{67}{3}\pi r^3$

15. In a marriage ceremony of her daughter Yamini. Mukesh has to make arrangements for the accomoadation of 180 persons. For this purpose, he plans to build a conical tent in such a way that each person have 5 m^2 of the space on the ground and 30 m^3 of air to breadth. Find the height of the conical tent.

(a) 20 m (b) 13 m (c) 18 m (d) 22 m

16. Water is flowing at the rate of 10 km/h through a pipe of diameter 28 cm into a rectangular tank which is 80 m long and 65 m wide. Determine the time in which the level of the water in the tank will rise by 9 cm.

(a) 44 min (b) 45.6 min

(c) 48 min (d) 40 min

17. A conical vessel of radius 6 cm and height 8 cm is completely filled with water. A metal sphere is now lowered into the water. The size of the sphere is such that when it touches the inner surface, it just get immersed. The fraction of water that overflows from the conical vessel is

(a) $\frac{3}{8}$ (b) $\frac{5}{8}$ (c) $\frac{7}{8}$ (d) $\frac{5}{16}$

18. A rectangular strip 16 cm × 3.5 cm is rotated about the longer side. What is the volume and the whole surface area of the solid thus generated.

(a) 612 cm^3, 429 cm^2

(b) 618 cm^3, 418 cm^2

(c) 616 cm^3, 429 cm^2

(d) 624 cm^3, 420 cm^2

19. A cylindrical can whose base is horizontal and of internal radius 3.5 cm contains sufficient water so that when a solid sphere is placed in the can, water just covers the sphere. Given that the sphere just fits in the can, find the depth of water in the can before the sphere was put into it.

(a) 2.3 cm (b) 5.1 cm
(c) 1.5 cm (d) 3.2 cm

2 Marks Questions

20. For a wooden article was made by scooping out a hemisphere from each end of a solid cylinder, as shown in Fig. If the height of the cylinder is 10 cm, and its base is of radius 3.5 cm, match the column.

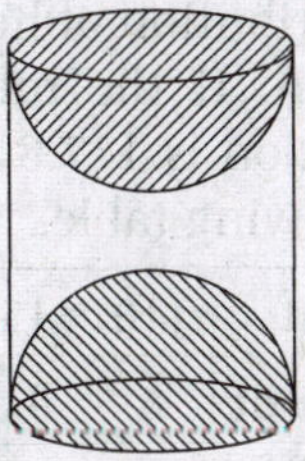

Match the following.

	List-I		List-II
A.	Volume of cylinder	i.	$\frac{196}{3}\pi$
B.	Total surface area	ii.	$122.5\ \pi$
C.	Volume of scoops	iii.	374
D.	Volume of the article	iv.	$171.5/3\ \pi$

Choose the correct option.

	A	B	C	D		A	B	C	D
(a)	iv	ii	i	iii	(b)	ii	iii	iv	i
(c)	iv	iii	i	ii	(d)	iii	iv	ii	i

21. A wall of diameter of 20 m is dug 10.5 m deep. The earth taken out of it is spread evenly all around to a width of 6 m to the form an embankment. Find the height of the embankment.

(a) 6.90 m (b) 6.73 m
(c) 7.80 m (d) None of these

22. Water is a conical, 8 m wide and 1.2 m deep, is flowing with a speed of 20 km/h. How much area will it irrigate in 45 min, if 10 cm standing water is needed?

(a) 140 hec (b) 144 hec
(c) 135 hec (d) 120 hec

23. From a solid cylinder whose height is 2.4 cm and diameter 1.4 cm, a conical cavity of the same height and same diameter is hollowed out. The total surface area of the remaining solid to the nearest cm^2 is

(a) 20 cm^2 (b) 19 cm^2
(c) 21 cm^2 (d) 18 cm^2

24. A solid consisting of a right circular cone of height 120 cm and radius 60 cm standing on a hemisphere of radius 60 cm in placed upright in a right circular cylinder full of water such that it touches the bottom. Find the volume of water left in the cylinder, if the radius of the cylinder is 60 cm and its height is 180 cm.

(a) 1.15 m^3 (b) 1.131 m^3
(c) 2.30 m^3 (d) 1.6 m^3

25. A right triangle whose sides are 3 cm and 4 cm (other than hypotenuse) is made to revolve about its hypotenuse. Find surface area of the double cone so formed.

(a) 56 cm^2 (b) 54 cm^2
(c) 52.8 cm^2 (d) 59 cm

Chapter 13

Statistics

1 Mark Questions

1. If the mean of terms 6, $6+2x$, 5 and $8+3x$ is 20. Then, x will be

(a) 11 (b) 33 (c) 22 (d) 55

2. The mean marks of 100 students were found to be 40. Later on, it was discovered that a score of 53 was misread as 83. Then, the correct mean will be

(a) 37.5 (b) 35.6 (c) 39.7 (d) 38.7

3. Find the mean of the following distribution.

x	10	30	50	70	89
f	7	8	10	15	10

(a) 50 (b) 55 (c) 58 (d) 60

4. The mean of a set of 20 observations is 19.3. The mean is reduced by 0.5 when a new observation is added to the set. The new observation is

(a) 19.8 (b) 9.8
(c) 9.2 (d) 8.8

5. If the sum of the deviations of a set of values $x_1, x_2, x_3, \ldots, x_n$ measured from 50 is (−10) and the sum of deviations of the values from 46 is 70. Then, the mean is

(a) 49 (b) 49.5
(c) 49.75 (d) 50

6. The distribution of height of 50 children are given. If the mean height for the distribution is 117.8 cm, then complete the following table.

Height	110	115	x_1	120	121	125
Number of students	6	8	14	f_1	4	3

(a) $x_1 = 118$, $f_1 = 15$ (b) $x_1 = 121$, $f_1 = 15$
(c) $x_1 = 118$, $f_1 = 8$ (d) None of these

7. The mean of three positive numbers is 10 more than the smallest of the numbers and 15 less than the largest of the three. If the median of the three number is 5, then the mean of squares of the numbers is?

(a) $108\frac{2}{3}$ (b) $216\frac{2}{3}$ (c) $208\frac{1}{3}$ (d) $116\frac{2}{3}$

8. The median of the observations 34, 32, 38, 48, 24, 30, 27, 21 and 35 is

(a) 31 (b) 32 (c) 27 (d) 38

9. The median of the variables $x+4$, $x-\frac{7}{2}$, $x-\frac{5}{2}$, $x-3$, $x-2$, $x+\frac{1}{2}$, $x-\frac{1}{2}$ and $x+5$, where $x>0$, is

(a) $x-3$ (b) $x-2$ (c) $x+\frac{5}{4}$ (d) $x-\frac{5}{4}$

10. The mean and median of the numbers 1, 2, 3, 4, y, 8, 9, 10, 12 and x written in increasing order are both 10, then the values of x and y are

(a) $x=15, y=36$ (b) $x=39, y=12$
(c) $x=15, y=36$ (d) $x=39, y=15$

11. If the median of the following frequency distribution is 40 and total frequency is 60, then find the missing frequencies.

Marks	0-10	10-30	30-60	60-80	80-90
Number of students	5	f_1	30	f_2	2

(a) $f_1=16, f_2=9$ (b) $f_1=15, f_2=8$
(c) $f_1=8, f_2=15$ (d) $f_1=18, f_2=7$

12. A survey regarding the heights (in cm) of 51 girls of class *X* of a school was conducted and the following data were obtained :

Height (in cm)	Number of girls
Less than 140	4
Less than 145	11
Less than 150	29
Less than 155	40
Less than 160	46
Less than 165	51

Find the median height

(a) 147.02 (b) 142.36
(c) 153.24 (d) 149.03

13. Consider the following table.

Fruits	Orange	Mango	Banana	Apple
Quantity (in kg)	4	7	9	3

A man bought fruits in the above quantity. The fruit which corresponds to the mode of the given data is

(a) Apple (b) Banana
(c) Mango (d) Orange

14. If the median and mean of a given data are 12 and 8 respectively, then the mode is

(a) 24 (b) 20 (c) 0 (d) 10

15. Age distribution of cases of a certain disease admitted during a year in a particular hospital.

Age (in yr)	Number of cases
5-14	6
15-24	11
25-34	21
35-44	23
45-54	14
55-64	5

The mode age of this distribution, is

(a) 36.31 (b) 36 (c) 37 (d) 37.31

16. The following is the distribution of height of students of a certain class in certain city name Kota?

Height (in cm)	150-152	153-155	156-158	159-161	162-164
Number of Students	15	118	142	127	18

Find the average height (in approx) of maximum number of students.

(a) 168.35 (b) 157.35
(c) 170.38 (d) None of these

Directions (Q. Nos. 17 and 18) *The following graph is a histogram representing the weight of 100 children.*

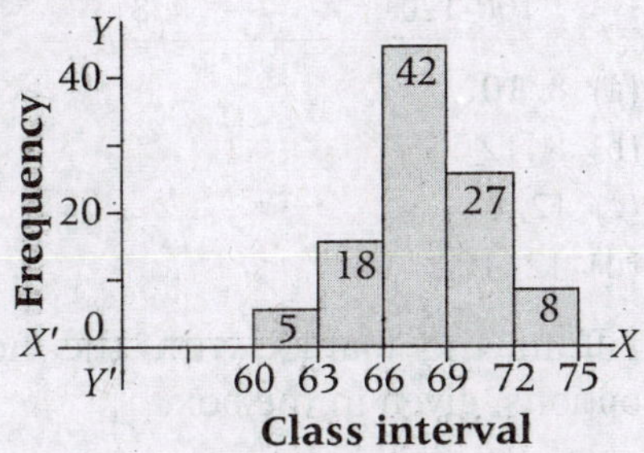

17. The median of the above data is

(a) 65.93 (b) 66.93
(c) 67.93 (d) 68.93

18. The mode class of the above data is

(a) 60-63 (b) 93-66
(c) 66-69 (d) 69-72

Directions (Q. Nos. 19-20) *Read the given information carefully and answer the following questions.*

In a project given in a school, Jessica has been asked to prepare a detail of the activities performed by her in a day. After analysing the hours spend by her in each activity like eating, sleeping, studying, etc., she prepared a pie chart to depict it. After depicting it in the form of pie chart, Jessica started making a bar graph with the help of this to make the project report more clear.

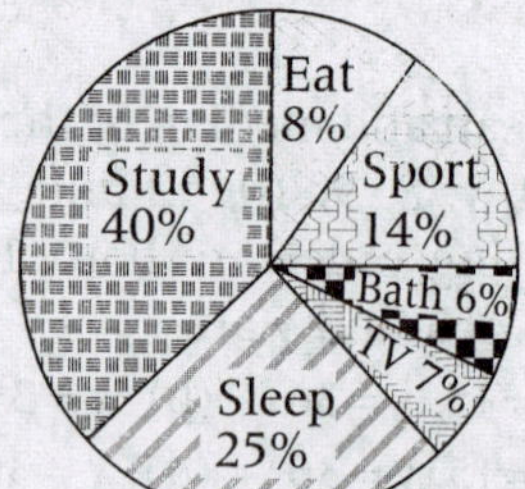

19. What is the average time spent by Jessica in sleeping and playing?

(a) 4.68 h (b) 5.68 h
(c) 4.69 h (d) 5.69 h

20. Which activity is acting as a mode in the information?

(a) Studying
(b) Sleeping
(c) Sports
(d) Eating

2 Marks Questions

21. If the mean of the following frequency distribution is 62.8 and the sum of all the frequencies is 50, then find the values of p and q, when $a = 70$, are respectively

Class Interval	Frequency
0-20	5
20-40	p
40-60	10
60-80	q
80-100	7
100-120	8

(a) 8, 10
(b) 8, 12
(c) 12, 8
(d) 12, 10

22. Fill in the blanks with the help of options, given in the box.

(i) $\frac{2x+2}{2}$, (ii) 10.5, (iii) $a\bar{x}$, (iv) 29,
(v) 11.5, (vi) 27, (vii) $\frac{a}{n}\bar{x}$,
(viii) $\frac{x+1}{2}$, (ix) $\frac{\Sigma f_i x_i}{\Sigma f_i}$, (x) $\frac{\Sigma f_i u_i}{\Sigma f_i}$

I. The arithmetic mean of 1, 2, 3,..., x is ________.

II. The mean of first 6 multiples of 3 is ____.

III. If mean of n observations is $\bar{x}$ and each value is multiplied by a, then the new mean will be ____.

IV. If $\mu_i = \frac{x_i - 25}{10}$, $\Sigma f_i u_i = 20$ and $\Sigma f_i = 100$. Then, $\bar{x}$ is ____.

Codes

	I	II	III	IV		I	II	III	IV
(a)	i	v	iii	iv	(b)	viii	ii	iii	vi
(c)	viii	v	vii	vi	(d)	i	ii	vii	vi

Chapter

14

Probability

1 Mark Questions

1. If a die is tossed once, then the probability of getting an even number is

(a) $\frac{1}{6}$ (b) $\frac{1}{3}$

(c) $\frac{1}{2}$ (d) $\frac{1}{4}$

2. If the probability of Manish winning a tennis match is 0.7, then the probability of his lossing the match is

(a) 0.4 (b) 0

(c) 0.2 (d) 0.3

3.

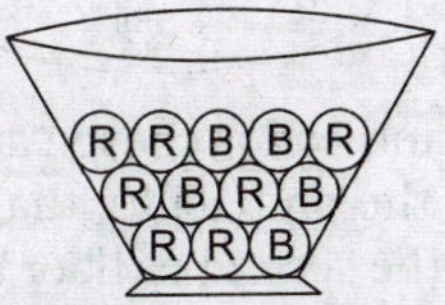

In the above figure, the probability of not getting a red ball from the bucket is

(a) $\frac{7}{12}$ (b) $\frac{5}{12}$

(c) 1 (d) 0

4. The probability that in a family of 3 children, there will be atleast one boy, is

(a) $\frac{1}{2}$ (b) $\frac{1}{8}$

(c) $\frac{7}{8}$ (d) $\frac{3}{4}$

5. If a bag contains 40 marbles, where the probability of drawing a green marble is $\frac{3}{5}$. Then, the number of green marbles in the bag is

(a) 12 (b) 24

(c) 36 (d) 6

6. A card is randomly drawn from a deck of 52 cards. The probability that this card bears an even number in black is

(a) 5/26 (b) 5/13

(c) 3/13 (d) 3/26

7. There are 45 tickets numbered as 1, 2, 3,..., 45 respectively. One ticket is drawn at random. If the ticket with a number as the multiple of 3 and 5 cost ₹ 50 and other tickets are for free, then the probability that a person buying the ticket needs to pay ₹ 50 is

(a) $\frac{1}{5}$ (b) $\frac{2}{15}$ (c) $\frac{1}{15}$ (d) $\frac{4}{15}$

8. If a letter is drawn at random from the letters in the word 'PRORATA', then the letters which have equal probability of being drawn are

(a) A and R (b) P, O and T

(c) R, O and A (d) Both (a) and (b)

9. If an year has 365 days, then the probability of having 53 Sundays in a leap year is

(a) $\frac{1}{7}$ (b) $\frac{2}{7}$

(c) $\frac{2}{365}$ (d) $\frac{1}{365}$

10. A bag contains 12 balls out of which x are black. If 6 more black balls are put in the bag, the probability of drawing a black ball will be doubled as that of earlier. Then, x is equal to

(a) 6 (b) 3

(c) 2 (d) None of these

11. A number x is selected from the numbers 1,2,4 and then a second number y is selected from the numbers 1, 4, 10. What is the probability that the product xy of the two selected numbers is less than 10?

(a) $\frac{4}{9}$ (b) $\frac{5}{9}$

(c) $\frac{7}{9}$ (d) 1

12.

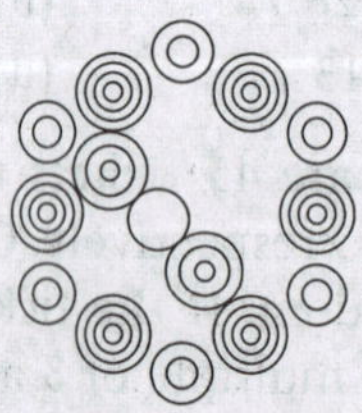

In the above figure, if Jamie made this design using fifteen discs. Then, the probability of designs having a combination of four concentric circles or two concentric circles is

(a) $\frac{2}{5}$ (b) $\frac{3}{5}$ (c) $\frac{4}{5}$ (d) 1

13. A game consists of tossing a one rupee coin 3 times and noting its outcome each time. Aryan wins if all the tosses give the same result i.e. three heads or three tails and loses otherwise. Then, the probability that Aryan will lose the game.

(a) 3/4 (b) 1/2

(c) 1 (d) 1/4

14. Tarun and bani are friends. What is the probability that both will have the same birthday?

(a) $\frac{2}{365}$ (b) $\frac{1}{5}$

(c) $\frac{1}{2}$ (d) $\frac{1}{365}$

15. The pictures show the packs of three sets of objects.

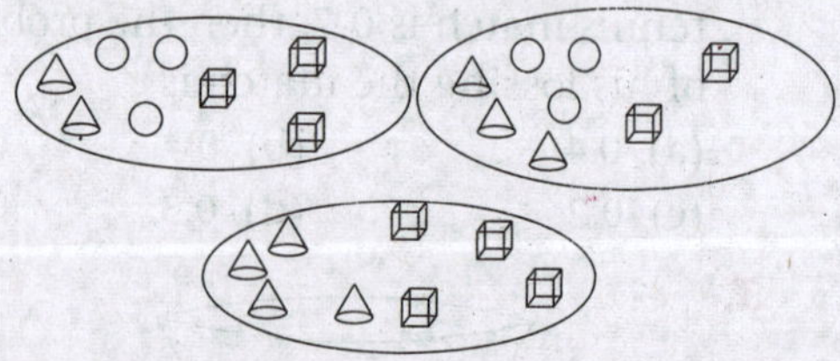

If a die and ball is chosen at random, then what is the probability that either the die is from the second pack or the ball is from the first pack?

(a) $\frac{2}{24}$ (b) $\frac{3}{24}$

(c) $\frac{4}{24}$ (d) $\frac{5}{8}$

2 Marks Questions

16. Fill in the blanks with the help of options, given in the box.

(i) 1 (ii) $\frac{1}{5}$ (iii) $\frac{2}{5}$ (iv) 5 (v) $\frac{1}{2}$
(vi) $\frac{\text{Total number of possible outcomes}}{\text{Number of favourable outcomes}}$
(vii) $\frac{\text{Number of favourable outcomes}}{\text{Total number of possible outcomes}}$
(viii) 0 (ix) $\frac{1}{4}$ (x) $\frac{1}{6}$

I. Probability of an event E, i.e. $P(E) =$ ___ .
II. The probability of an impossible event is ___ .
III. $P(E) + P(\bar{E}) =$ ___ .
IV. Probability of getting an E by selecting a vowel at random from set of vowels is ___ .
V. Probability of getting a red card from the well shuffled deck of 52 cards is ___ .
VI. Two dice are thrown simultaneously. The probability of getting a doublet is ___ .

Codes

	I	II	III	IV	V	VI
(a)	vi	ii	iv	ii,	iii	viii
(b)	vii	viii	i	ii	v	x
(c)	vii	i	iv	viii	v	ii
(d)	vi	ii	iv	viii	iii	v

17. State 'T' for true and 'F' for false.

I. In a throw of a die, the probability of getting a prime number is $\frac{1}{2}$.
II. When two dice are thrown, the probability of getting not equal number on both dice is $\frac{1}{36}$.
III. The probability of getting a face card from a deck of 52 cards is $\frac{3}{13}$.
IV. The probability of getting two heads in tossing two coins simultaneously is $\frac{1}{4}$.

Codes

	I	II	III	IV
(a)	T	F	T	T
(b)	T	T	F	T
(c)	F	T	T	T
(d)	T	F	F	T

18. Match the following.

List I	List II
A. A die is thrown once, the probability of getting a number 3, 4 or 5 is	i. $\frac{1}{2}$
B. A die is thrown once, the probability of getting a number divisible by 3 and 5	ii. 0
C. When two dice are thrown together, the probability of getting a number always greater than 4 on the second die	iii. $\frac{1}{3}$

Codes

	A	B	C
(a)	i	ii	iii
(b)	iii	i	ii
(c)	i	iii	ii
(d)	ii	iii	i

19. From a pack of 52 cards, a black jack, a red queen and two black kings fell down. A card was drawn from the remaining pack at random.

On the basis of above information, which statement/es is/are correct?

I. The probability that the card drawn is a black card, is $\frac{23}{48}$
II. The probability of getting a king or a red queen will be $\frac{1}{24}$

(a) Only statement I
(b) Only statement II
(c) Both statement I and statement
(d) Neither statement II nor statement II.

PRACTICE SET 01

1 Mark Questions

1. Four positive integers sum to 125. If the first of these numbers is increased by 4, the second is decreased by 4, the third is multiplied by 4 and the fourth is divided by 4 we find four equal numbers, then four original integers are

(a) 16, 24, 5, 40 (b) 8, 12, 5, 40
(c) 12, 20, 5, 72 (d) 16, 24, 5, 80

2. ₹ 3000 were divided among 100 children. If each girl gets ₹ 50 and each boy gets ₹ 25, then the number of boys is

(a) 20 (b) 40
(c) 60 (d) 80

3. If LCM of two numbers is 48, then which of the following cannot be their HCF?

(a) 9 (b) 8 (c) 6 (d) 3

4. The value of

$$\frac{x+\sqrt{x^2-y^2}}{x-\sqrt{x^2-y^2}}+\frac{x-\sqrt{x^2-y^2}}{x+\sqrt{x^2-y^2}} \text{ is}$$

(a) $\frac{x^2}{y^2}$ (b) y^2/x^2

(c) $\frac{x}{y}$ (d) $\frac{2(2x^2-y^2)}{y^2}$

5. The value of $\sqrt{\frac{4+2\sqrt{3}}{7+4\sqrt{3}}}$ is

(a) $\sqrt{1-\sqrt{3}}$

(b) $\sqrt{1+\sqrt{3}}$

(c) $\sqrt{2+\sqrt{3}}$

(d) None of the above

6. If $x^2-3x+1=0$, then the value of $\left(x^2+\frac{1}{x^2}\right)$ is

(a) 7 (b) −7
(c) 3 (d) −3

7. If r and s are zeroes of the polynomial t^2-4t+3, then $\frac{1}{r}+\frac{1}{s}-2rs+\frac{14}{3}$ is equal to

(a) 0 (b) 1
(c) 2 (d) −1

8. Lara baked 30 oatmeal cookies and 42 chocolate chip cookies to package in plastic containers for her teacher friends at school. She wants to divide the cookies into identical containers, so that each container has the same number of each kind of cookie. If she wants each container to have the greatest number of cookies possible, how many plastic containers does she needs?

(a) 12 (b) 7
(c) 5 (d) 13

9. If α and β are the zeroes of the polynomial $3x^2-11x+6$, then the value of $\frac{\alpha}{\beta}+\frac{\beta}{\alpha}+2\left(\frac{1}{\alpha}+\frac{1}{\beta}\right)+3\alpha\beta$ is

(a) 18/259

(b) $\frac{259}{9}$

(c) $\frac{259}{18}$

(d) $\frac{9}{259}$

10. In the given figure, find the values of a, b and c.

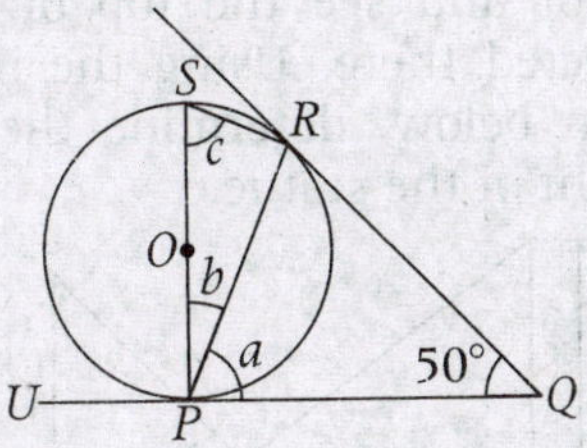

(a) 40°, 25°, 65° (b) 25°, 65°, 25°
(c) 25°, 65°, 65° (d) 65°, 25°, 65°

11. For the given cyclic quadrilateral $ABCD$, find the value of $\angle BCE$.

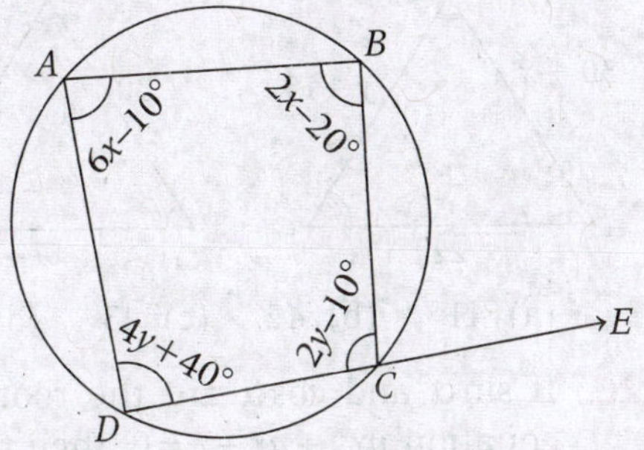

(a) 40° (b) 140°
(c) 70° (d) 110°

12. If the equation $(p^2+r^2)x^2-2r(p+q)x+r^2+q^2=0$ has equal roots, then

(a) $2r=p+q$ (b) $r^2=pq$
(c) $r=\frac{2pq}{p+q}$ (d) $r=pq$

13. The point which is equidistant from the points (0, 0) (0, 4) and (2, 3) is

(a) $\left(\frac{1}{4},2\right)$
(b) (2, 1/4)
(c) (2, 1/2)
(d) (1/2, 2)

14. Due to increase in price of a commodity by ₹ 45. Mr. Rakesh could now buy 15 kg less for ₹ 300, then find the new quantity of the commodity bought.

(a) 5 kg (b) 10 kg
(c) 15 kg (d) 20 kg

15. The sum of a two-digit number and the number formed by interchanging its digits, is 132. If 15 is subtracted from the first number, then the new number is 6 more than 3 times the sum of the digits of the first number. Then, the original number is

(a) 75 (b) 57
(c) 63 (d) 59

16. The solution of the given system of equations is

$$3(ax-by)+(a+6b)=0$$
$$3(bx+ay)+(b-6a)=0$$

(a) $x=2, y=\frac{1}{3}$ (b) $x=-2, y=\frac{-1}{3}$
(c) $x=\frac{-1}{3}, y=2$ (d) $x=\frac{-1}{3}, y=-2$

17. Mrs Evan has 120 crayons and 30 pieces of paper to give her students. What is the maximum number of the students she can have in her class, so that each student gets equal number of crayons and equal number of papers?

(a) 30 (b) 40
(c) 35 (d) 45

18. The expression equivalent to $\sqrt{\frac{1+\sin\theta}{1-\sin\theta}}$

(a) $\tan\theta+\operatorname{cosec}\theta$
(b) $\tan\theta+\sec\theta$
(c) $\cot\theta+\operatorname{cosec}\theta$
(d) $\cot\theta+\sec\theta$

19. If α and β are the zeroes of the polynomial $f(x) = x^2 - p(2x+4) - 4c$, then $\frac{(\alpha+2)(\beta+2)}{4}$ is

(a) $1+c$ (b) $\frac{1}{c}$

(c) $1-c$ (d) c

20. The line segment joining the points (a, b) and (c, d) subtends an angle θ at the origin such that $ac + bd = 0$, then measure of angle θ is

(a) 60° (b) 30°

(c) 45° (d) 90°

21. If two circles are such that the centre of one lies on the circumference of the other having equal radius, then the ratio of the common chord of the two circles to the diameter of one of the circles is

(a) 2:1 (b) $\sqrt{3}:2$

(c) $\sqrt{5}:2$ (d) $2\sqrt{3}:1$

22. Tyres from two different automobiles are shown below:

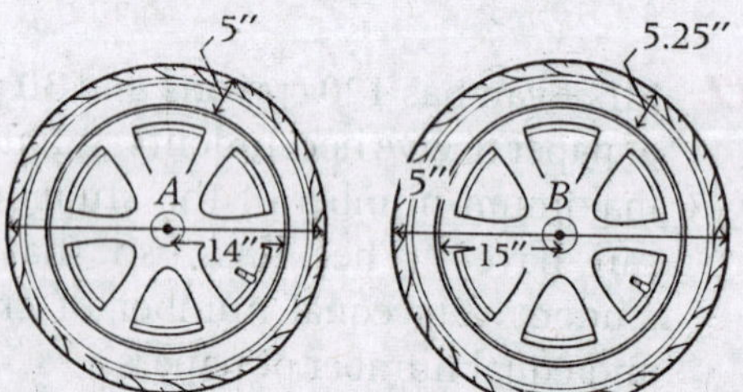

How many revolutions does each tyre makes while travelling 200 ft? (Take $\pi = 22/7$)

(a) $A = 32, B = 30$ (b) $A = 42, B = 30$

(c) $A = 32, B = 40$ (d) $A = 42, B = 40$

23. A single letter is selected at random from the word 'CHAMPION'. The probability that it is a vowel, is

(a) 1/4 (b) 3/8

(c) 1/2 (d) 3/4

24. A statue of a freedom fighter is located in a museum. A student looks into a mirror and see the top of the statue reflected there. Using the information given below, determine the unknown height of the statue.

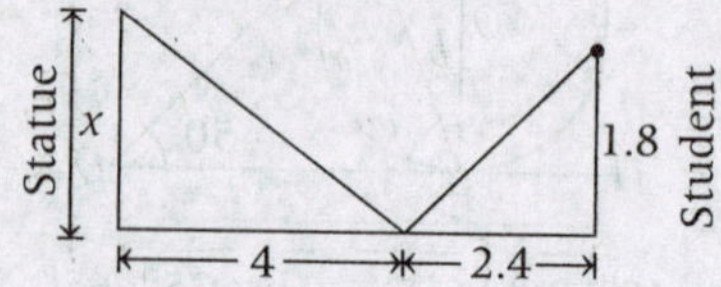

(a) 2 m (b) 3 m (c) 4 m (d) 5 m

25. If the given triangles are similar, then the value of $x + y$ is (approximately)

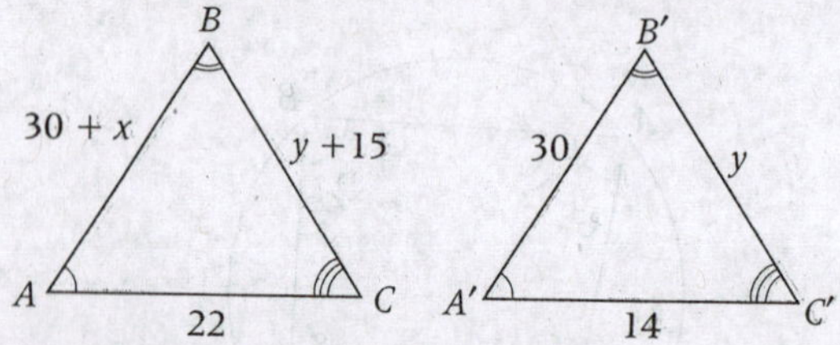

(a) 41 (b) 42 (c) 43 (d) 44

26. If $\sin\alpha$ and $\cos\alpha$ are the roots of the equation $px^2 + qx + r = 0$, then the value of $p^2 - q^2 + 2rp$ is

(a) 1 (b) −1

(c) 0 (d) None of these

27. Anmol is covering a circular pool with a heavy duty cover for the winter. The pool has a diameter of 24 ft. If the cover extends 24 inch beyond the edge of the pool and a rope runs along the edge of the cover to secure the cover place. Then, the length of the rope required is

(a) 44 ft (b) 88 ft (c) 80 ft (d) 99 ft

28. The area left after cutting out the largest circle that can be inscribed in a square of length $2a$ units, is

(a) $(4\pi + a^2)$ sq units

(b) $(4\pi - a^2)$ sq units

(c) $a^2(4-\pi)$ sq units

(d) $a^2(2-\pi)$ sq units

29. If a coin is tossed three times in succession, then the number of sample points in sample space is

(a) 8 (b) 3
(c) 6 (d) 9

30. In the given expression $(pr+q)^{(p-q)}$, p, q and r can be any positive integer greater than 1 and less than 5. What is largest possible value of the expression?

(a) 64
(b) 256
(c) 324
(d) Can't be determined

31. If Dev is standing 100 ft from the tower and sees a bird on the top of the tower. Then, what is the angle of elevation of the bird?

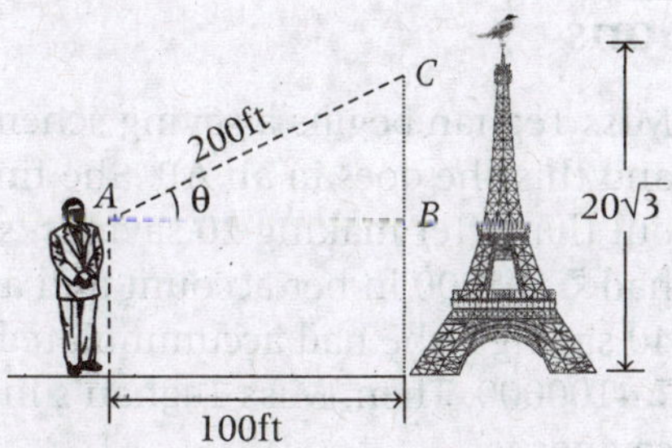

(a) 30° (b) 45° (c) 60° (d) 90°

32. Two ships move towards a light house with angle of elevation from the top of the light house be α and β (where, α > β) respectively and at a distance a and b from the light house. Then, the distance between the ships is

(a) $\dfrac{h(\cos\beta\sin\alpha-\sin\beta\cos\alpha)}{\sin\beta\sin\alpha}$

(b) $\dfrac{h(\sin\beta\cos\alpha-\cos\beta\sin\alpha)}{\sin\beta\sin\alpha}$

(c) $\dfrac{h(\sin\beta\cos\alpha-\cos\beta\sin\alpha)}{\cos\alpha\cos\beta}$

(d) $\dfrac{h(\sin\alpha\cos\beta-\sin\beta\cos\alpha)}{\cos\alpha\cos\beta}$

33. Simplify

$$\frac{8x^3-y^3+z^3+6xy}{a^3-8b^3+27c^3+18abc} \div \frac{4x^2+y^2+z^2+2xy+yz-2xz}{a^2+4b^2+9c^2+2ab+6bc-3ac}.$$

(a) $\dfrac{2x+y+z}{a+b+c}$ (b) 1

(c) 0 (d) $\dfrac{2x-y+z}{a-2b+3c}$

34. In the given figure, if O is the centre of a circle, RTS is its tangent and $\angle LTS=34°$, then measure of the reflex $\angle TOL$ is

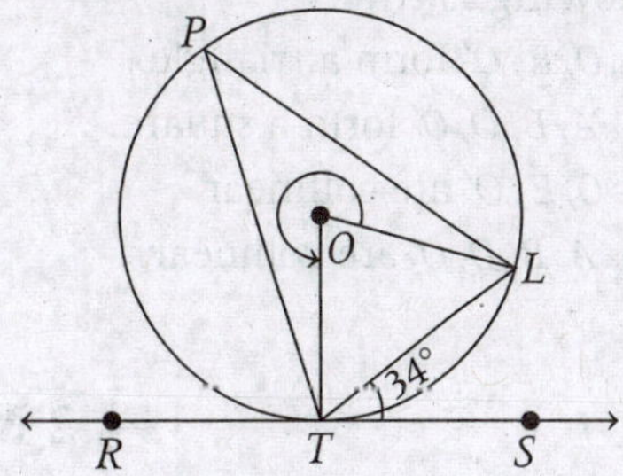

(a) 74° (b) 292° (c) 272° (d) 282°

35. A Mathematician randomly selects a number from 1 to 100 to test the validity of a result. What is the probability that the selected number is an odd prime number?

(a) 1/5 (b) 3/25 (c) 6/25 (d) 2/25

36. The track has six lanes. Each lane is 1.25 m wide. There is a 180° arc at each end of the track. If the radii for the arcs in the first two lanes are given. Then, the difference of the distance around lane 2 and lane 1 approximately is

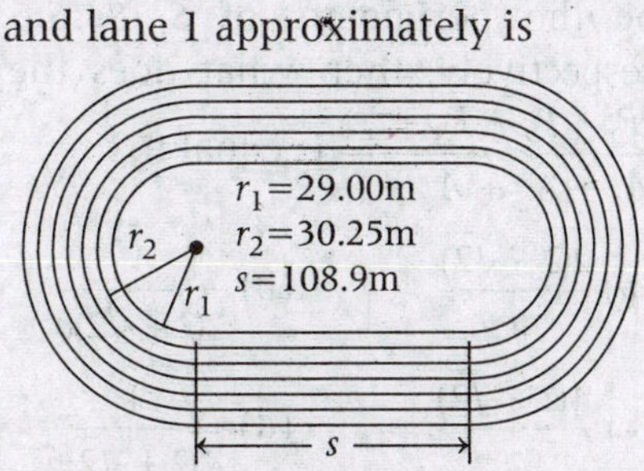

(a) 8 m (b) 10 m (c) 12 m (d) 14 m

37. A die is loaded in such a manner that for $n = 1, 2, 3, 4, 5, 6$, the probability of the face marked n, showing up when the die is rolled, is proportional to n. Find the probability that the number 5 will appear on tossing the die.

(a) 5/21 (b) 4/19
(c) 3/11 (d) 2/21

38. If the common tangents AB and CD of two circles with centres O and O' intersect at E, then which of the following is true?

(a) O, E, O' form a triangle.
(b) A, B, O, O' form a square.
(c) O, E, O' are collinear.
(d) A, B, O, O' are collinear.

39. The present age difference between father and son is 21 and the ratio of their age will be 7 : 3 after 7 yr. How old is son now?

(a) 8 yr
(b) 8 yr 6 month
(c) 8 yr 9 month
(d) 10 yr

40. There are three sets of key rings A, B and C, for a house. The first set has five keys, the second has seven and the third has eight, of which only one key in each set opens the door to the storeroom.

What is the probability that key doesn't open the door in third set?

(a) 5/24 (b) 6/24
(c) 7/8 (d) 8/24

2 Marks Questions

41. The average, median and mode are calculated for the list 4, 4, 8, 11, 13. If the number 2 is added to the list, then which of the following will not change?

(a) The average (b) The median
(c) The mode (d) None of the above

42. Let S_1 be a square of side a another square S_2 is formed by joining the mid-points of the sides of S_1. The same process is applied to S_2 to form yet another square S_3 and so on. If A_1, A_2, A_3, ... be the areas and P_1, P_2, P_3 ...... be the perimeters of S_1, S_2, S_3, ... respectively, then what does the ratio $\frac{P_1 + P_2 + P_3 + \dots}{A_1 + A_2 + A_3 + \dots}$ is equal to?

(a) $\frac{2(2+\sqrt{2})}{a}$ (b) $\frac{1}{2(2+\sqrt{2})a}$

(c) $\frac{4(2+\sqrt{2})}{a}$ (d) $\frac{1}{4(2+\sqrt{2})a}$

43. Miss Teghan begins a saving scheme and this she does in an AP. She finds out that after making 20 savings, she had ₹ 105000 in her account and after 40 savings, she had accummulated ₹ 4100000. Then, Miss Teghan's initial savings is

(a) ₹ 5000 (b) ₹ 10000
(c) ₹ 15000 (d) ₹ 20000

44. At a display booth in an amusement park, every visitor gets a gift bag. Some of the bags have items in them as shown in the table given below.

Items	Bags
Hat	Every 3rd visitor
Shirt	Every 5th visitor
Backpack	Every 12th visitor

4 bags contain all the three items, if it is a multiple of 3, 5 and 12.

How often will a bag contain all three items, if the total number of gift bags are 1200?

(a) 20 (b) 30

(c) 60 (d) 120

45. In the given figure, if AD is the bisector of $\angle BAC$, if $AB = 8$ cm, $AC = 16$ cm and $BC = 6$ cm, then the value of BD and DC are.

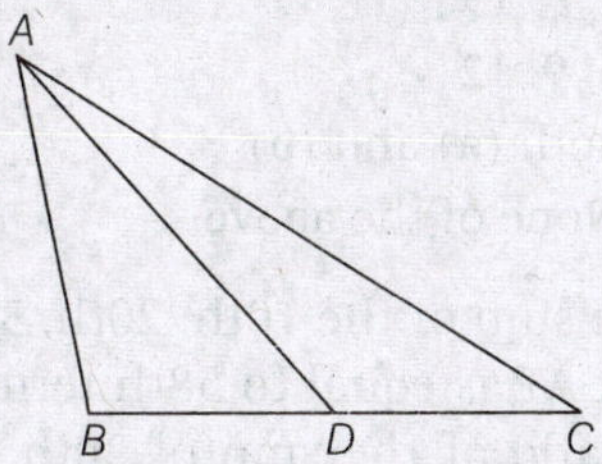

(a) 4 cm, 2 cm (b) 4 cm, 8 cm

(c) 1 cm, 2 cm (d) 2 cm, 4 cm

46. Suppore p is price of commodity and q is the quantity. If the demand equation for a commodity is $p(q+4) = 400$ and the supply equation is $2p - q = 38$. Find units of commodity sold at equilibrium price.

(a) 14 units

(b) 12 units

(c) 10 units

(d) 8 units

47. If α, β, and γ are the zeroes of the polynomial $f(x) = px^3 + qx^2 + rx + s$, then $\frac{1}{\alpha} + \frac{1}{\beta} + \frac{1}{\gamma} =$

(a) r/s (b) $-r/s$

(c) $-q/s$ (d) p/s

48. The angle of depression of a girl from an aeroplane at a point of time is α. After 1.5 h, the angle of depression become $\beta\ (\beta > \alpha)$. If the aeroplane is flying at a speed of 200 km/h.

Then, what would be the distance covered by the aeroplane, if its directly above the girl, from its second position?

(a) $\frac{200 \tan\alpha}{\tan\beta - \tan\alpha}$ (b) $\frac{200 \tan\alpha}{\tan\alpha - \tan\beta}$

(c) $\frac{300 \tan\alpha}{\tan\beta - \tan\alpha}$ (d) $\frac{300 \tan\alpha}{\tan\alpha - \tan\beta}$

49. The point P (4, 3) is reflected on the X-axis as $P'(x, y)$ and O' is the image of O (the origin) when reflected on the line PP'. Find the lengths of the segments PP' and OO'.

(a) 8 units, 6 units

(b) 6 units, 8 units

(c) 64 units, 36 units

(d) 36 units, 64 units

50. Match the following:

List I	List II
A. $3^{2x+2} = 82(3^x - 1) + 73$	i. 8
B. $\sqrt{16 + 6\sqrt{16 + 6\sqrt{16 + \ldots\infty}}}$	ii. $\{-2, 2\}$
C. $4\left(x^2 + \frac{1}{x^2}\right) + 4\left(x + \frac{1}{x}\right) - 7 = 0,\ x \neq 0$	iii. $\left\{-2, \frac{-1}{2}\right\}$

	A	B	C
(a)	ii	i	iii
(b)	i	ii	iii
(c)	iii	i	ii
(d)	iii	ii	i

PRACTICE SET 02

1 Mark Questions

1. Simplify : $\dfrac{(x+1/y)^p \times (x-1/y)^q}{(y+1/x)^p \times \left(y-\dfrac{1}{x}\right)^q}$

(a) $(x/y)^{p-q}$ (b) $(x/y)^{p+q}$

(c) $\left(\dfrac{y}{x}\right)^{p/q}$ (d) $\left(\dfrac{y}{x}\right)^{pq}$

2. Sum of digits of a two-digit number is 6 and product is 5 (if $x > y$), then the number formed by interchanging the digits, is

(a) 15 (b) 51 (c) 23 (d) 32

3. In a seminar, the number of participants in subject quizer Math, Physics and Chemistry are 65, 91, 143 respectively. Find the number of rooms required, if in each room the same number of participants, and to be seated and all of them being in the same subject.

(a) 21 (b) 23 (c) 12 (d) 10

4. If the zeroes of the polynomial $f(x) = x^3 - px^2 + qx + r$ are in arithmetic progression, then

(a) $p^3 + 9pq + 27r = 0$

(b) $2p^3 + 9pq + 27r = 0$

(c) $2p^3 - 9pq - 27r = 0$

(d) $p^3 - 9pq - 27r = 0$

5. A manufacturer of AC produced 620 sets in 4th yr and 720 sets in the 9th yr. If the production increase uniformly by a fixed number every year, then the total production in first 10 yr is

(a) 6200 (b) 6400

(c) 6500 (d) 6600

6. If the sum of three numbers in AP is 27 and their product is 405, then the numbers are

(a) 3, 9, 15

(b) 6, 9, 12

(c) Both (a) and (b)

(d) None of the above

7. If the sum of the 10th, 20th, 30th terms of an AP is equal to 58th term. What is the ratio of the sum of 20th, 30th and 40th terms to the sum of 5th, 10th and 15th terms?

(a) 2:1 (b) 20:9

(c) 29:9 (d) 19:9

8. The second negative term of the AP sequence $20, 19\frac{1}{4}, 18\frac{1}{2}, 17\frac{3}{4}, \ldots$ is

(a) 27th (b) 28th

(c) 30th (d) 29th

9. If a and b are zeroes of the polynomial $3x^2 + 13x + 4$, then $\frac{a}{b} + \frac{b}{a}$ is equal to

(a) $\dfrac{169}{12}$ (b) $\dfrac{145}{12}$

(c) $\dfrac{144}{12}$ (d) $\dfrac{167}{12}$

10. *A* and *B* are friends and their ages differ by 2 yr. *A*'s father *D* is twice as old as *A* and *B* is twice as old as his sister *C*. The age of *D* and *C* differ by 40 yr. Find the ages of *A* and *B*.

(a) 28 yr and 26 yr (b) 26 yr and 24 yr

(c) 30 yr and 28 yr (d) None of these

11. On dividing $x^4 - 5x + 6$ by a polynomial $g(x)$, the quotient and remainder were $-x^2 - 2$ and $-5x + 10$ respectively, then $g(x)$ is

(a) $x^2 - 2$ (b) $2 - x^2$
(c) $(x^2 + 2)$ (d) $-(x^2 + 2)$

12. Y-axis divides the line joining the points $A(-6, 3)$ and $(12, 3)$ in the ratio.

(a) 1 : 4 (b) 2 : 1
(c) 4 : 1 (d) 1 : 2

13. If α and β are the zeroes of the quadratic polynomial $g(x) = 2x^2 + 5x + k$ such that $\alpha^2 + \beta^2 + \alpha\beta = 21/4$, then the value of k is

(a) 2 (b) 4
(c) −2 (d) −4

14. In the given figure, if $AB \parallel CD$, $\angle DCE = x$ and $\angle ABE = y$, then $\angle CEB$ is equal to

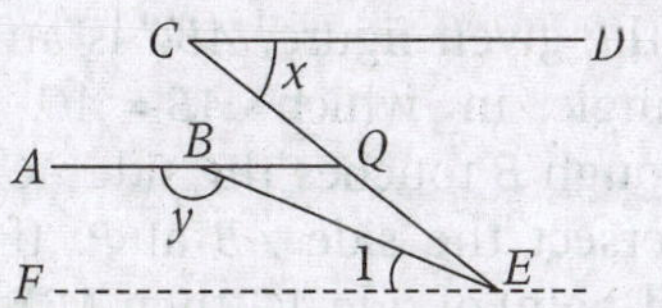

(a) $\angle y - \angle x$ (b) $\dfrac{\angle x + \angle y}{2}$
(c) $(\angle x + \angle y) - \pi/2$ (d) $\angle x + \angle y - \pi$

15. In ΔPQR, $PQ = PR$ and $QR = 12$ cm. S is a point on side PR such that $PS = 10$ cm and $RS = 8$ cm, then

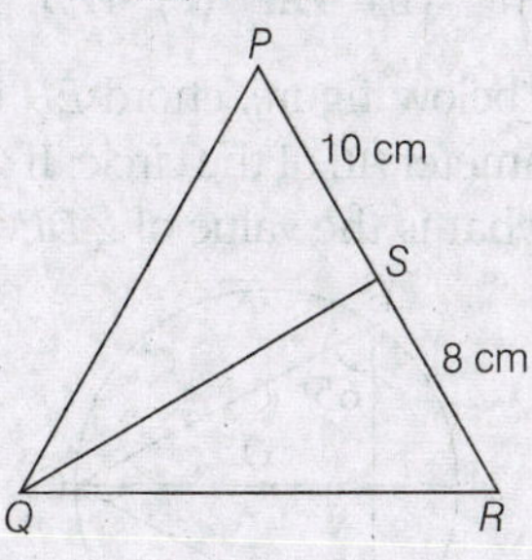

(a) $\Delta QRS \sim \Delta PRQ$
(b) $QS = 12$ cm
(c) Both (a) and (b)
(d) None of the above

16. In the given figure, l and m are two parallel tangents at A and B. If the tangent at C makes an intercept DE between the tangents l and m. Then, $\angle DFE$ is equal to

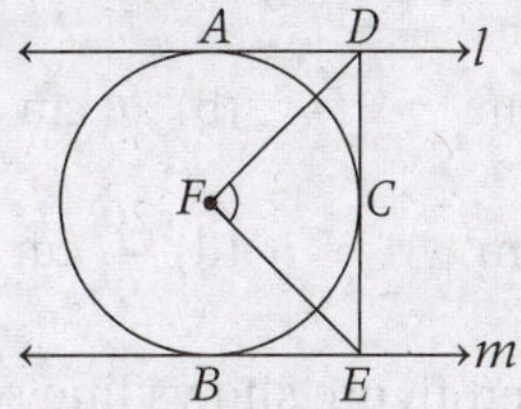

(a) 90° (b) 60° (c) 75° (d) 45°

17. A circle with diameter AD of length $2a$ units is drawn. Then, what will be the area of $EFCD$ (in sq units), if ΔEAD is an equilateral triangle and $ABCD$ is a square?

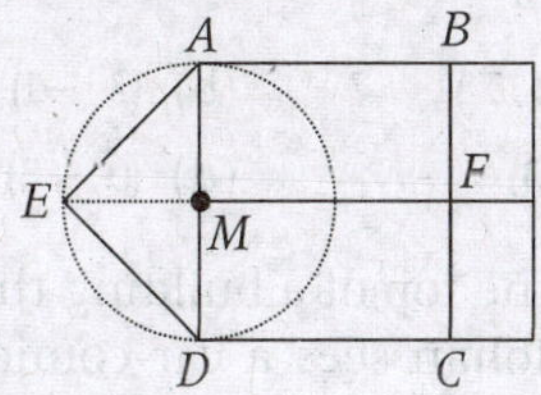

(a) $(4 + \sqrt{3})\dfrac{a^2}{2}$
(b) $(8 + \sqrt{3})\dfrac{a^3}{2}$
(c) $4a^2 + \sqrt{3}a^3$
(d) $8a^3 + \sqrt{3}a^2$

18. In the given figure, AOB is a diameter of a circle with centre O. If $\angle BOD = 150°$, find $\angle ACD$.

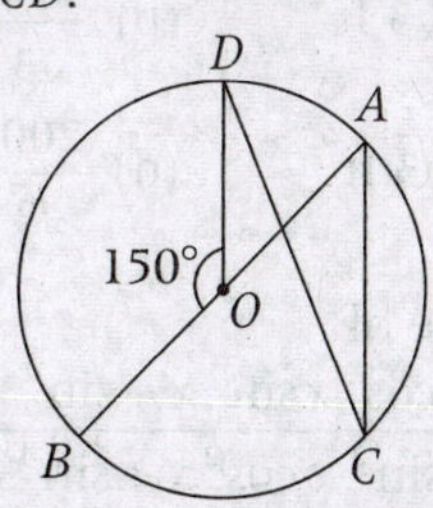

(a) 15° (b) 60°
(c) 30° (d) 90°

19. O is the centre of a circle of radius 5 cm. T is a point such that $OT = 13$ cm and OT intersects the circle at E. If AB is the tangent to the circle at E, find length of AB.

(a) $\frac{20}{3}$ cm (b) 20 cm
(c) $\frac{20}{7}$ cm (d) $\frac{20}{9}$ cm

20. The given figure shows line segment AB. P and Q are points on AB such that $AP : PQ : QB = 3 : 4 : 5$. What are the coordinates of mid-point of line segment PQ?

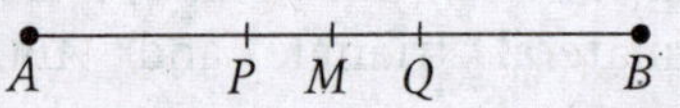

(a) $(-2, 7)$ (b) $(2, -1)$
(c) $(0, 3)$ (d) $(0, -3)$

21. From the top of a building that is 200 ft tall, Mohan sees a car coming towards the building with angle of depression being 30° and 60°, respectively. How far did the car travel initially?

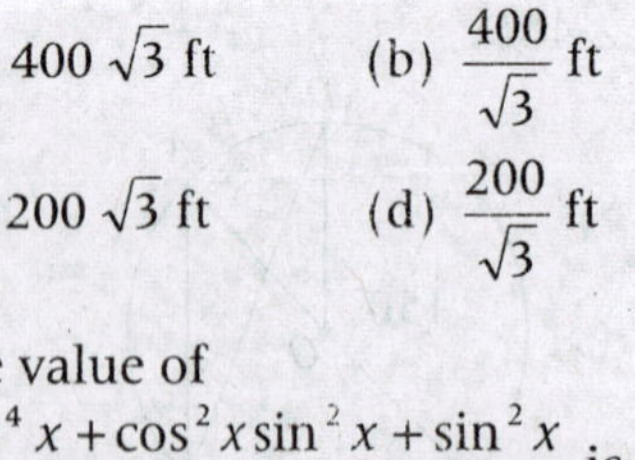

(a) $400\sqrt{3}$ ft (b) $\frac{400}{\sqrt{3}}$ ft
(c) $200\sqrt{3}$ ft (d) $\frac{200}{\sqrt{3}}$ ft

22. The value of $\dfrac{\cos^4 x + \cos^2 x \sin^2 x + \sin^2 x}{\cos^2 x + \sin^2 x \cos^2 x + \sin^4 x}$ is

(a) 2 (b) 1
(c) 3 (d) 0

23. The relation obtained by eliminating θ from the equation $x = r\cos\theta + s\sin\theta$ and $y = r\sin\theta - s\cos\theta$ will be

(a) $x^2 + y^2 = 0$ (b) $x^2 + y^2 = r^2 + s^2$
(c) $x^2 + y^2 = r^2$ (d) $x^2 + y^2 = s^2$

24. The sum of the circumference of four semi-circles, if the radius of first arc is r and next each arc is increased by 1, is

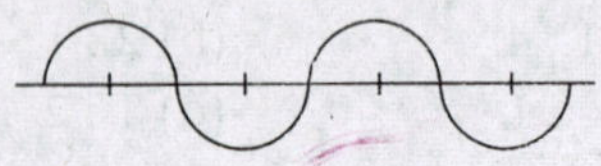

(a) $4\pi r + 2\pi r$ (b) $4\pi r$
(c) $4\pi r + 6\pi$ (d) $8\pi r$

25. A regular polygon is inscribed in a circle. If each side subtends an angle of 36° at the centre, then the number of sides in the polygon are

(a) 10 (b) 12 (c) 11 (d) 14

26. In the given figure, ABC is an isosceles triangle in which $AB = AC$. A circle through B touches the side AC at D and intersect the side AB at P. If D is the mid-point of side AC, then AB is equal to

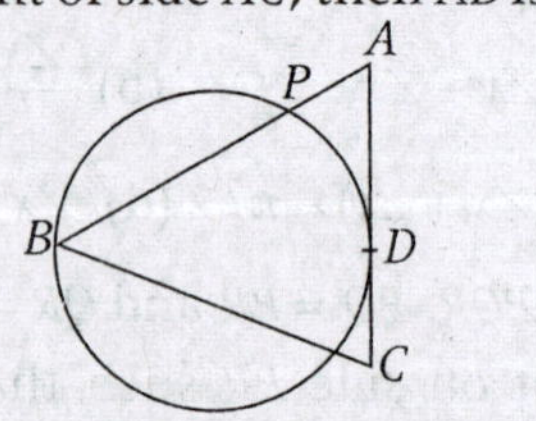

(a) $4AD$ (b) $4AP$ (c) $4PB$ (d) $4DC$

27. In the below figure, chord ED is parallel to the diameter AC of the circle. If $\angle CBE = 65°$, then what is the value of $\angle DEC$?

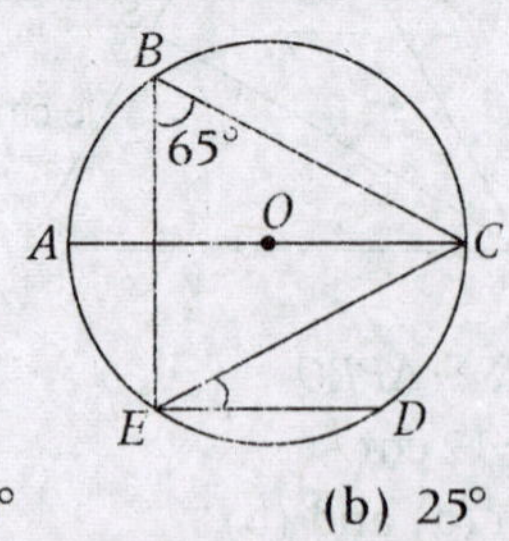

(a) 35° (b) 25°
(c) 45° (d) 55°

28. **Assertion** (A) If the roots of the equation $ax^2 - 2\sqrt{2}x + c = 0$ are real and equal, then $ac = \frac{1}{2}$.

Reason (R) If the discriminant of a quadratic equation is zero, then roots are real and equal.

Which of the following statements is true?

(a) (A) is true and (R) is correct explanation of (A)
(b) (A) is false and (R) is true
(c) (A) is true and (R) is false
(d) Both (A) and (R) are false

29. If $\tan\theta + \sin\theta = m$ and $\tan\theta - \sin\theta = n$ then

(a) $(m^2 - n^2)^2 = 16\,mn$
(b) $(m^2 - n^2) = 4\sqrt{mn}$
(c) Both (a) and (b)
(d) $m^2 - n^2 = 16\sqrt{mn}$

30. A motorboat is pulling a parasailer. The line to the parasailer is 800 ft long. The angle between the line and the water is about 30°. How high is the parasailer?

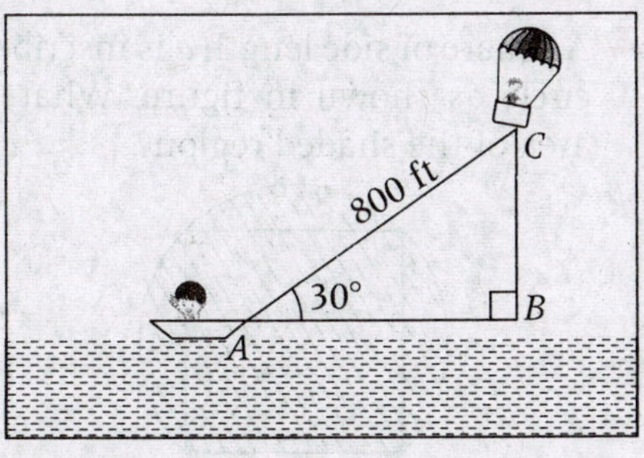

(a) 300 ft
(b) 350 ft
(c) $300\sqrt{3}$ ft
(d) 400 ft

31. The value of $\log\cos 0° + \log\cos 1° + \log\cos 2° + \ldots + \log\cos 90°$ is

(a) 0 (b) 1
(c) −1 (d) Undefined

32. The median of the following information is

Height	151	152	153	154	155	156	157
Number of plants	6	4	11	9	16	12	2

(a) 154 (b) 154.5
(c) 153.5 (d) 153

33. The mode of the following distribution is

Height	30-40	40-50	50-60	60-70	70-80	80-90
Number of trees	4	3	8	11	6	2

(a) 63 (b) 63.75
(c) 65 (d) 66

34. Which of the following geometrical figure is formed by the coordinates of the points $A(5,6)$, $B(1,5)$, $C(2,1)$ and $D(6,2)$?

(a) Rhombus (b) Parallelogram
(c) Square (d) Rectangle

35. A dentist records the number of cavities in 100 children from a school. The information obtained is summarised in the following table:

Number of cavities (x_i)	f_i	n_i
0	25	0.25
1	20	0.2
2	x	z
3	15	0.15
4	y	0.05

The mean of the cavities is

(a) 1.55 (b) 2.55 (c) 3.55 (d) 4.55

36. Two dice P and Q have their respective faces marked as

P	2	2	4	4	9	9
Q	1	1	6	6	8	8

The probability that die P rolls a higher number than Q is

(a) 4/9 (b) 1/3
(c) 2/3 (d) 5/9

37. A circular pond is to be constructed inside a circular park having origin as the same centre such that the circumference of the pond passes through the point $(5, 2\sqrt{6})$ and the remaining area of the park is 462 sq. units, then which of the following point lies on the circumference of the park?

(a) $(10, 4\sqrt{6})$
(b) $(15, 6\sqrt{6})$
(c) $(5, 4\sqrt{6})$
(d) $(10, 5\sqrt{6})$

38. There are 20 red balls and 15 green balls in a box. If only red balls are to be subtracted from the box so that the probability of randomly drawing a red ball becomes 2/5, then how many red balls must be subtracted from the box?

(a) 5 (b) 10 (c) 12 (d) 15

39. If a number y is chosen at random from the numbers $-5, -4, -2, -1, 0, 1, 2, 4, 5.$ then the probability that $y^2 \leq 4$ is

(a) $\frac{1}{3}$ (b) $\frac{1}{2}$ (c) $\frac{1}{10}$ (d) $\frac{1}{8}$

40. Given two squares $ABCD$ and $PQRS$ such that $PQRS$ is inscribed in $ABCD$. Then, the area of the given figure $ABCD$ is

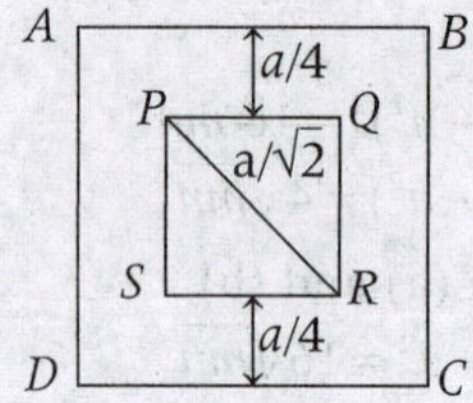

(a) $\frac{a^2}{4}$ (b) a^2 (c) $2a^2$ (d) $\frac{a^2}{2}$

2 Marks Questions

41. Solve the following and choose the correct option.

$$\frac{1}{2(3x+2y)} + \frac{12}{5(2x-3y)} = \frac{34}{10}$$

and $$\frac{5}{6(3x+2y)} + \frac{25}{12(2x-3y)} = \frac{15}{4}$$

(a) $x = \frac{7}{26}, y = \frac{-2}{13}$

(b) $x = \frac{5}{26}, y = \frac{-2}{13}$

(c) $x = \frac{7}{26}, y = \frac{-1}{13}$ (d) $x = \frac{5}{26}, y = \frac{-1}{13}$

42. A square of side length a is inscribed in a circle as shown in figure. What is the area of the shaded region?

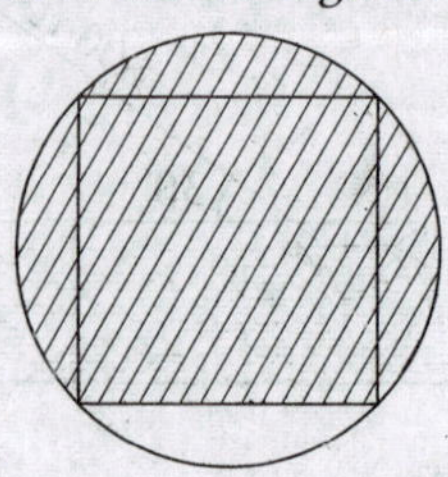

(a) $\frac{(3\pi+2)}{8}a^2$ (b) $\frac{(3\pi+2)}{4}a^2$

(c) $\frac{(3\pi-2)}{4}a^2$ (d) $\frac{(3\pi+2)a^2}{8}$

43. Solve the following and choose the correct option.

$$x\left(a-b+\frac{ab}{a-b}\right)=y\left(a+b-\frac{ab}{a+b}\right)$$

$$x+y=2a^2$$

(a) $x=\frac{a^3-b^3}{a}, y=\frac{a^2-b^2}{b}$

(b) $x=\frac{a^2-b^2}{a}, y=\frac{a^2-b^2}{b}$

(c) $x=\frac{a^3-b^3}{a}, y=\frac{a^3+b^3}{a}$

(d) None of the above

44. A research team wishes to determine the altitude of a mountain. They use a light source L mounted on a structure of height 2 m, to shine a beam of light through the top of a pole P' to the top of the mountain M'. The height of the pole is 20 m. The distance between the altitude of the mountain and the pole is 1000 m.

The distance between the pole and the light source is 10 m. Assuming that the light source, the pole and the altitude of the mountain are in the same plane. Then, altitude h of the mountain is

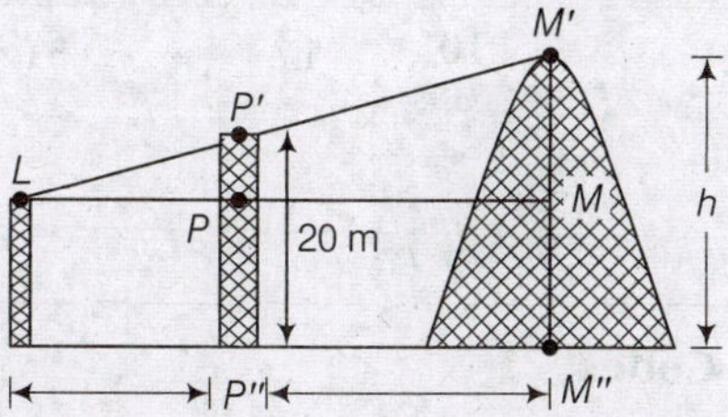

(a) 1800 m (b) 1810 m

(c) 1820 m (d) 1840 m

45. 92% and 95% pure acid solution are mixed to obtain 14 l of 94% pure acid solution. Find the amount of each type of acid to be mixed to form the mixture.

(a) $14/3\ l$ and $\frac{28}{3}\ l$ (b) $7/3\ l$ and $14/3$

(c) $\frac{28}{3}\ l$ and $14/3\ l$ (d) $14/3\ l$ and $7/3\ l$

46. Match the following.

	List I	List II
A.	The volume of a cube, which curved surface area is 384 cm^2.	(i) 462 cm^2
B.	The total surface area of a hemisphere with radius is 7 cm.	(ii) 66 cm^3
C.	The volume of a cone with radius is 3 cm and height is 7 cm.	(iii) 512 cm^3
D.	The volume of a right circular cylinder with base area is 154 cm^2 and height is 10 cm.	(iv) 1540 cm^3

(a) (A) → (i), (B) → (ii), (C) → (iii), (D) → (iv)

(b) (A) → (ii), (B) → (iv), (C) → (iii), (D) → (i)

(c) (A) → (iii), (B) → (i), (C) → (ii), (D) → (iv)

(d) (A) → (ii), (B) → (iii), (C) → (i), (D) → (iv)

47. Global Tea Estate began production in 1999, it produced 8000 cartons of tea, it is projected that production will increase by 50 cartons each year. Also, the production cost for first year was ₹ 70 per carton which reduced by ₹ 2 each successive year and the selling price of each carton increases by 10% of the production cost of year 1999.

Find the total production from start when it has just increased production by 30% over the initial figure.

(a) 450000

(b) 480000

(c) 480500

(d) 450800

48. Consider the following statistical table:

$$\left(\Sigma n_i = 1 \text{ and } \frac{f_i}{N} = n_i\right)$$

x_i	f_i	cf	n_i
1	4	4	0.08
2	4	8	
3		16	0.16
4	7	23	0.14
5	5	28	
6		38	
7	7	45	0.14
8			0.1

Completing the above statistical table, match the following:

	List I		List II
A.	Mode	i.	4.76
B.	Median	ii.	6
C.	Mean	iii.	5

Codes

	A	B	C		A	B	C
(a)	i	ii	iii	(b)	ii	iii	i
(c)	iii	i	ii	(d)	ii	i	iii

49. The coordinates of the vertices after a dilation with a scale factor of 1/5, centred at the origin.

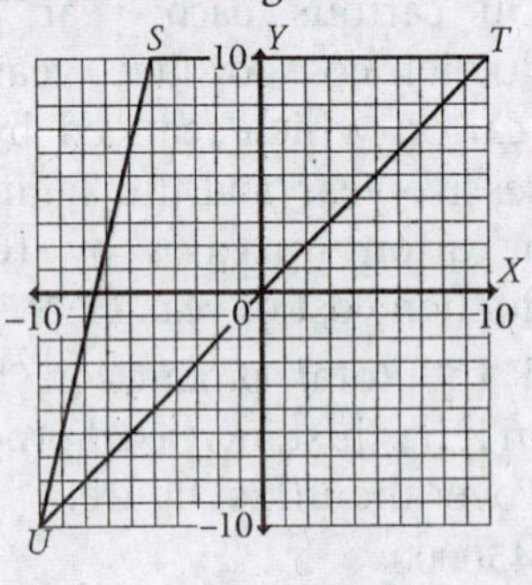

$S(-5,10) \rightarrow S'(\square, \square)$

$T(10,10) \rightarrow T'(\square, \square)$

$U(-10,-10) \rightarrow U'(\square, \square)$

(a) $S'(-1,2), T'(2,2), U'(-2,-2)$

(b) $S'(1,-2), T'(2,2), U'(-2,-2)$

(c) $S'(-1,2), T'(-2,-2), U'(-2,2)$

(d) None of the above

50. Match the following cans with each can's circumference:

	List I		List II
A.	$5\frac{1}{4}$ 	i.	11 units
B.	175 	ii.	16.5 units
C.	10 	iii.	31.4 units

Codes

	A	B	C
(a)	i	ii	iii
(b)	ii	i	iii
(c)	i	iii	ii
(d)	iii	ii	i

HINTS & SOLUTIONS

Chapter 1 : Real Numbers

1. *(d)* For number of rows to be the least, the number of students in each row must be the highest. The number of students in each row is a highest common factor of 44 and 32. The highest common factor value is the HCF of 44 and 32 which is 4.

$\therefore$ Minimum numbers of rows

$$= \frac{44}{4} + \frac{32}{4}$$

$= 11 + 8 = 19$ rows

2. *(d)* Here, $108 = 2^2 \times 3^3$

and $288 = 2^5 \times 3^2$

$\therefore$ HCF $(108, 288) = 2^2 \times 3^2$

$= 4 \times 9 = 36$

3. *(a)* Each student to have same number of pens and pencils

$=$ HCF $(1001, 910)$

$=$ HCF $(11 \times 91, 10 \times 91) = 91$

4. *(c)* Let the three numbers be x, y and z.

Now, according to the question,

$x \times y = 42$

and $y \times z = 78$

$\Rightarrow x \times y \times y \times z = 42 \times 78$

$\Rightarrow x \times y^2 \times z = 7 \times 6 \times 6 \times 13$

$= 7 \times 6^2 \times 13$

$\therefore$ $x = 7$, $y = 6$ and $z = 13$

Now, $x + y + z = 7 + 6 + 13$

$= 26$

5. *(a)* Required number

$=$ HCF $\{(4665 - 1305), (6905 - 4665), (6905 - 1305)\}$

$=$ HCF $(3360, 2240, 5600)$

$=$ HCF $(2^5 \times 5 \times 3 \times 7, 2^6 \times 5 \times 7, 2^5 \times 5^2 \times 7)$

$= 2^5 \times 5 \times 7 = 1120$

$\therefore$ Sum of digits $= 1 + 1 + 2 + 0$

$= 4$

6. *(a)* If two co-prime numbers are a and b, their ratio in simplest form $= \frac{a}{b}$, because HCF of two co-prime numbers is always 1. e.g. 6 and 7 are co-primes, their ratio $= \frac{6}{7}$.

7. *(b)* Prime factorisation of 1314,

2	1314
3	657
3	219
	73

$\therefore$ $a = 3, b = 73$

8. *(d)* The least five-digit number

$= 10000$

Now, LCM $(12, 15, 18) = 180$

We have,

```
180) 10000 (55
      900
     1000
      900
      100
```

Difference $= (180 - 100) = 80$

$\therefore$ Required smallest 5 digit number divisible by 12, 15 and 18

$= 10000 + 80$

$= 10080$

9. *(c)* HCF of 720 and 405 is,

```
405)720(1
    405
    315)405(1
        315
         90)315(3
            270
             45)90(2
                90
                 ×
```

$\therefore$ Minimum number of glasses

$$= \frac{720}{45} + \frac{405}{45}$$

$$= \frac{1125}{45} = 25$$

10. *(b)* Given, fractions are $\frac{17}{18}, \frac{43}{45}, \frac{59}{60}$ and $\frac{31}{36}$.

Here, LCM $(18, 45, 60, 36) = 180$

We get, $\frac{170}{180}, \frac{172}{180}, \frac{177}{180}, \frac{155}{180}$

$\therefore$ $\frac{155}{180} < \frac{177}{180} < \frac{172}{180} < \frac{170}{180}$

$\therefore$ $\frac{31}{36} < \frac{17}{18} < \frac{43}{45} < \frac{59}{60}$

11. *(d)* (i) HCF below two $(2, 12)$ $\times$ LCM of above $(4, 6)$

$= 2 \times 12$

$= 24$

(ii) HCF $\times$ LCM $= a \times b$

$\Rightarrow$ $2 \times$ LCM $= 6 \times 10$

$\Rightarrow$ LCM $= 30$

(iii) HCF $\times$ LCM $- a \times b$

$\Rightarrow$ HCF $\times 12 = 4 \times 12$

$\Rightarrow$ HCF $= 4$

12. *(d)* Since, we know that product of two numbers

$=$ (HCF $\times$ LCM)

$\therefore$ Sumit's score $\times 144$

$= 5040 \times 12$

$\therefore$ Sumit's score

$$= \frac{5040 \times 12}{144} = 420$$

13. *(c)* Since, $1.43\overline{28} = 1.432828...$ is a non-terminating and repeating decimal i.e. an irrational number.

14. *(a)* $\sqrt{9} = \pm\ 3$is a rational number and others are irrational.

$\therefore$ $\sqrt{9}$ is odd one here.

15. *(b)* Let $x = \sqrt{6 + \sqrt{6 + \sqrt{6 + \ldots}}}$

$x^2 = 6 + \sqrt{6 + \sqrt{6 + \ldots}}$

$\Rightarrow$ $x^2 = 6 + x$

$\Rightarrow$ $(x + 2)(x - 3) = 0$

$\Rightarrow$ $x = 3, -2$

$\therefore$ $x = 3$

[$\because x$ can not be negative]

16. (c) Taking numbers $5+\sqrt{3}$ and $5-\sqrt{3}$

Now, their sum
$=5+\sqrt{3}+5-\sqrt{3}=10$, rational

Now, their product
$=(5+\sqrt{3})(5-\sqrt{3})=(5)^2-(\sqrt{3})^2$
$=25-3=22$, rational

17. (b) $a=\sqrt{11}+\sqrt{3}$
$\Rightarrow a^2=(\sqrt{11}+\sqrt{3})^2$
$=11+3+2\sqrt{33}$
$=14+2\sqrt{33}$
$b=\sqrt{12}+\sqrt{2}$
$\Rightarrow b^2=(\sqrt{12}+\sqrt{2})^2$
$=14+2\sqrt{24}$
As, $\sqrt{33}>\sqrt{24}, a^2>b^2$, hence $a>b$.
$c=\sqrt{6}+\sqrt{4}$
$\Rightarrow c^2=(\sqrt{6}+\sqrt{4})^2$
$=10+2\sqrt{24}$
As $14>10, b^2>c^2$, hence $b>c$
Hence, $a>b>c$

18. (a) $\dfrac{1}{\sqrt{9}+\sqrt{10}}$
$=\dfrac{\sqrt{9}-\sqrt{10}}{(\sqrt{9}+\sqrt{10})(\sqrt{9}-\sqrt{10})}$
(By multiplying both its numerator and denominator by $\sqrt{9}-\sqrt{10}$)
Hence,
$\dfrac{1}{\sqrt{9}+\sqrt{10}}=\dfrac{\sqrt{9}-\sqrt{10}}{(\sqrt{9})^2-(\sqrt{10})^2}$
$=\dfrac{\sqrt{9}-\sqrt{10}}{-1}$
By multiplying numerator and denominator of each term by the conjugate of their denominators, the given expression becomes
$\dfrac{\sqrt{9}-\sqrt{10}}{-1}+\dfrac{\sqrt{10}-\sqrt{11}}{-1}$
$+\dfrac{\sqrt{11}-\sqrt{12}}{-1}+\dots\dfrac{\sqrt{99}-\sqrt{100}}{-1}$
$=\dfrac{\sqrt{9}-\sqrt{100}}{-1}=7$

19. (b) By inspection, we can reject ab and cd.
$ab=\sqrt[4]{6}-\sqrt[4]{5}$
$\therefore \quad abd=\sqrt{6}-\sqrt{5}$
and $abde=6-5=1$
$\therefore$ $abde$ is a rational number.

20. (d) Given,
$7\times13+13=104=2^3\times13$
The product of two prime numbers is composite.

21. (c) A. LCM of two coprime numbers
= Product of numbers = 117
B. LCM $(a,b)\times$ HCF (a,b)
= Product of a and $b=1$
$\Rightarrow ab=1$
$\Rightarrow a=\dfrac{1}{b}$
C. LCM $\left(\dfrac{2}{3},\dfrac{3}{5},\dfrac{4}{7}\text{ and }\dfrac{9}{13}\right)$
$=\dfrac{\text{LCM }(2,3,4,9)}{\text{HCF }(3,5,7,13)}=\dfrac{36}{1}=36$

22. (c)
A. Smallest composite number = 4
Smallest prime number = 2
HCF of 2 and 4 = 2
B. HCF of 32 and 54 is
$32=2\times2\times2\times2\times2$
$54=2\times3\times3\times3$
HCF = 2
C. HCF of 336 and 54
$336=2\times2\times2\times2\times3\times7$
$54=2\times3\times3\times3$
HCF $=2\times3=6$
D. HCF of 475 and 495
$475=5\times5\times19$
$495=3\times3\times5\times11$
HCF = 5

23. (c) $(x^2-4x+4)(x+3)$
$=(x-2)^2(x+3)$
$[\because (a-b)^2=a^2+b^2-2ab]$
$(x^2+2x-3)(x-2)$
$=(x^2+3x-x-3)(x-2)$
$=\{x(x+3)-1(x+3)\}(x-2)$
$=\{(x-1)(x+3)\}(x-2)$
$\therefore$ HCF of $(x^2-4x+4)(x+3)$ and $(x^2+2x-3)(x-2)$ is $(x+3)(x-2)$

24. (b) Given, $l\times b=2028$
where, $l=13a$ and $b=13b$
$\Rightarrow \quad 13a\times13b=2028$
$\Rightarrow 169ab=2028\Rightarrow ab=12$
$\therefore$ The suitable pairs are (1, 12) and (3, 4).
So, required pairs are
$(13\times1, 13\times12)$ and $(13\times3, 13\times4)$
i.e. (13, 156) and (39, 52).

25. (a) $x=28+(1\times2\times3\times\dots\times16\times28)$
$x=28\,[1+(1\times2\times3\times\dots\times16)]$
$\therefore x$ is a composite number.
$y=17+(1\times2\times3\times4\times\dots\times17)$
$=17\,[1+(1\times2\times3\times\dots\times16)]$
$\therefore y$ is a composite number.
Now,
$x-y=[1+(1\times2\times3\times\dots\times16)]\,(28-17)$
$=11\,[1+(1\times2\times3\times\dots\times16)]$
$\therefore x-y$ is a composite number.
$x+y=[1+(1\times2\times3\times\dots\times16)]\,(28+17)$
$=45\,[1+(1\times2\times3\dots\times16)]$
$\therefore x+y$ is a composite number.

26. (a) LCM (11, 91) = 1001
By hit and trial method, we get
$1001\times88=\underline{8}\,\underline{8}\,\underline{0}\,\underline{8}\,\underline{8}$
$\therefore$ Third digit from the left is '0'.

27. (d) Required time
= LCM (252, 308, 198)
= 2772 s
Now, 1 min = 60 s
$\Rightarrow$ 1 s = 1/60 min
$\therefore$ 2772 s $=\dfrac{2772}{60}$ min
= 46 min 12 s

28. (c) Number of toys distributed by Aisha = 40 − 5 = 35
and number of toys distributed by Succhi = 61 − 5 = 56
$\therefore$ Number of toys received by each child = HCF (35, 56) = 7
Now, number of children whom Aisha distributed the toys $=\dfrac{35}{7}=5$

and number of children whom Succhi distributed the toys

$= \frac{56}{7} = 8$

$\therefore$ Total number of children

$= 5 + 8 = 13$

29. *(a)* (A) We know HCF (28, 16, 12)

$= 2 \times 2 = 4$

$\therefore$ Number of books each student got = 4

(B) Number of students who got Maths books $= \frac{28}{4} = 7$

Number of students who got Science books $= \frac{16}{4} = 4$

Number of students who got Social Science books $= \frac{12}{4} = 3$

$\therefore$ Total number of students who got books $= 7 + 4 + 3 = 14$

30. *(d)* Given, total distance

$= 360$ km

Speed of Sumeet = 12 km/h

Number of hours taken by Sumeet to complete

1 round $= \frac{\text{Distance}}{\text{Speed}} = \frac{360}{12}$

$= 30$ h

and speed of John = 15 km/h

Number of hours taken by John to complete 1 round

$= \frac{\text{Distance}}{\text{speed}} = \frac{360}{15} = 24$ h

Thus, Sumeet and John complete 1 round in 30 h and 24 h, respectively.

Now, to find required hours, we find the LCM of 30 and 24

$30 = 2 \times 3 \times 5$

$24 = 2 \times 2 \times 2 \times 3$

Then, LCM (30, 24)

$= 2 \times 2 \times 2 \times 3 \times 5 = 120$

Hence, Sumeet and John will meet each other again after 120 h.

Chapter 2 : Polynomials

1. *(c)* $f(2) = 2^2 - 4 \times 2 + k$

$\Rightarrow 2^2 - 4 \times 2 + k = 0$

$\Rightarrow \quad 4 - 8 + k = 0$

$\Rightarrow \quad k = 4$

2. *(b)* Here, $\alpha + \beta = \frac{2}{3} - \frac{1}{4} = \frac{5}{12}$

and $\alpha\beta = \left(\frac{2}{3}\right)\left(-\frac{1}{4}\right) = -\frac{1}{6}$

$\therefore$ Required polynomial

$= x^2 - \frac{5}{12}x - \frac{1}{6}$

$= \frac{1}{12}(12x^2 - 5x - 2)$

3. *(b)* Since the graph cuts the X-axis at -2, 1 and 3.

$\therefore$ Zeroes of the polynomial are -2, 1 and 3.

4. *(b)* Given, $2x^2 + 14x + 20 = 0$

$\Rightarrow \quad x^2 + 7x + 10 = 0$

$\Rightarrow \quad (x + 2)(x + 5) = 0$

$\Rightarrow \quad x = -2$ and -5

5. *(d)* Since, $(x + 1)$ is a factor. We have, $f(-1) - 0$

$\Rightarrow a_0(-1)^n + a_1(-1)^{n-1} + a_2(-1)^{n-2} + \ldots + a_n = 0$

$\Rightarrow a_0 + a_2 + a_4 + \ldots + a_n = a_1 + a_3 + a_5 + \ldots + a_n$

where, n is even or odd number whatever it may be.

6. *(b)* $\because \quad f(-4) = 0$

$\Rightarrow (-4)^2 - (-4) - (2k + 2) = 0$

$\Rightarrow \quad -(2k + 2) = -20$

$\Rightarrow \quad k + 1 = 10$

$\therefore \quad k = 9$

7. *(d)* $\because \quad f(2) = 0$

$\Rightarrow (2)^2 + (a + 1) \times 2 + b = 0$

$\Rightarrow \quad 6 + 2a + b = 0 \quad \ldots$(i)

and $\quad f(-3) = 0$

$\Rightarrow (-3)^2 + (a + 1) \times (-3) + b = 0$

$\Rightarrow \quad 6 - 3a + b = 0 \quad \ldots$(ii)

On subtracting Eq. (ii) from Eq. (i), we get

$5a = 0 \Rightarrow a = 0$

$\therefore \quad b = -6$ [from Eq. (i)]

Hence, $a = 0$ and $b = -6$

8. *(b)* Given, HCF (6, 12) = 6 is one of the zeroes.

$\therefore \quad f(6) = 0$

$\Rightarrow \quad (6)^2 - 8 \times 6 + k = 0$

$\Rightarrow \quad k = 12$

9. *(a)* Here, $l + m + n = p$, $lmn = r$

Now, $\frac{1}{lm} + \frac{1}{lm} + \frac{1}{nl}$

$= \frac{n + l + m}{lmn} = \frac{p}{r}$

10. *(d)* Let zeroes be α and $\frac{1}{\alpha}$

$\therefore$ Product of zeroes $= \alpha \times \frac{1}{\alpha} = 1$

But product of zeroes $= \frac{6m}{m^2 + 9}$

$\Rightarrow \quad 1 = \frac{6m}{m^2 + 9}$

$\Rightarrow \quad m^2 - 6m + 9 = 0$

$\Rightarrow \quad (m - 3)^2 = 0$

$\Rightarrow \quad m = 3$

11. *(c)* Missing term

= Sum of zeroes

$= -\frac{b}{a}$ in $ax^2 + bx + c$

$\therefore$ Missing term $= -\frac{7}{2}$

12. *(d)* Here, $\quad \alpha + \beta = \frac{-(-8)}{1} = 8$

$\Rightarrow \quad \alpha + \beta = 8 \quad \ldots$(i)

Also given, $\alpha - \beta = 2 \quad \ldots$(ii)

On adding Eqs. (i) and (ii), we get

$2\alpha = 10 \Rightarrow \alpha = 5$

$\Rightarrow \quad \beta = 3$

$\therefore \quad \gamma = \alpha\beta = 15$

13. *(a)* Given,

$\alpha^2 + \beta^2 = 25 \quad \ldots$(i)

and $\quad \alpha + \beta = -7 \quad \ldots$(ii)

We know, k = Product of roots

$= \alpha\beta$

From Eqs. (i) and (ii), we have

$(\alpha + \beta)^2 = \alpha^2 + \beta^2 + 2\alpha\beta$

$\Rightarrow \quad (-7)^2 = 25 + 2\alpha\beta$

$\Rightarrow \quad 49 - 25 = 2\alpha\beta$

$24 = 2\alpha\beta \Rightarrow \alpha\beta = 12$

$\therefore \quad k = 12$

14. *(a)* Let α and β be the zeroes of equation $lx^2 + nx + n = 0$.

$$\Rightarrow \quad \alpha + \beta = -\frac{n}{l} \quad \ldots\text{(i)}$$

and $$\alpha\beta = \frac{n}{l} \quad \ldots\text{(ii)}$$

Given $\frac{\alpha}{\beta} = \frac{p}{q} \Rightarrow \alpha = \frac{p}{q}\beta$

Substitute in Eq. (ii), $\frac{p}{q}.\beta^2 = \frac{n}{l}$

$$\beta^2 = \frac{n}{l} \times \frac{q}{p}$$

$$\Rightarrow \quad \beta = \sqrt{\frac{n}{l}} \times \frac{\sqrt{q}}{\sqrt{p}}$$

$$\therefore \quad \alpha = \frac{p}{q}\frac{\sqrt{n}}{\sqrt{l}}\frac{\sqrt{q}}{\sqrt{p}} = \frac{\sqrt{p}}{\sqrt{q}}\frac{\sqrt{n}}{\sqrt{l}}$$

Substitute α and β in Eq. (i)

$$\frac{\sqrt{p}}{\sqrt{q}}\frac{\sqrt{n}}{\sqrt{l}} + \frac{\sqrt{n}}{\sqrt{l}}\frac{\sqrt{q}}{\sqrt{p}} = -\frac{n}{l}$$

$$\Rightarrow \quad \frac{\sqrt{n}}{\sqrt{l}}\left(\frac{\sqrt{p}}{\sqrt{q}} + \frac{\sqrt{q}}{\sqrt{p}}\right) = -\frac{n}{l}$$

$$\Rightarrow \quad \frac{\sqrt{p}}{\sqrt{q}} + \frac{\sqrt{q}}{\sqrt{p}} = -\frac{n}{l} \times \sqrt{\frac{l}{n}}$$

$$\therefore \quad \sqrt{\frac{p}{q}} + \sqrt{\frac{q}{p}} + \sqrt{\frac{n}{l}} = 0$$

15. *(b)* Let the two zeroes of the given polynomial be α and β.

Then, $\alpha = \frac{\sqrt{3}}{4}$ and $\alpha \cdot \beta = -\frac{1}{2}$

$$\therefore \quad \beta = -\frac{1}{2} \times \frac{4}{\sqrt{3}} = \frac{-2\sqrt{3}}{3}$$

$$\therefore \text{Sum of zeroes} = \frac{\sqrt{3}}{4} + \left(\frac{-2\sqrt{3}}{3}\right)$$

$$= -\frac{5\sqrt{3}}{12}$$

∴ Required quadratic equation

$$= x^2 - \left(\frac{-5\sqrt{3}}{12}\right)x + \left(\frac{-1}{2}\right)$$

$$= x^2 + \frac{5x}{4\sqrt{3}} - \frac{1}{2}$$

16. *(a)* We have, $p(-1) = 0$

$$\Rightarrow (-1)^3 + 3(-1)^2 - 2P(-1) + Q = 0$$

$$\Rightarrow \quad 2 + 2P + Q = 0 \quad \ldots\text{(i)}$$

Also, $p(-2) = 0$

$$\Rightarrow (-2)^3 + 3(-2)^2 - 2P(-2) + Q = 0$$

$$\Rightarrow \quad 4 + 4P + Q = 0 \quad \ldots\text{(ii)}$$

On subtracting Eq. (i) from Eq. (ii), we get

$$2 + 2P = 0$$

$$\Rightarrow \quad P = -1$$

$$\Rightarrow \quad Q = 0 \quad \text{[from Eq. (i)]}$$

17. *(c)* $f(x) = x^2 - 3x + 2$

$$= (x - 2)(x - 1)$$

$$\alpha = 2 \text{ and } \beta = 1$$

$$\therefore \quad \frac{2\alpha}{\beta} = \frac{2 \times 2}{1} = 4$$

and $$\frac{2\beta}{\alpha} = \frac{2 \times 1}{2} = 1$$

∴ The new quadratic polynomial

$$= x^2 - \left(\frac{2\alpha}{\beta} + \frac{2\beta}{\alpha}\right)x + \frac{2\alpha}{\beta} \times \frac{2\beta}{\alpha}$$

$$= x^2 - (4+1)x + 4 \times 1$$

$$= x^2 - 5x + 4$$

18. *(a)* $\alpha + \beta + \gamma = 2 = \frac{-b}{a}$

$$\Rightarrow \quad b = -2a$$

$$\alpha\beta + \beta\gamma + \gamma\alpha = -7 = \frac{c}{a}$$

$$\Rightarrow \quad c = -7a$$

and $$\alpha\beta\gamma = -14 = \frac{-d}{a}$$

$$\Rightarrow \quad d = 14a$$

$$b : c : d = -2 : -7 : 14$$

Cubic polynomial is $k(x^3 - 2x^2 - 7x + 14)$

19. *(a)* ∵ $p(-a) = 0$

$$\Rightarrow a^2(-a) + 2a(-a)^2 - b^3 = 0$$

$$\Rightarrow \quad -a^3 + 2a^3 - b^3 = 0$$

$$\Rightarrow \quad a^3 - b^3 = 0$$

$$\Rightarrow \quad a^3 = b^3 \Rightarrow a = b$$

20. *(b)* In figure (A), curve intersects X-axis at two times. Hence, it has two zeroes.

In figure (B), curve touches X-axis at one time. Hence, it has one zero.

In figure (C), curve doesn't intersect/touch X-axis. Hence, it has no zero.

21. *(c)* $\therefore \frac{P(x)}{Q(x)} = \dfrac{\frac{1+5x}{1-5x}}{\frac{1-5x}{1+5x}}$

$$= \frac{(1+5x)(1+5x)}{(1-5x)(1-5x)} = \frac{(1+5x)^2}{(1-5x)^2}$$

22. *(a)* $f(x) = x^2 + 6x + a$

$$g(x) = x^2 + 4x + b$$

$$h(x) = x^2 + 14x + c$$

$$\text{LCM} = (x+8)(x-2)(x+6)$$

As three given polynomials are quadratic and their LCM is cubic, each polynomial is the product of two factors of LCM. By inspection methods,

$$f(x) = x^2 + 6x + a$$

$$= (x+8)(x-2)$$

$$\Rightarrow a = -16$$

$$g(x) = x^2 + 4x + b$$

$$= (x-2)(x+6)$$

$$\Rightarrow b = -12$$

$$h(x) = x^2 + 14x + c$$

$$= (x+8)(x+6)$$

$$\Rightarrow c = 48$$

$$\therefore a + b + c = -16 - 12 + 48 = 20$$

23. *(b)* Let A be the required expression

$$\frac{1}{x-2} + \frac{1}{x+2} + A = \frac{4x^3}{x^4 - 16}$$

$$\therefore A = \frac{4x^3}{x^4 - 16} - \left(\frac{1}{(x-2)} + \frac{1}{x+2}\right)$$

$$= \frac{4x^3}{x^4 - 16} - \frac{2x}{x^2 - 4}$$

$$= \frac{2x}{x^2 - 4}\left[\frac{2x^2}{x^2 + 4} - 1\right]$$

$$= \frac{2x}{x^2 - 4}\left[\frac{2x^2 - x^2 - 4}{x^2 + 4}\right]$$

$$= \frac{2x}{x^2 + 4}$$

24. *(b)* Given, Length of the garden $= (2x^3 + 5x^2 - 7)$ m

We know, Perimeter of the garden $= 2 \times (\text{length} + \text{breadth})$

$\therefore 4x^3 - 2x^2 + 4$
$= 2(2x^3 + 5x^2 - 7 + \text{breadth})$
$\Rightarrow 2x^3 - x^2 + 2$
$= (2x^3 + 5x^2 - 7) + \text{breadth}$

So, breadth of the rectangle
$= 2x^3 - x^2 + 2 - 2x^3 - 5x^2 + 7$
$= (-6x^2 + 9)$ m

25. (a) $P(x)$
$= (x+1)(x-3)(2x^2 + ax - 2)$
As, $\text{HCF} = (x-3)(x+2)$
$\therefore P(-2) = 0$
or $x = -2$ is the zero.
$\Rightarrow [(-2+1)(-2-3)\{2\times 4 + a(-2) - 2\}] = 0$
$\Rightarrow (-1)(-5)(8 - 2a - 2) = 0$
$\Rightarrow 5(6 - 2a) = 0 \Rightarrow a = 3$
Also, $Q(x)$
$= (x-1)(x+2)(3x^2 + bx - 3)$
As, $\text{HCF} = (x-3)(x+2)$
$\therefore Q(3) = 0$
or $x = 3$ is the zero.
$\Rightarrow (3-1)(3+2)(3\times 9 + 3b - 3) = 0$
$\Rightarrow 10(24 + 3b) = 0$
$\Rightarrow b = -8$

26. (b) Here,
$\alpha + \beta = \frac{-10}{4}$ and $\alpha\beta = \frac{k}{4}$
$\alpha^2 + \beta^2 + \alpha\beta = \frac{21}{4}$
$\Rightarrow (\alpha+\beta)^2 - 2\alpha\beta + \alpha\beta = \frac{21}{4}$
$\Rightarrow \left(\frac{-10}{4}\right)^2 - \alpha\beta = \frac{21}{4}$
$\Rightarrow \frac{100 - 4k}{16} = \frac{21}{4}$
$\Rightarrow 100 - 84 = 4k$
$\Rightarrow 16 = 4k \Rightarrow k = 4$

27. (c) $2x^2 - 5x - (2k+1)$
Then, $2\alpha^2 - 5\alpha - (2k+1) = 0$
and $2(2\alpha)^2 - 5(2\alpha) - (2k+1) = 0$
$2\alpha^2 - 5\alpha = 2k+1$ ...(i)
$8\alpha^2 - 10\alpha = 2k+1$ ...(ii)
From Eqs. (i) and (ii), we get
$2\alpha^2 - 5\alpha = 8\alpha^2 - 10\alpha$
$\Rightarrow 6\alpha^2 = 5\alpha$
$\Rightarrow \alpha = \frac{5}{6}$ $[\because \alpha \neq 0]$
$\Rightarrow 2\alpha = \frac{5}{6} \times 2 = \frac{5}{3}$
Thus, the zeroes of the polynomial are $\frac{5}{6}$ and $\frac{5}{3}$. Now, substituting $\alpha = \frac{5}{6}$ in Eq. (i),
we get
$2\times\frac{25}{36} - \frac{25}{6} = 2k+1$
$2k + 1 = \frac{50-150}{36}$
$\Rightarrow 2k+1 = \frac{-100}{36}$
$2k = \frac{-100}{36} - 1$
$\Rightarrow 2k = \frac{-136}{36}$
$k = \frac{-68}{36} = \frac{-17}{9}$

28. (c) Here, $\alpha + \beta = \frac{8}{2} = 4$
and $\alpha\beta = \frac{4}{2} = 2$
Now,
$\frac{\alpha}{\beta} + \frac{\beta}{\alpha} + 2\left(\frac{1}{\alpha} + \frac{1}{\beta}\right) + 3\alpha\beta$
$= \frac{\alpha^2 + \beta^2}{\alpha\beta} + 2\left(\frac{\alpha+\beta}{\alpha\beta}\right) + 3\alpha\beta$
$= \frac{(\alpha+\beta)^2 - 2\alpha\beta}{\alpha\beta} + 2\left(\frac{\alpha+\beta}{\alpha\beta}\right) + 3\alpha\beta$
$= \frac{(4)^2 - 2\times 2}{2} + 2\left(\frac{4}{2}\right) + 3\times 2$
$= 6 + 4 + 6 = 16$

29. (d) I. True,
Since, $(\alpha+\beta)^2 = 4\alpha\beta$
$\Rightarrow \alpha^2 + \beta^2 - 2\alpha\beta = 0$
$\Rightarrow (\alpha - \beta)^2 = 0$
$\Rightarrow \alpha = \beta$
II. True,
Given, $\alpha + \beta = 0$
$4 + \beta = 0$
$\Rightarrow \beta = -4$
$\therefore$ Coefficient of linear term
$= \alpha + \beta = 0$
$\therefore x^2 - (\alpha+\beta)x + \alpha\beta = x^2 - 16$
III. False,
$\alpha + \beta + \gamma = 5$
and $\alpha\beta + \beta\gamma + \alpha\gamma = 8$
Now, $(\alpha+\beta+\gamma)^2 = \alpha^2 + \beta^2 + \gamma^2 + 2(\alpha\beta + \beta\gamma + \alpha\gamma)$
$\Rightarrow 25 = \alpha^2 + \beta^2 + \gamma^2 + 2\times 8$
$\Rightarrow 9 = \alpha^2 + \beta^2 + \gamma^2$

Chapter 3 : Pair of Linear Equations in Two Variables

1. (d) Consider $4x^2 - 9y^2 = 0$
$\Rightarrow (2x - 3y)(2x + 3y) = 0$
$\Rightarrow 2x - 3y = 0$ and $2x + 3y = 0$

2. (b) Let the number of questions which are correct be x and the questions which is wrong be y.
$\because x + y = 50$ ...(i)
$2x - \frac{y}{2} = 40$
$4x - y = 80$ ...(ii)
From Eqs. (i) and (ii), we have
$5x = 130$
$x = 26$
$y = 24$
$\therefore$ Questions which is correctly attempted is 26.

3. (d) Semi-perimeter of a triangle$(s) = \frac{a+b+c}{2}$
$a + 5 = s; b + 3 = s; c + 2 = s$
Perimeter of triangle
$= a + b + c$
$2s = s - 5 + s - 3 + s - 2$
$-10 = s$
$\therefore$ Perimeter of triangle $(2s) = 20$

4. (c) Let the number of cows be x and let the number of hens be y.
So, $4x + 2y = 92$ ...(i)
$x + y = 29$ ...(ii)
By multiplying Eq. (ii) by 2, we get
$2x + 2y = 58$ ...(iii)

Now, on subtracting Eqs. (i) and (iii), we get

$2x = 34$

$\Rightarrow \quad x = 17$

$\therefore$ Number of cows in his shed $= 17$

5. (*d*) Let the number of lux cakes be x and dove cakes be y.

Given, $30x + 40y = 360$

$3x + 4y = 36$

$\Rightarrow \quad x = \frac{36 - 4y}{3}$

$\Rightarrow \quad x = 12 - \frac{4y}{3}$

As x and y are positive integers, $y = 3$ or 6

$\Rightarrow \quad x = 8, 1$

There are two combinations.

6. (*d*) Let there are x boys and y girls in the class.

Case I

$12x + 6y = 900$

$2x + y = 150 \quad \ldots(i)$

Case II

$5x + 10y = 900$

$x + 2y = 180 \quad \ldots(ii)$

By mutiplying Eqs. (ii) by 2 and subtracting both equation, we get

$2x + y = 150$

$2x + 4y = 360$

$- \quad - \quad -$

$-3y = -210$

$y = 70$

Put $y = 70$ in Eq. (ii), we get

$x = 40$

$\therefore$ Total number of students of the class $= 110$

7. (*c*) Let there be n students in the class. The total weight of the students after the eight new students join the class.

$60n + 64(8) = 62(n + 8)$

$\Rightarrow 60n + 64(8) = 62n + 62(8)$

$\Rightarrow \quad 62n - 60n = 64(8) - 62(8)$

$\Rightarrow \quad 2n = 8(2)$

$\Rightarrow \quad n = 8$

$\therefore$ Initially, there were 8 students in the class.

8. (*b*) Given,

$x + 2y = -1 \quad \ldots(i)$

and $\quad 2x - 3y = 12 \quad \ldots(ii)$

From Eq. (i), we get

$x = -1 - 2y \quad \ldots(iii)$

Putting the value in Eq. (ii) from Eq. (iii), we get

$2(-1 - 2y) - 3y = 12$

$\Rightarrow \quad -7y = 14$

$\Rightarrow \quad y = -2$

Now, $x = -1 - 2y = -1 - 2(-2)$

$= -1 + 4 = 3$

$\therefore \quad x = 3, y = -2$

9. (*d*) Let the monthly income of X and Y be $3x$, $4x$ and montly expenditures be $5y$, $7y$.

Saving $(X) = 3x - 5y$

Saving $(Y) = 4x - 7y$

Given, $\frac{3x - 5y}{4x - 7y} = \frac{3}{2}$

$\Rightarrow 6x - 10y = 12x - 21y$

$\Rightarrow 6x - 11y = 0 \quad \ldots(i)$

and $(3x - 5y) - (4x - 7y) = 500$

$\Rightarrow -x + 2y = 500 \quad \ldots(ii)$

Solving Eqs. (i) and (ii), we get $y = 3000$ and $x = 5500$

$\therefore$ Monthly income of Mr. Y

$= 4x = ₹\, 22000$

10. (*d*) Let the length and breadth of the rectangle be x unit and y unit respectively.

$\therefore$ According to the first condition,

$(x + 2)(y + 2) = xy + 76$

$xy + 2x + 2y + 4 = xy + 76$

$2x + 2y = 72$

$x + y = \frac{72}{2} = 36$

11. (*b*) Let the numerator and denominator be x and y respectively.

According to the question,

$\frac{x + 1}{y + 1} = \frac{4}{5}$

$\Rightarrow \quad 5(x + 1) = 4(y + 1)$

$\Rightarrow \quad 5x - 4y = -1 \quad \ldots(i)$

and $\quad \frac{x - 5}{y - 5} = \frac{1}{2}$

$\Rightarrow \quad 2x - 10 = y - 5$

$\Rightarrow \quad 2x - y = 5 \quad \ldots(ii)$

Solving Eqs. (i) and (ii), we get

$x = 7$

$\therefore$ Numerator $= 7$

12. (*a*) Let the number of 50 paise coins and 40 paise coins be x and y respectively. Then

$x + y = 50 \quad \ldots(i)$

and $0.5x + 0.4y = 22$

$\Rightarrow \quad 5x + 4y = 220 \quad \ldots(ii)$

Solving Eqs. (i) and (ii), we get $x = 20$ and $y = 30$

13. (*c*) Given, $x + y = a + b \quad \ldots(i)$

and $\quad ax - by = a^2 - b^2 \quad \ldots(ii)$

By using elimination method, we get

$ax + ay = a^2 + ab$

$ax - by = a^2 - b^2$

$- \quad + \quad - \quad +$

$(a + b)\, y = b^2 + ab$

$\Rightarrow \quad (a + b)\, y = b\,(a + b)$

$\Rightarrow \quad y = b$

$\therefore \quad x = a \quad$ [from Eq. (i)]

14. (*d*) Let depreciation on machinery be ₹ x and depreciation on equipment be ₹ y. Then,

$x + y = 8000 \quad \ldots(i)$

Also, $\quad \frac{x}{y} = \frac{1}{3}$

$\Rightarrow \quad 3x = y \quad \ldots(ii)$

From Eqs. (i) and (ii), we get

$x + 3x = 8000$

$\Rightarrow \quad 4x = 8000 \Rightarrow x = \frac{8000}{4}$

$\therefore \quad x = ₹\, 2000$

Depreciation on equipment

$= 3x = ₹\, 6000$

$\therefore$ Rate of depreciation on equipment $= \frac{6000}{8000} \times 100 = 75\%$

15. (*a*) In a cyclic quadrilateral, sum of opposite angles is 180°.

$\therefore 3y - 5 - 4x + 5 = 180°$

$\Rightarrow \quad 3y - 4x = 180° \quad \ldots(i)$

and $\quad 2y + 15 - 4x + 5 = 180°$

$\Rightarrow \quad 2y - 4x = 160° \quad \ldots(ii)$

On solving Eqs. (i) and (ii), we get

$x = -30°$ and $y = 20°$

$A = 2y + 15 = 2 \times 20° + 15 = 55°$

$B = -4x + 5$

$= -4 \times (-30) + 5 = 125°$

$C = -4x + 5 = -4 \times 30° + 5$

$= 125°$

$D = 3y - 5 = 3 \times 20 - 5 = 55°$

16. (c) $3x + 7y = 32$ ...(i)

$7x + 3y = 48$ ...(ii)

Step 1 Adding both the equations, we get

$10x + 10y = 80$

$\Rightarrow 10(x + y) = 80$

$x + y = 8$ ...(iii)

Step 2 Subtracting Eq. (i) from Eq. (ii), we have

$(7x + 3y) - (3x + 7y) = 48 - 32$

$\Rightarrow 4x - 4y = 16$

$\Rightarrow 4(x - y) = 4 \times 4$

$x - y = 4$ ...(iv)

Step 3 Adding the Eqs. (iii) and (iv), we have

$x + y + x - y = 12$

$\Rightarrow 2x = 12$

$\Rightarrow x = 6$

Substituting $x = 6$ in any of the Eqs. (i), (ii), (iii) or (iv), we get $y = 2$

$\therefore$ The solution of the pair of equations is

$x = 6, y = 2$

17. (a) Let x, y be the tens and units digits respectively.

According to question,

$10x + y = x + y + 4 + 10y + x$

$\Rightarrow 8x - 10y = 4$

$\Rightarrow 4x - 5y = 2$ ...(i)

$\Rightarrow 10x + y = 10y + x + 18$

$x - y = 2$ ...(ii)

Multiply Eq. (ii) by 4, we have

$4x - 4y = 8$ ...(iii)

Subtracting Eq. (i) from Eq. (iii), we get

$y = 6$

Substitute $y = 6$ in Eq. (ii), we have

$x = 8$

$\therefore$ Product of the digits

$= xy = 48$

18. (c) Let the present age of father and son be x and y years respectively. Then,

$(x - 2) = 5(y - 2)$

$\Rightarrow x - 2 = 5y - 10$

$\Rightarrow x - 5y + 8 = 0$ ...(i)

and $x + 2 = 3(y + 2) + 8$

$\Rightarrow x + 2 = 3y + 6 + 8$

$\Rightarrow x - 3y - 12 = 0$ ...(ii)

Solving Eqs. (i) and (ii), we get

$x = 42$ yr and $y = 10$ yr

19. (a) By cross-multiplication,

we have $\frac{x}{\{b \times -(1 + c)\} - a \times -c}$

$= \frac{-y}{\{a \times -(1 + c)\} - b \times -c}$

$= \frac{1}{(a \times a) - b \times b}$

$\Rightarrow \frac{x}{ac - bc - b}$

$= \frac{y}{ac - bc + a} = \frac{1}{a^2 - b^2}$

$\Rightarrow \frac{x}{c(a - b) - b} = \frac{y}{c(a - b) + a}$

$= \frac{1}{(a - b)(a + b)}$

$\Rightarrow x = \frac{c(a - b) - b}{(a - b)(a + b)}$

and $y = \frac{c(a - b) + a}{(a - b)(a + b)}$

Hence, $x = \frac{c}{a + b} - \frac{b}{a^2 - b^2}$

and $y = \frac{c}{a + b} + \frac{a}{a^2 - b^2}$

20. (a) Let the person invested ₹ x at the rate of 12% SI and ₹ y at the rate of 10% SI, then according to the question,

$\frac{12x}{100} + \frac{10y}{100} = 130$

$\Rightarrow 12x + 10y = 13000$

$\Rightarrow 6x + 5y = 6500$ ...(i)

and $\frac{10x}{100} + \frac{12y}{100} = 134$

$\Rightarrow 10x + 12y = 13400$

$\Rightarrow 5x + 6y = 6700$ ...(ii)

On solving Eqs. (i) and (ii), we get

$x = 500$ and $y = 700$

$\therefore$ Original interest

$= 12\%$ of $500 + 10\%$ of 700

$= 60 + 70 = 130$

Hence, total amount

$= 1200 + 130 =$ ₹1330

21. (b) Let Mr Linda invested ₹x at 9% and ₹y at 8%.

According to the question,

$x + y = 40000$ ... (i)

and $\frac{9}{100} \times 2 \times x + \frac{8}{100} \times 2 \times y$

$= 7000$

$\Rightarrow 18x + 16y = 700000$ ...(ii)

$\Rightarrow x =$ ₹ 30000

and $y =$ ₹ 10000

Now, interest earned if amount invested is interchanged

$= \frac{30000 \times 2 \times 8}{100} + \frac{10000 \times 2 \times 9}{100}$

$= 4800 + 1800 =$ ₹6600

22. (b) Consider $\frac{2}{x} + \frac{2}{3y} = \frac{1}{6}$ ...(i)

and $\frac{3}{x} + \frac{2}{y} = 0$ ...(ii)

Put $x = 6, y = -4$ in Eq. (i), we get

$\text{LHS} = \frac{2}{6} + \frac{2}{3 \times -4} = \frac{2}{6} - \frac{2}{12}$

$= \frac{4 - 2}{12} = \frac{2}{12} = \frac{1}{6} = \text{RHS}$

Put $x = 6, y = -4$ in Eq. (ii),

$\text{LHS} = \frac{3}{6} + \frac{2}{(-4)}$

$= \frac{3}{6} - \frac{2}{4} = \frac{1}{2} - \frac{1}{2} = 0 = \text{RHS}$

Hence, it is a solution of the given equations.

23. (c) Given,

$\left(\frac{1 + b}{b}\right)x + \left(\frac{1 + a}{a}\right)y = b - a$

...(i)

and $\frac{1}{b}x - \frac{4}{a}y = 5$ ... (ii)

On multiplying Eq. (i) by $\frac{4}{a}$ and Eq. (ii) by $\left(\frac{1 + a}{a}\right)$, and adding, we get

$\frac{4}{a}\left(\frac{1+b}{b}\right)x+\frac{1}{b}\left(\frac{1+a}{a}\right)x$

$=\frac{4}{a}(b-a)+5\left(\frac{1+a}{a}\right)$

$\Rightarrow \left\{\frac{4}{a}\frac{(1+b)}{b}+\frac{(1+a)}{ab}\right\}x = \frac{4(b-a)}{a}+\frac{5(a+1)}{a}$

$\Rightarrow \left(\frac{a+5+4b}{ab}\right)x=\frac{a+5+4b}{a}$

$\Rightarrow \quad x=b$

On putting $x=b$ in Eq. (ii), we get

$1-\frac{4}{a}y=5 \Rightarrow \quad y=-a$

24. (b) $2x-3y=18$ ...(i)

$4x-y=16$ ...(ii)

By multiplying Eq. (i) by 2 and subtracting, we get

$4x-6y=36$
$4x-y=16$
$- \quad + \quad -$
$-5y=+20$
$y=-4$

Put $y=-4$ in Eq. (i), we get

$2x-3(-4)=18$

$\Rightarrow \quad 2x=6 \Rightarrow x=3$

Now, put $x=3$ and $y=-4$ in given equation

$5x-py-23=0$

$\Rightarrow 5(3)-p(-4)-23=0$

$\Rightarrow \quad +4p=8$

$\Rightarrow \quad p=2$

25. (b) Let the age of mother be x years and age of her son by y years.

$x+y=2(x-12)$

$\Rightarrow x+y=2x-24$

$\Rightarrow \quad y=x-24$ ...(i)

$\Rightarrow (x+9)+(y+9)=3(x-14)$

$\Rightarrow x+y+18=3x-42$

Put the value of y from Eq. (i),

$x+x-24+18=3x-42$

$\Rightarrow \quad 36=x$

$\therefore \quad x=36$ yr

Now, put the value of x in Eq. (i),

$y=12$ yr

Hence, her son's present age is 12 yr.

Chapter 4 : Quadratic Equations

1. (d) Given equation

$=ax^m+bx^n+c=0$

For $m=1$ and $n=2$,

$ax+bx^2+c=0$

$\Rightarrow \quad bx^2+ax+c=0$ ...(i)

For $m=2$ and $n=1$,

$ax^2+bx+c=0$ ...(ii)

Both Eqs. (i) and (ii) are quadratic.

2. (d) Let Rakhi's age be x yr, then Rakhi's mother's age be $(x+26)$ yr.

According to the question,

$(x+3)(x+29)=360$

$\Rightarrow \quad x^2+32x+87=360$

$\Rightarrow \quad x^2+32x-273=0$

3. (c) Given, $\frac{x+3}{x+2}=\frac{3x-7}{2x-3}$

$(x+3)(2x-3)=(3x-7)(x+2)$

$\Rightarrow 2x^2+3x-9=3x^2-x-14$

$\Rightarrow \quad x^2-4x-5=0$

By factorization,

$x^2-5x+x-5=0$

$\Rightarrow \quad x(x-5)+1(x-5)=0$

$\Rightarrow \quad (x-5)(x+1)=0$

$\Rightarrow \quad x=5,-1$

4. (a) Given, equation is

$17a^2-20a+10=10a^2+2a+7$

$\Rightarrow \quad 7a^2-22a+3=0$

$\Rightarrow \quad 7a^2-21a-a+3=0$

$\Rightarrow 7a(a-3)-1(a-3)=0$

$\therefore \quad a=3$ or $a=\frac{1}{7}$

Roots of the given equation

$=3,\frac{1}{7}$

5. (a) Given,

$x^2-120x+2000=0$

$\Rightarrow x^2-2\times 60x+2000 + 3600-3600=0$

$\Rightarrow \quad (x-60)^2=1600$

$\Rightarrow \quad (x-60)^2=(40)^2$ ...(i)

Comparing Eq. (i) with $(x+\alpha)^2=c^2$, we get

$\alpha=-60$ and $c=40$

6. (b) The required equation is

x^2-(Sum of roots) $x+$ Product of roots $=0$

$\Rightarrow x^2-[7+(-3)]x+(7)(-3)=0$

$\Rightarrow \quad x^2-4x-21=0$

7. (b) Given, one of the root of the equation,

$x=3+2\sqrt{3} \Rightarrow x-3=2\sqrt{3}$

Squaring on both sides,

$(x-3)^2=(2\sqrt{3})^2$

$x^2+9-6x=12$

$x^2-6x-3=0$

8. (b) For equal roots, $D=0$

i.e. $\quad b^2-4ac=0$

$\therefore \quad (k-2)^2-4\times(k-2)\times 2=0$

$\Rightarrow \quad k^2+4-4k-8(k-2)=0$

$\Rightarrow \quad k^2+4-4k-8k+16=0$

$\Rightarrow \quad k^2-12k+20=0$

$\Rightarrow \quad (k-10)(k-2)=0$

$\Rightarrow \quad k=2$ or $k=10$

But $k=2$ will make the equation non-quadratic.

$\therefore k=10$ is the possible answer.

9. (a) Given, equation

$mx^2+nx-10=0$

Putting roots $x=\frac{-2}{5}$ and $x=\frac{5}{3}$

$4m-10n=250$ ...(i)

and $25m+15m=90$ ...(ii)

On solving,

$m=15$ and $n=-19$

10. (c) (ii) $9x^2+3kx+4=0$

Since, $D=0$ [equal roots]

i.e. $\quad b^2-4ac=0$

$\Rightarrow (3k)^2-4\times 9\times 4=0$

$\Rightarrow \quad k^2-16=0$

$\Rightarrow \quad k=\pm 4$

(iii) $(k+4)x^2+(k+1)x+1=0$

Since, $b^2-4ac=0$

$\Rightarrow \quad (k+1)^2-4(k+4)=0$

$\Rightarrow k^2+1+2k-4k-16=0$

$\Rightarrow \quad k^2-2k-15=0$

$\Rightarrow \quad (k-5)(k+3)=0$

$\Rightarrow \quad k = 5 \text{ and } -3$

(iv) $5x^2 - kx + 1 = 0$

$\because \quad b^2 - 4ac = 0$

$\Rightarrow k^2 - 4 \times 5 = 0 \Rightarrow k^2 = 20$

$\Rightarrow \quad k = \pm\sqrt{20}$

11. (b) A. $\because D = b^2 - 4ac$

$= 1 - 4 \times 2 \times (-1)$

$= 1 + 8 = 9 > 0$

Real and distinct.

B. $\because \quad D = b^2 - 4ac$

$= (-4)^2 - 4 \times 4 \times 1$

$= 16 - 16 = 0$

Real and equal.

C. $\because \quad D = (5)^2 - 4 \times 2 \times 5$

$= 25 - 40 = -15 < 0$

Not real.

12. (d) For no real roots,

$b^2 - 4ac < 0,$

$[2(ac+bd)]^2 - 4(a^2+b^2)(c^2+d^2) < 0$

$\Rightarrow 4(a^2c^2 + b^2d^2 + 2abcd) - 4(a^2c^2 + a^2d^2 + b^2c^2 + b^2d^2) < 0$

$\Rightarrow -4(a^2d^2 + b^2c^2 - 2abcd) < 0$

$\Rightarrow \quad (a^2d^2 + b^2c^2 - 2abcd) > 0$

$\Rightarrow \quad (ad - bc)^2 > 0$

$\Rightarrow \quad ad > bc \Rightarrow ad \neq bc$

13. (a) For non-real roots,

$b^2 - 4ac < 0 \Rightarrow b^2 - 64 < 0$

$\Rightarrow \quad b^2 < 64 \Rightarrow |b| < 8$

$\Rightarrow \quad b < 8$ and $b > -8$

$\therefore \quad -8 < b < 8$

14. (a) We have $x^2 - px + q = 0$

Let α and β are two real roots.

So, $\alpha + \beta = p, \alpha\beta = q$

Given, $\alpha - \beta = 1$

$\therefore \quad 2\alpha = p + 1 \Rightarrow \alpha = \frac{p+1}{2}$

Now $\beta = p - \alpha = p - \frac{p+1}{2}$

$= \frac{2p - p - 1}{2} = \frac{p-1}{2}$

and $\alpha\beta = q$

$\left(\frac{p+1}{2}\right)\left(\frac{p-1}{2}\right) = q$

$\Rightarrow p^2 - 1 = 4q \Rightarrow p^2 - 4q = 1$

15. (a) Let the length of each side of the square A be x m.

Then, its perimeter will be $4x$ m. Therefore, perimeter of square B will be $(24 + 4x)$ m.

$\Rightarrow$ Side of square $B = \frac{24 + 4x}{4}$

$= (6 + x)$ m

According to the question,

$x^2 + (6+x)^2 = 468$

$\Rightarrow x^2 + 36 + x^2 + 12x = 468$

$\Rightarrow \quad 2x^2 + 12x - 432 = 0$

$\Rightarrow \quad x^2 + 6x - 216 = 0$

16. (a) Let the digit at ten's place be x and one's place be y.

Then, the number $= 10x + y$

According to the question,

$10x + y = 4(x + y)$

$\Rightarrow \quad 6x - 3y = 0$

$\Rightarrow \quad y = 2x$ ...(i)

and $\quad 10x + y = 3xy$

$\Rightarrow 10x + 2x = 3x \times 2x$ [from Eq. (i)]

$\Rightarrow \quad 6x^2 - 12x = 0$

$\Rightarrow \quad 6x(x-2) = 0$

$\therefore \quad x = 2$ and $y = 4$

Hence, the number

$= 10 \times 2 + 4 = 24$

17. (c) Given, $\frac{n}{2}(n-3) = 90$

$\Rightarrow \quad n(n-3) = 180$

$\Rightarrow \quad n^2 - 3n - 180 = 0$

$\Rightarrow \quad n = 15, -12 \Rightarrow n = 15$

[$\because$ side can not be negative]

18. (b) Let the present age of son be x yr.

$\therefore$ Present age of man $= x^2$ yr

According to the question,

$x^2 - 1 = 8(x-1)$

$\Rightarrow \quad x^2 - 8x + 7 = 0$

$\therefore \quad x = 1$ or $x = 7$

Neglect $x = 1$, as this can't be possible.

$\therefore$ Present age of the man

$= (7)^2 = 49$ yr

19. (b) Let the number of persons be x, then gifts distributed by each member is $x - 1$.

According to the question,

$x(x-1) = 1980$

$\Rightarrow \quad x^2 - x - 1980 = 0$

By factorisation,

$x^2 - 45x + 44x - 1980 = 0$

$\Rightarrow x(x-45) + 44(x-45) = 0$

$\Rightarrow \quad (x-45)(x+44) = 0$

$\Rightarrow \quad x = 45, -44$

[$\because$ x can not be negative]

and number of gifts distributed by each member

$= x - 1 = 45 - 1 = 44$

20. (c) Let the average speed be x km/h and time taken be y h.

According to the question,

$xy = 1500 \Rightarrow y = \frac{1500}{x}$ ...(i)

and $(x + 250)\left(y - \frac{1}{2}\right) = 1500$

$\Rightarrow xy - \frac{1}{2}x + 250y - \frac{250}{2} = 1500$

$\Rightarrow 1500 - \frac{x}{2} + 250y - \frac{250}{2} = 1500$

$-\frac{1}{2}x + 250y - 125 = 0$

Put the value of y from Eq. (i),

$x^2 + 250x - 750000 = 0$

[By factorisation]

On solving, $x = -1000$ km/h

or $\quad x = 750$ km/h.

Negative value is neglected.

$\therefore$ Average speed $= 750$ km/h

21. (a) Let the two consecutive positive even numbers be x and $(x + 2)$ respectively.

According to the question,

$x^2 + (x+2)^2 = 340$

$x^2 + x^2 + 4 + 4x = 340$

$x^2 + 2x - 168 = 0$

[By factorisation]

$\therefore \quad x = -14$ or $x = 12$

Negative value is eliminated

$\therefore$ Consecutive numbers are 12 and 14.

22. (a) According to the question,

$(3k+1)(2k-1) = 144$

$6k^2 - k - 145 = 0$

On solving, $k = -\frac{29}{6}$ or $k = 5$

Negative value is neglected.

$\therefore$ Perimeter $= 2[3k+1+2k-1]$
$= 2[5k] = 10\times 5 = 50$ cm

23. (*d*) Let the shortest side be x m, then the hypotenuse $= (2x-1)$ m and the third side $= (x+1)$ m

According to the question,

$(2x-1)^2 = x^2 + (x+1)^2$

$[\because H^2 = P^2 + B^2$, in a right $\Delta ABC]$

$\Rightarrow 4x^2 + 1 - 4x = x^2 + x^2 + 1 + 2x$

$\Rightarrow 2x^2 - 6x = 0 \Rightarrow x^2 - 3x = 0$

$\Rightarrow \quad x(x-3) = 0$

$\Rightarrow \; x = 0$ and $3 \Rightarrow x = 3$

[$\because$ 0 is not possible]

$\therefore$ Shortest side $= 3$ m,
Hypotenuse $= 2\times 3 - 1 = 5$ m
and third side $= 3+1 = 4$ m

$\therefore$ Area of triangle $= \frac{1}{2}\times b\times h$

$= \frac{1}{2}\times 3\times 4 = 6\ \text{m}^2$

24. (*b*) Let the time taken by B be x days.

$\therefore$ The time taken by A be $(x-6)$ days.

$\Rightarrow$ B's one day's work $= \frac{1}{x}$

and A's one day's work $= \frac{1}{x-6}$

$\therefore$ A and B's one day's work

$= \frac{1}{x} + \frac{1}{x-6} = \frac{2x-6}{x^2-6x}$

According to the question,

$\frac{2x-6}{x^2-6x} = \frac{1}{4}$

$\Rightarrow \quad 8x - 24 = x^2 - 6x$

$\Rightarrow \quad x^2 - 14x + 24 = 0$

$\Rightarrow x^2 - 12x - 2x + 24 = 0$

$\Rightarrow x(x-12) - 2(x-12) = 0$

$\Rightarrow \quad x = 12$ and 2

Since, $x = 2$ is not suitable.

$\therefore$ Required number of days by $B = 12$

25. (*d*) $\because \quad f(-2) = 0$

$\therefore (-2)^2 + (-2)p - 2 = 0$

$\Rightarrow \quad 4 - 2p - 2 = 0 \Rightarrow p = 1$

Now, for $x^2 + px + k = 0$ having equal roots,

$p^2 - 4k = 0 \Rightarrow 1 - 4k = 0$

[since, $p = 1$]

$\Rightarrow \quad k = \frac{1}{4}$

26. (*c*) Let three consecutive numbers be $x-1, x, x+1$.

According to the question,

$x^2 = [(x+1)^2 - (x-1)^2] + 60$

$\Rightarrow x^2 = [x^2 + 1 + 2x - x^2 - 1 + 2x] + 60$

$\Rightarrow \quad x^2 = 4x + 60$

$\Rightarrow x^2 - 4x - 60 = 0$

By factorisation,

$x^2 - 10x + 6x - 60 = 0$

$\Rightarrow \quad x(x-10) + 6(x-10) = 0$

$\Rightarrow \quad (x-10)(x+6) = 0$

$\Rightarrow \quad x = 10, -6$

[$\because$ x cannot be negative]

$\therefore$ The sequence of numbers $= 9$, 10 and 11

Hence, the sum $= 9 + 10 + 11 = 30$

27. (*b*) Let the time taken to reach be x h.

Total distance $= 150$ km

According to the question,

$\frac{150}{x} - \frac{150}{x+1} = 5$

$\Rightarrow 150x + 150 - 150x = 5x^2 + 5x$

$\Rightarrow \quad 5x^2 + 5x - 150 = 0$

$\Rightarrow \quad x^2 + x - 30 = 0$

By factorisation,

$x^2 + 6x - 5x - 60 = 0$

$\Rightarrow \quad x(x+6) - 5(x+6) = 0$

$\Rightarrow \quad (x+6)(x-5) = 0$

$\Rightarrow \quad x = -6, 5$

[$\because$ x cannot be negative]

$\Rightarrow \quad x = 5$

$\therefore$ Time taken to return $= 5 + 1 = 6$ h

28. (*b*) $x^2 + 2cx + ab = 0 \quad \ldots$(i)

$x^2 - 2(a+b)x + a^2 + b^2 + 2c^2 = 0 \quad \ldots$(ii)

On comparing above equations with

$A_1x^2 + B_1x + c_1 = 0$ and
$A_2x^2 + B_2x + C_2 = 0$
respectively, we get

$A_1 = 1, B_1 = 2c, C_1 = ab$
$A_2 = 1, B_2 = -2(a+b)$,
$C_2 = a^2 + b^2 + 2c^2$

Let D_1 and D_2 be the discriminant of Eqs. (i) and (ii), respectively.

$D_1 = (2c)^2 - 4\times 1\times ab$
$= 4c^2 - 4ab = 4(c^2 - ab)$

and $D_2 = [-2(a+b)]^2 - 4\times 1 \times(a^2 + b^2 + 2c^2)$

$= 4(a+b)^2 - 4(a^2 + b^2 + 2c^2)$

$= 4(2ab - 2c^2) = -8(c^2 - ab)$

Since, the roots of Eq. (i) are real and unequal.

$D_1 > 0 \Rightarrow (c^2 - ab) > 0$

$c^2 - ab > 0 \Rightarrow -8(c^2 - ab) < 0$

$D_2 < 0$

Hence, roots of Eq. (ii) are not real.

29. (*c*) Given, distance travelled by car A per litre is x km.

Distance travelled by car B travels per litre is $(x+5)$ km.

According to the question,

$\frac{400}{x} - \frac{400}{x+5} = 4$

$\Rightarrow \quad \frac{100}{x} - \frac{100}{x+5} = 1$

$\Rightarrow 100(x+5) - 100x = x^2 + 5x$

$\Rightarrow 100x + 500 - 100x = x^2 + 5x$

$\Rightarrow \quad x^2 + 5x - 500 = 0$

By factorisation,

$x^2 + 25x - 20x - 500 = 0$

$\Rightarrow x(x+25) - 20(x+5) = 0$

$\Rightarrow \quad (x+25)(x-20) = 0$

$\Rightarrow \quad x = -25, 20$

$\Rightarrow \quad x = 20$

[$\because$ x cannot be negative]

$\therefore$ Distance travelled per litre by B is $(x+5)$ km $= 25$ km

$\therefore$ Petrol usage by car $B = \frac{400}{25} = 16$ L

$\therefore$ Both the statements are required to answer the question.

30. (d) Let P be the initial profit (2 yr ago) and the increase in profit every year be $x\%$.

Then, profit at the end of first year

$$= P + \frac{Px}{100} = P\left(1 + \frac{x}{100}\right)$$

Profit at the end of the second year

$$= P\left(1+\frac{x}{100}\right)\left(1+\frac{x}{100}\right)$$

$$= P\left(1+\frac{x}{100}\right)^2$$

Since, profit is 4 times in last two years.

$$\therefore P\left(1+\frac{x}{100}\right)^2 = 4P$$

$$\Rightarrow \left(1+\frac{x}{100}\right)^2 = 4$$

$$\Rightarrow (100 + x)^2 = 4 \times (100)^2$$

$$\Rightarrow (100)^2 + x^2 + 200x = 40000$$

$$\Rightarrow x^2 + 200x - 30000 = 0$$

By factorisation,

$$x^2 + 300x - 100x - 30000 = 0$$

$$\Rightarrow x(x + 300) - 100(x + 300) = 0$$

$$\Rightarrow (x + 300)(x - 100) = 0$$

$$\Rightarrow x = -300, 100$$

[for increasing profit take '+' sign only]

$= 100\%$

Chapter 5 : Arithmetic Progressions

1. (a) Here, First term, $a = \frac{-3}{2}$

and common difference,

$$d = \frac{-1}{2} - \left(\frac{-3}{2}\right)$$

$$= \frac{-1}{2} + \frac{3}{2} = \frac{-1+3}{2} = 1$$

2. (b) Given, $A = (a - b)^2$

$$= a^2 + b^2 - 2ab$$

and $A + d = a^2 + b^2$

Now, $A + d - A = a^2 + b^2 - a^2 - b^2 + 2ab$

$\Rightarrow d = 2ab$

The next term $= A + 2d$

$$= a^2 + b^2 - 2ab + 4ab$$

$$\therefore T_3 = a^2 + b^2 + 2ab = (a + b)^2$$

3. (c) Given, a, b, c, d, e are in AP.

We have, $a = A \Rightarrow b = A + d$

$c = A + 2d \Rightarrow d = A + 3d$

and $e = A + 4d$

Consider, $a - 4b + 6c - 4d + e$

$$= A - 4(A + d) + 6(A + 2d) - 4(A + 3d) + A + 4d$$

$$= A - 4A - 4d + 6A + 12d - 4A - 12d + A + 4d$$

$$= 0$$

4. (c) Here, we see that 8th terms of given series $T_8 = 26$ and $T'_8 = 17$

The required term is the 8th term of the AP where,

$$a = \frac{-1}{3} \quad \text{and} \quad d = \frac{1}{3}$$

$$\therefore a_8 = a + 7d$$

$$= \frac{-1}{3} + \frac{7}{3}$$

$$= \frac{6}{3} = 2$$

5. (a) Let the numbers be $a - d$, $a, a + d$. Then,

$$a - d + a + a + d = 12$$

$$\Rightarrow 3a = 12 \Rightarrow a = 4 \text{ and}$$

$$(a - d)^3 + a^3 + (a + d)^3 = 288$$

$$a^3 - d^3 - 3ad(a - d) + a^3 + a^3 + d^3 + 3ad(a + d) = 288$$

$$\Rightarrow 3a^3 + 6ad^2 = 288$$

$$\Rightarrow 3 \times 4^3 + 6 \times 4 \times d^2 = 288$$

$$\Rightarrow 24d^2 = 288 - 192$$

$$\Rightarrow d^2 = \frac{96}{24} = 4 \Rightarrow d = \pm 2$$

The numbers are, $4 - 2, 4, 4 + 2$ i.e. 2, 4, 6

6. (d) The arrangement of apples form a sequence with terms 1,4,7,10,... with a (first term) = 1 and d (common difference)

$$= 4 - 1 = 3.$$

$\therefore$ Number of apples required to make a pile of 10th layer is

$$T_{10} = a + (10 - 1)a$$

$$= 1 + 9d$$

$$= 1 + 9 \times 3 = 28$$

7. (b) The arithmetic mean of p and q is $\frac{p+q}{2}$.

$$\therefore \frac{p^{n+1} + q^{n+1}}{p^n + q^n} = \frac{p+q}{2}$$

$$\Rightarrow 2p^{n+1} + 2q^{n+1} = p^{n+1} + p^n q + q^n p + q^{n+1}$$

$$\Rightarrow p^{n+1} + q^{n+1} = p^n q + q^n p$$

$$\Rightarrow p^n(p - q) = q^n(p - q)$$

$$\Rightarrow p^n = q^n \Rightarrow \left(\frac{p}{q}\right)^n = 1$$

$$\Rightarrow n = 0 \quad [\because a^0 = 1]$$

8. (c) Given, Radius of the first circle = r and then it is increased by 1 cm successively.

$\therefore r, r + 1, r + 2, r + 3, r + 4$ are radii of 5 circles respectively.

$\therefore$ Total length of wire required to make 5 such circles.

$$= 2\pi r + 2\pi(r + 1) + 2\pi(r + 2) + 2\pi(r + 3) + 2\pi(r + 4)$$

$$= 2\pi[r + r + 1 + r + 2 + r + 3 + r + 4]$$

$$= 2\pi\,[5r + 10] = 2 \times 5 \times \pi[r + 2]$$

$$= 10\pi(r + 2) \text{ cm}$$

9. (b) Given,

$$\text{AP} = \frac{1}{1\cdot 2}, \frac{1}{2\cdot 3}, \frac{1}{3\cdot 4}, \ldots$$

$\therefore n$th term of the AP.

$$= \frac{1}{n(n + 1)}$$

10. (b) Given, $a = 3$ ...(i)

$a + d = 7$ ...(ii)

and $a + (n - 1)d = 47$ ...(iii)

From Eqs. (i) and (ii), we get

$$a + d - a = 7 - 3 \Rightarrow d = 4$$

Using Eq. (iii), we get

$$3 + (n - 1)4 = 47$$

$$\Rightarrow (n - 1)4 = 44$$

$$\therefore n = 12$$

11. (b) Given,

$a_t = a + (t - 1)d = s$ ...(i)

and $a_s = a + (s - 1)d = t$ ...(ii)

Now, $(t - s) = a + (s - 1)d - a - (t - 1)d$

$$\Rightarrow t - s = (s - t)d$$

[from Eqs. (i) and (ii)]

$$\Rightarrow (t - s) = -(t - s)d$$

$\Rightarrow \quad d = -1$

From Eq. (i), we get

$a + (t-1)(-1) = s$

$\Rightarrow \quad a = s + t - 1$

Now, $\quad a_n = a + (n-1)d$

$= s + t - 1 + (n-1) \times (-1)$

$= s + t - 1 - n + 1$

$\therefore a_n = s + t - n$

12. (a) Let the sides of pentagon be, $a - 2d, a - d, a, a + d, a + 2d$.

Given, perimeter of pentagon $= 100$

$\therefore a - 2d + a - d + a + a + d + a + 2d = 100$

$\Rightarrow \quad 5a = 100 \Rightarrow a = 20$

Then, $a + 2d + a - 2d = 2a$

$= 2 \times 20 = 40$

13. (a) Let the common difference of two AP's be d_a and d_b.

Then, $\quad d_a = d_b \quad$ [given]

Now, $a_2 = 3 + d_a \quad$ ... (i)

and $\quad b_2 = 8 + d_b \quad$ ...(ii)

From Eqs. (i) and (ii), we get

$a_2 - b_2 = 3 - 8 + d_a - d_b = -5$

$[\because d_a = d_b]$

14. (b) According to the question,

$a_1 = 25 \Rightarrow a_2 = 22$

$a_3 = 19$ and so on.

So, $\quad d = 22 - 25 = -3$

Now, given $a_n = 7$

$\therefore \quad 7 = 25 + (n-1)(-3)$

$[\because a_n = a + (n-1)d]$

$\Rightarrow \quad -18 = (n-1)(-3)$

$\Rightarrow \quad n - 1 = 6 \Rightarrow n = 7$

15. (c) Given, $8a_8 = 15a_{15}$

$8[a + (8-1)d] = 15[a + (15-1)d]$

$\Rightarrow \quad 8a + 56d = 15a + 210d$

$\Rightarrow \quad 7a + 154d = 0$

$\Rightarrow \quad a + 22d = 0$

$\Rightarrow \quad a + (23-1)d = 0$

16. (c) Given, the rate of interest form an AP

10%, 11.5%, 13%, ...

Here, $a = 10\%$ and $d = 1.5\%$

Now, rate of interest for 11th year,

$a_{11} = 10\% + (11-1)1.5\%$

$= 10\% + 10 \times 1.5\%$

$= 10\% + 15\% = 25\%$

$\therefore \quad I = \frac{P \times R \times T}{100}$

$= \frac{1000 \times 25 \times 11}{100} = ₹\ 2750$

$\therefore$ Amount $= P + I$

$= 1000 + 2750 = ₹3750$

17. (c) Given an AP, with first term = 3.2

and common difference = 0.2

To find the nth term such that

$a_n = 6$

$\therefore \quad 6 = 3.2 + (n-1)(0.2)$

$\Rightarrow \quad 2.8 = (n-1)(0.2)$

$\Rightarrow \quad \frac{2.8}{0.2} = n - 1$

$\Rightarrow \quad n - 1 = 14 \Rightarrow n = 15$

18. (d) Number of workers left on 10th day $= 48 + (10-1)(-4)$

$[\because a = 48, d = -4]$

$= 48 + 9 \times (-4)$

$= 48 - 36 = 12$

Now, work done by 48 workers in 1 day $= \frac{1}{11}$

$\therefore$ Work done by 1 worker in 1 day $= \frac{1}{11 \times 48}$

$\therefore$ Work done by 12 workers in 1 day $= \frac{12}{11 \times 48} = \frac{1}{44}$

Then, time taken by the workers left, to complete the entire work, is 44 days.

19. (b) Given series is 1,7,13,...

i.e. $a = 1$ and $d = 7 - 1 = 6$

We know that,

$S_n = \frac{n}{2}[2a + (n-1)d]$

$\Rightarrow \quad 1160 = \frac{n}{2}[2 \times 1 + (n-1)6]$

$\Rightarrow \quad 1160 = n[1 + 3n - 3]$

$\Rightarrow \quad 3n^2 - 2n - 1160 = 0$

$\Rightarrow 3n^2 - 60n + 58n - 1160 = 0$

$\Rightarrow \quad (n-20)(3n+58) = 0$

$\Rightarrow \quad n = 20$

$[\because n$ can not be in fraction$]$

20. (d) Given, $S_m : S_n = 1 : 1$

$\therefore \frac{m}{2}[2a + (m-1)d] : \frac{n}{2}[2a + (n-1)d] = 1 : 1$

$\Rightarrow \quad \frac{m[2a + (m-1)d]}{n[2a + (n-1)d]} = \frac{1}{1}$

$\Rightarrow \quad m[2a + (m-1)d] = n[2a + (n-1)d]$

$\Rightarrow 2a(m-n) = d[(n-m)(n+m) - (n-m)]$

$\Rightarrow 2a(m-n) = d(n-m)(n+m-1)$

$\Rightarrow 2a + d(m+n-1) = 0$

21. (c) $S_m = \frac{m}{2}[2a + (m-1)d] = n$

$2am + m(m-1)d = 2n \quad$ ...(i)

and $S_n = \frac{n}{2}[2a + (n-1)d] = m$

$2an + n(n-1)d = 2m \quad$ ...(ii)

Subtracting Eq. (ii) from Eq. (i), we get

$2a(m-n) + [(m^2 - n^2) - (m-n)]d = 2(n-m)$

$\Rightarrow (m-n)[2a + (m+n-1)d] = -2(n-m)$

$\Rightarrow 2a + (m+n-1)d = -2$

$\therefore S_{m+n} = \frac{m+n}{2}[2a + (m+n-1)d]$

$= \frac{m+n}{2} \times -2 = -(m+n)$

22. (b) $\frac{S_n}{S'_n} = \frac{\frac{n}{2}[2a_1 + (n-1)d_1]}{\frac{n}{2}[2b_1 + (n-1)d_2]}$

$= \frac{5n+9}{9n+6}$

$\Rightarrow \quad \frac{2a_1 + (n-1)d_1}{2b_1 + (n-1)d_2} = \frac{5n+9}{9n+6}$

For the ratio of mth term, put $n = 2m - 1$, we get

$\frac{2a_1 + (2m-1-1)d_1}{2b_1 + (2m-1-1)d_2} = \frac{5(2m-1)+9}{9(2m-1)+6}$

$\Rightarrow \dfrac{a_1 + (m-1)d_1}{b_1 + (m-1)d_2} = \dfrac{10m+4}{18m-3}$

For $m = 18$, we have

$\dfrac{a_1 + 17d_1}{b_1 + 17d_2} = \dfrac{184}{321}$

23. (a) $S_1 = \dfrac{n}{2}[2\times 1 + (n-1)1]$

$S_1 = \dfrac{n}{2}(n+1)$

$S_2 = \dfrac{n}{2}[2\times 1 + (n-1)2]$

$= \dfrac{n}{2}[2 + 2n - 2] = n^2$

$S_3 = \dfrac{n}{2}[2\times 1 + (n-1)3]$

$= \dfrac{n}{2}[2 + 3n - 3] = \dfrac{n}{2}[3n-1]$

Now $S_1 + S_3 = \dfrac{n}{2}[n+1+3n-1]$

$= \dfrac{n}{2}\times 4n = 2n^2 = 2S_2$

24. (a) According to the question,

$a_m = 2a_n$

$\Rightarrow a + (m-1)d = 2[a + (n-1)d]$

$\Rightarrow a + md - d = 2a + 2nd - 2d$

$\Rightarrow \quad a = (m - 2n + 1)d$ ...(i)

Now, $a_n = 3a_p$

$\Rightarrow a + (n-1)d = 3[a + (p-1)d]$

$\Rightarrow \quad 2a = (n - 1 - 3p + 3)d$

$\Rightarrow \quad 2a = (n - 3p + 2)d$

From Eq. (i), we have

$2(m - 2n + 1)d = (n - 3p + 2)d$

$\Rightarrow \quad 2m - 5n + 3p = 0$

25. (b) SI for 1 yr,

$SI = \dfrac{P \times R \times T_1}{100}$

$= \dfrac{2000\times 4\times 1}{100} = ₹\,80$

SI for 2 yr,

$SI = \dfrac{2000\times 4\times 2}{100} = ₹160$

SI for 3 yr,

$SI = \dfrac{2000\times 4\times 3}{100} = ₹240$

and so on.

So, SI forms an AP

80, 160, 240, 320, ...

with $a = 80$ and $d = 80$

$\therefore$ Total interest for 30 yr,

$T_{30} = a + (n-1)d$

$= 80 + (30-1)80$

$= 80(30) = ₹2400$

26. (c)

$S_{2n} - S_n = \dfrac{2n}{2}[2a + (2n-1)d] - \dfrac{n}{2}[2a + (n-1)d]$

$= \dfrac{n}{2}[4a + 4nd - 2d - 2a - nd + d]$

$= \dfrac{n}{2}[2a + 3nd - d]$

$= \dfrac{n}{2}[2a + (3n-1)d]$

Now,

$\dfrac{S_{2n} - S_n}{S_{3n}} = \dfrac{\dfrac{n}{2}[2a + (3n-1)d]}{\dfrac{3n}{2}[2a + (3n-1)d]}$

$= \dfrac{1}{3}$

27. (c) Given, p, a, b, q are in AP.

$\therefore \quad 2a = p + b$ ...(i)

and $\quad 2b = a + q$ ...(ii)

From Eqs. (i) and (ii), we get

$2(b-a) = q + a - p - b$

$\Rightarrow \quad 2(b-a) - (a-b) = q - p$

$\Rightarrow \quad 3(b-a) = q - p$

$\Rightarrow \quad b - a = \dfrac{q-p}{3}$ ...(iii)

Now, consider p, m, n, q are in AP.

Similarly, we have

$2m = n + p$ ...(iv)

and $\quad 2n = m + q$ ...(v)

From Eqs.(iv) and (v), we get

$2(n-m) = m - n + q - p$

$\Rightarrow \quad 3(n-m) = q - p$

$\Rightarrow \quad n - m = \dfrac{q-p}{3}$ ...(vi)

From Eqs. (iii) and (vi),

$\dfrac{b-a}{n-m} = \dfrac{\dfrac{q-p}{3}}{\dfrac{q-p}{3}} = 1$

28. (a) We have,

d_1 = distance travelled to pick up the first flag

$= 10 + 10 = 2\times 10 = 20\text{ m}$

d_2 = distance travelled to pick up the second flag

$= 2\times(10+6) = 32\text{ m}$

$\vdots \qquad \vdots$

d_{10} = distance travelled to pick up 10th flag

$= 2\times[10 + (10-1)\times 6]\text{ m}$

$\therefore$ Total distance travelled

$= d_1 + d_2 + d_3 + \ldots + d_{10}$

$= \dfrac{10}{2}[2\times 20 + (10-1)12]$

$= 5(40 + 108) = 5\times 148 = 740\text{ m}$

29. (d) Given, series

$45^2 - 43^2 + 44^2 - 42^2 + 43^2 - 41^2 + \ldots$ 15 terms

$= (45^2 - 43^2) + (44^2 - 42^2) + (43^2 - 41^2) + \ldots$ 15 terms

$= (45+43)(45-43) + (44+42)(44-42) + (43+41)(43-41) + \ldots$ 15 terms

$= (45+43)(2) + (44+42)(2) + (43+41)(2) + \ldots$ 15 terms

$= 2[(45 + 44 + 43 + \ldots$ 15 terms$) + (43 + 42 + 41 + \ldots$ 15 terms$)]$

$= 2\times\dfrac{15}{2}[2\times 45 + (15-1)(-1)] + 2\times\dfrac{15}{2}[2\times 43 + (15-1)(-1)]$

$= 15(90-14) + 15(86-14)$

$= 15(76) + 15(72) = 2220$

30. (c) Let the digits of the number be $a-d, a, a+d$ (ones, tens and hundred, respectively), then the number so formed

$= 100(a+d) + 10\times a + 1(a-d)$

$= 100a + 100d + 10a + a - d$

$= 111a + 99d$ ...(i)

Number formed by reversing the digits

$= 100(a-d) + 10\times a + 1(a+d)$

$= 100a - 100d + 10a + a + d$

$= 111a - 99d$ ...(ii)

Now, according to the question,

$a + d + a + a - d = 21$

$\Rightarrow \quad 3a = 21 \quad \Rightarrow \quad a = 7$

Also,

$111a + 99d = 111a - 99d + 396$

[from Eqs. (i) and (ii)]

$\Rightarrow \quad 198d = 396 \Rightarrow d = 2$

$\therefore$ The number is

$111 \times 7 + 99 \times 2$

$= 777 + 198 = 975$

[from Eq. (i)]

31. (d) The first sequence of numbers satisfying the given statement is

4, 11, 18, 25, 32, 39, 46, $\boxed{53}$

and so on.

Which turns into an AP with $a_1 = 4$ and $d_1 = 7$.

The second sequence of numbers satisfying the given statement is

9, 20, 31, 42, $\boxed{53}$ and so on.

$\therefore$ The first common term of the required AP is 53.

difference 7 and of second sequence it is 11.

$\therefore$ Common difference

$= \text{LCM}(7, 11) = 77$

$\therefore$ The next term of the required sequence will be

$a + d = 53 + 77 = 130$

The expression for the terms of the required AP is $77k + 53$, $k = 0$ to 12.

[$\because$ for $k = 13$, $77 \times 13 = 1001$, which is not required]

$\therefore$ Total number of terms = 13

Chapter 6 : Similarity of Triangles

1. (c) Given, $\Delta ABC \sim \Delta PQR$

$\therefore \quad \frac{AB}{PQ} = \frac{BC}{QR} = \frac{AC}{PR}$

$\frac{AB}{PQ} = \frac{AC}{PR} \Rightarrow \frac{1}{1.5} = \frac{2}{PR}$

$\Rightarrow \quad PR = 3\,\text{cm}$

2. (d) We have, $\frac{BC}{DE} = \frac{2}{1}$

[by basic proportionality theorem]

$\Rightarrow \quad BC = 2DE$

$\Rightarrow \quad z - 33 = 2(z - 37)$

$\Rightarrow \quad z = 41$

$\therefore \quad BC = z - 33$

$= 41 - 33 = 8$

3. (c) Given, $DE \,||\, AB$

In ΔCDE and ΔCAB,

$\frac{CD}{CA} = \frac{CE}{CB} \Rightarrow \frac{CA}{CD} = \frac{CB}{CE}$

$\Rightarrow \quad \frac{CD + AD}{CD} = \frac{CE + EB}{CE}$

$\Rightarrow \quad 1 + \frac{AD}{CD} = 1 + \frac{EB}{CE}$

4. (b) $\because \quad \Delta ABC \sim \Delta DFE$

$\therefore \quad \frac{AB}{DF} = \frac{AC}{DE} \Rightarrow \frac{5}{7.5} = \frac{8}{DE}$

$\Rightarrow DE = 12\,\text{cm}$

and $\angle ABC = \angle DFE$

$= 180° - (50° + 30°) = 100°$

5. (a) Given, $LM \,||\, AB$

$\Rightarrow \quad \frac{LC}{AL} = \frac{MC}{MB}$

$\Rightarrow \quad \frac{LC}{AL} + 1 = \frac{MC}{MB} + 1$

$\Rightarrow \frac{LC + AL}{AL} = \frac{MC + MB}{MB}$

$\Rightarrow \quad \frac{AC}{AL} = \frac{BC}{BM}$

$\Rightarrow \quad \frac{4x}{2x + 4} = \frac{2x + 3}{x + 2}$

$\Rightarrow 4x^2 + 8x = 4x^2 + 8x + 6x + 12$

$\Rightarrow \quad 6x = -12$

$\Rightarrow \quad x = -2$

Neglecting the '–' sign.

$\therefore \quad x = 2$

6. (c) Since, ΔADE and ΔACB, is similar

$\frac{AD}{AC} = \frac{AE}{AB}$

$\angle A = \angle A$

and $\angle ACB = \angle ADE = 65°$

Also, $\angle AED = \angle ABC$

$= 180° - 105° = 75°$

In ΔADE,

$\angle ADE + \angle AED + \angle DAE = 180°$

$\Rightarrow \quad 65° + 75° + \angle DAE = 180°$

$\Rightarrow \quad \angle DAE = 180° - 140° = 40°$

7. (a) Given, $PQRS$ is a parallelogram.

$\Rightarrow \quad PQ \,||\, RS$ or $PQ \,||\, BS$

$\Rightarrow \angle APQ = \angle ABR$

[alternate angles]

$\angle PAQ = \angle BAR$

[vertically opposite angles]

$\Rightarrow \Delta APQ \sim \Delta ABR$

[by AA similarity]

$\Rightarrow \quad \frac{AP}{AB} = \frac{PQ}{BR}$

$\Rightarrow \quad \frac{AP}{AB} = \frac{x}{x} \Rightarrow \frac{AP}{AB} = 1$

[as $PQ = SR = x$]

8. (c) In ΔBAC, $DE \,||\, AC$

$\Rightarrow \quad \frac{BE}{EC} = \frac{BD}{DA}$ ...(i)

Also, in ΔBAP, $DC \,||\, AP$

$\Rightarrow \quad \frac{BC}{CP} = \frac{BD}{DA}$ ...(ii)

From Eqs. (i) and (ii), we get

$\frac{BE}{EC} = \frac{BC}{CP} \Rightarrow \frac{BE}{CE} = \frac{BC}{BP - BC}$

$\Rightarrow \quad \frac{BE}{CE} = \frac{4}{6 - 4} = \frac{2}{1}$

9. (c) Now, $\frac{AR}{RB} = \frac{AQ}{QC}$

$\Rightarrow \quad RQ \,||\, BC$

and $\quad RQ = \frac{1}{2} BC$

Similarly, we have

$PR = \frac{1}{2} AC,\ PQ = \frac{1}{2} AB$

$\Rightarrow RQ = PR = PQ$

[since, $BC = AC = AB$]

$\therefore PQR$ is an equilateral triangle.

Hence, $PQ + QR + RP$

$= \frac{1}{2}(AB + BC + CA)$

10. (b) In ΔAPB and ΔEPC,

$\angle APB = \angle CPE$

[vertically opposite angles]

$\angle PCE = \angle 3 = \angle PBA$ [given]

$\therefore \quad \Delta APB \sim \Delta EPC$

[by AA similarity]

$\Rightarrow \quad \angle PEC = \angle 1$ ...(i)

Similarly, is ΔFQD and ΔBQA, is similar

$\Rightarrow \quad \angle QFD = \angle 2 \quad \ldots(ii)$

From Eqs. (i) and (ii), we get

$\angle PEC = \angle QFD$

[$\because \angle 1 = \angle 2$, given]

$\Rightarrow \quad \angle OFE = \angle OEF$

$\Rightarrow \quad OF = OE$

$\therefore \Delta OFE$ is an isosceles triangle.

11. (a) Given,

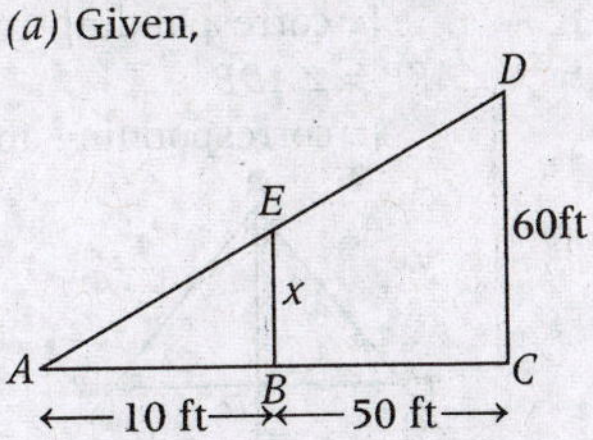

Let the height of the person be x ft.

We have, $\Delta ABE \sim \Delta ACD$

$\therefore \quad \frac{x}{10} = \frac{60}{60} \Rightarrow x = 10$ ft

12. (b)

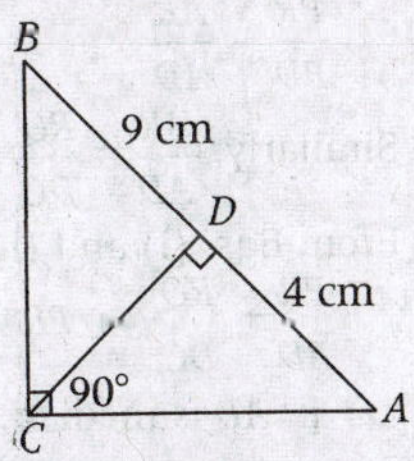

In ΔACB and ΔADC,

$\angle A = \angle A$ [common angles]

$\angle ACB = \angle ADC$ [each 90°]

$\therefore \quad \Delta ACB \sim \Delta ADC$ [by AA similarity]

$\Rightarrow \quad \angle ABC = \angle ACD \quad \ldots(i)$

Now, in ΔADC and ΔCDB,

$\angle ADC = \angle CDB$ [each = 90°]

$\angle ACD = \angle DBC$ [from Eq. (i)]

$\therefore \quad \Delta ADC \sim \Delta CDB$ [by AA similarity]

Now, $\frac{AD}{DC} = \frac{CD}{DB}$

$\Rightarrow AD \cdot DB = CD^2$

$\Rightarrow \quad 9 \times 4 = CD^2$

$\Rightarrow \quad CD = 3 \times 2 = 6$ cm

13. (b) Since, $PD \parallel BC$

[By Basic proportionality theorem]

$\frac{AD}{DC} = \frac{AP}{PB} \quad \ldots(i)$

Given, $\frac{AD}{DC} = \frac{CE}{BE} \quad \ldots(ii)$

[from Eqs. (i) and (ii),]

$\frac{AD}{DC} = \frac{AP}{PB} = \frac{CE}{BE}$

[By converse of basic proportionality theorem]

$PE \parallel AC$

14. (a) Since, $CE \parallel AD$

$\Rightarrow \angle 2 = \angle 4$ and $\angle 3 = \angle 1$

But $\angle 1 = \angle 2 \Rightarrow \angle 3 = \angle 4$

In ΔACE,

$\angle 3 = \angle 4 \Rightarrow AE = AC \quad \ldots(i)$

[$\because$ sides opposite to equal angles in a triangle are equal]

Now, in ΔBAD,

$EC \parallel AD \Rightarrow \frac{BD}{CD} = \frac{BA}{EA}$

[by basic proportionality theorem]

$\Rightarrow \frac{BD}{CD} = \frac{AB}{AC}$ [from Eq. (i)]

15. (c) $AB = 6.5$ cm

and $PQ = 10.4$ cm

$\because \Delta ABC \sim \Delta PQR$

$\frac{AB}{PQ} = \frac{BC}{QR} = \frac{AC}{PR} = \frac{6.5}{10.4} = \frac{65}{104}$

[$\because$ corresponding sides of similar triangles are proportional]

i.e. $AB = \frac{65}{104} PQ$, $BC = \frac{65}{104} QR$

$AC = \frac{65}{104} PR$

Also, given perimeter of $\Delta ABC = 60$ cm

$\therefore AB + BC + AC = 60$

$\Rightarrow \frac{65}{104}(PQ + QR + PR) = 60$

$\Rightarrow \quad PQ + QR + PR = \frac{60 \times 104}{65}$

$= 96$ cm

$\therefore$ Hence, perimeter of ΔPQR is 96 cm.

16. (b) Since, $\Delta ABC \sim \Delta EDF$

$\frac{AB}{ED} = \frac{AC}{EF} = \frac{BC}{DF}$

[$\because$ corresponding sides of similar triangles are proportional]

$\Rightarrow \frac{5}{12} = \frac{7}{EF} = \frac{BC}{15}$

On taking first and second terms, we get, $\frac{5}{12} = \frac{7}{EF}$

$\Rightarrow EF = \frac{7 \times 12}{5} = 16.8$ cm

On taking first and third terms, we get

$\frac{5}{12} = \frac{BC}{15} \Rightarrow BC = \frac{5 \times 15}{12}$

$= 6.25$ cm

Hence, the length of remaining sides of the triangles are $EF = 16.8$ cm and $BC = 6.25$ cm

17. (c) Given, $AM : MC = 3 : 4$

$BP : PM = 3 : 2$ and $BN = 12$ cm.

Draw $MR \parallel CN$, which meets AB at the point R, consider ΔBMR

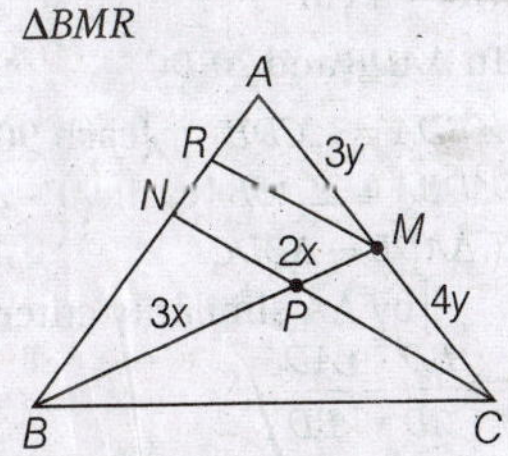

$PN \parallel MR$ (construction)

By BPT,

$\frac{BN}{NR} = \frac{BP}{PM} \Rightarrow \frac{12}{NR} = \frac{3}{2}$

$NR = 8$ cm

Consider ΔANC, $RM \parallel NC$

(By construction by BPT)

$\frac{AR}{RN} = \frac{AM}{MC} \Rightarrow \frac{AR}{8} = \frac{3}{4}$

$\Rightarrow AR = 6$ cm

$\therefore AN = AR + RN = 6 + 8$

$= 14$ cm

18. (a) In ΔABC,

$DE \parallel AC$

$\therefore \frac{BD}{DA} = \frac{BE}{EC}$

[basic proportionality theorem]

$$\frac{2x+10}{3x} = \frac{x+7}{2x}$$

$\Rightarrow 2x(2x+10) = 3x(x+7)$

$\Rightarrow 4x^2 + 20x = 3x^2 + 21x$

$\Rightarrow x^2 - x = 0$

$\Rightarrow x(x-1) = 0$

$\Rightarrow x - 1 = 0 \quad x = 0$ not possible

$x = 1$

19. (d) Given, $ST \parallel QR$, $PS \parallel SQ = \frac{3}{5}$ and $PR = 28$ cm

By using Basic proportionality theorem, we get

$$\frac{PS}{SQ} = \frac{PT}{TR} \Rightarrow \frac{PS}{SQ} = \frac{PT}{PR - PT}$$

$\Rightarrow \frac{3}{5} = \frac{PT}{28 - PT}$

$\Rightarrow 3(28 - PT) = 5PT$

$\Rightarrow 84 = 5PT + 3PT$

$PT = \frac{84}{8}$

$\Rightarrow PT = 10.5$ cm

Hence, the length of PT is 10.5 cm.

20. (c) Given, $BD = 8$ cm and $AD = 4$ cm

In ΔADB and ΔBDC,

$\angle BDA = \angle CDB$ [each 90°]

$\angle DBA = \angle DCB$ [each 90°–$\angle A$]

$\therefore \Delta ADB \sim \Delta BDC$

[by AA similarity criterion]

$\Rightarrow \frac{BD}{CD} = \frac{AD}{BD}$

[$\because$ corresponding sides of similar triangles are proportional]

$\Rightarrow CD = \frac{BD^2}{AD} = \frac{8^2}{4}$

$= \frac{64}{4} = 16$ cm

21. (d) Given $\angle LPQ = \angle QRP$ and $\angle RPM = \angle RQP$

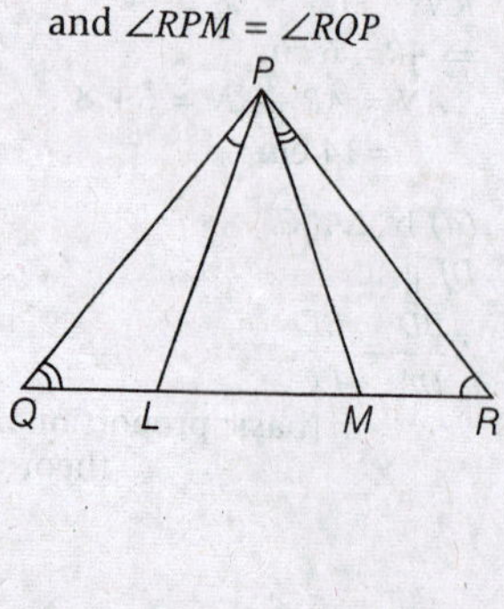

In ΔPQL and ΔRPM,

$\angle LPQ = \angle MRP$

[$\because \angle LPQ = \angle QRP$, given]

and $\angle LQP = \angle RPM$

[$\because \angle RQP = \angle RPM$, given]

$\therefore \Delta PQL \sim \Delta RPM$

[by AA similarity criterion]

Since, $\Delta PQL \sim \Delta RPM$

$\therefore \frac{QL}{PM} = \frac{PL}{RM}$

$\Rightarrow QL \times RM = PL \times PM$

In ΔPQL and ΔRQP

$\angle PQL = \angle RQP$

[common angle]

and $\angle QPL = \angle QRP$

[given]

$\therefore \Delta PQL \sim \Delta RQP$

[by AA similarity criterion]

Then, $\frac{PQ}{QR} = \frac{QL}{PQ}$

$\Rightarrow PQ^2 = QR \times QL$

22. (b) Given, height of boy $(BC) = 90$ cm $= 0.9$ m

Height of lamp-post $(PQ) = 3.6$ m

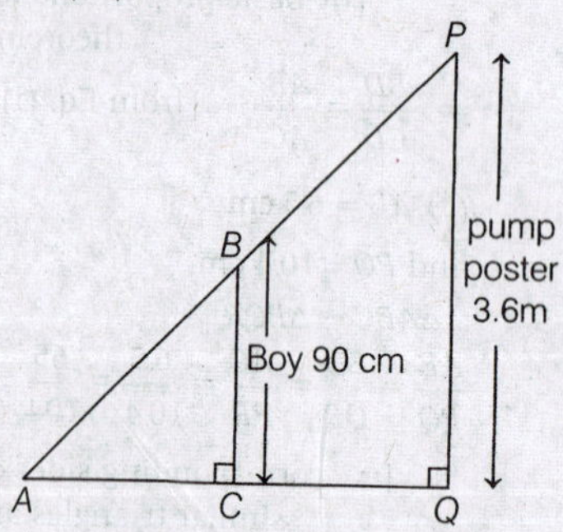

Speed of boy $= 1.2$ m/s

Time taken = 6 sec

$\therefore$ Distance moved by boy (CQ)

= Speed × Time

$= 1.2 \times 6 = 7.2$ m

Let length of shadow be $AC = x$ m

In ΔABC and ΔAPQ,

$\angle ACB = \angle AQP$ [each 90°]

and $\angle BAC = \angle PAQ$

[common angle]

$\Delta ABC \sim \Delta APQ$

[by AA similarity criterion]

Then, $\frac{AC}{AQ} = \frac{BC}{PQ}$

$\Rightarrow \frac{x}{x + 7.2} = \frac{0.9}{3.6}$

$\Rightarrow \frac{x}{x + 7.2} = \frac{1}{4}$

$\Rightarrow 4x = x + 7.2$

$\Rightarrow 4x - x = 7.2 \Rightarrow 3x = 7.2$

$x = 2.4$

23. (c) In ΔAPR and ΔABD

$\angle APR = \angle ABD$

[$\because$ corresponding angles]

$\angle ARP = \angle ADB$

[$\because$ corresponding angles]

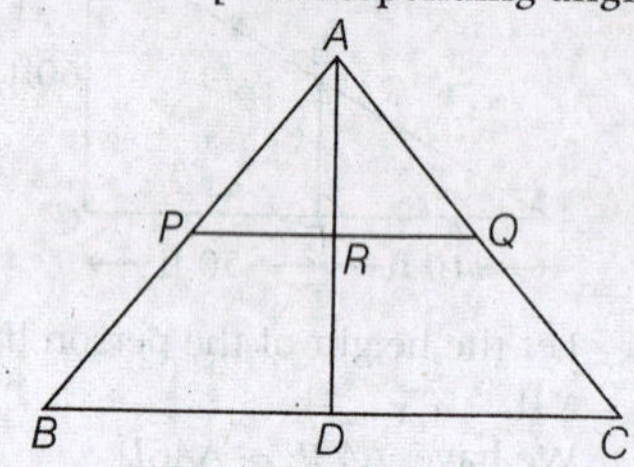

$\therefore \Delta APR \sim \Delta ABD$

[by AA similarity criterion]

$\frac{PR}{BD} = \frac{AR}{AD}$ ...(i)

Similarly, $\frac{AR}{AD} = \frac{RQ}{DC}$ ...(ii)

From Eqs. (i) and (ii), we get

$\frac{PR}{BD} = \frac{RQ}{DC} \Rightarrow PR = RQ$

[$\because AD$ is median, $BD = DC$]

24. (c) In ΔABC and ΔEBD, we have

$\angle ACB = \angle EDB$ [given]

$\angle ABC = \angle EBD$

[common angle]

$\therefore \Delta ABC \sim \Delta EBD$

[by AA similarity criterion]

Since, $\Delta ABC \sim \Delta EBD$

$\therefore \frac{AB}{EB} = \frac{BC}{BD} = \frac{AC}{ED}$

Now, taking first two terms, we get

$\frac{AB}{EB} = \frac{BC}{BD}$

$\frac{AB}{6} = \frac{BE + EC}{5}$

$\Rightarrow \frac{AB}{6} = \frac{6+4}{5}$

$\Rightarrow AB = \frac{60}{5} = 12$ cm

25. (a) In ΔABC,

$$\frac{AP}{PB} = \frac{AQ}{QC}$$

$\Rightarrow$ $PQ \parallel BC = PT \parallel BC$

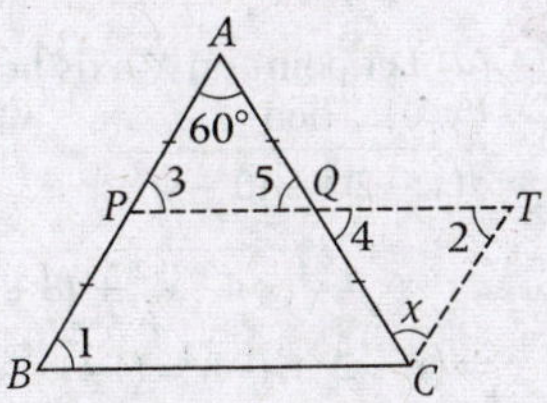

Also, $PT = BC$

$\therefore$ $PTCB$ is a parallelogram.

$\Rightarrow$ $\angle 1 = \angle 2$ ...(i)

Also, in ΔABC,

$$\frac{AP}{PB} = \frac{AQ}{QC}$$

$\Rightarrow$ $\Delta APQ \sim \Delta ABC$ [by SAS similarity]

$\therefore$ $\angle 1 = \angle 3$ ...(ii)

From Eqs. (i) and (ii), we have

$\angle 3 = \angle 2$ ...(iii)

In ΔAPQ and ΔCTQ,

$\angle 2 = \angle 3$ [from Eq. (iii)]

$\angle 4 = \angle 5$ [vertically opposite angles]

$\therefore$ $\Delta APQ \sim \Delta CTQ$ [by AA similarity]

$\Rightarrow$ $\angle x = \angle PAQ$

$\Rightarrow$ $\angle x = 60°$

26. (d) In ΔAPC and ΔBQC,

$\angle ACP = \angle BCQ$ [common angle]

$\angle PAC = \angle QBC$ [each 90°]

$\therefore$ $\Delta APC \sim \Delta BQC$ [by AA similarity]

$$\Rightarrow \quad \frac{AP}{BQ} = \frac{AC}{BC}$$

$$\Rightarrow \quad \frac{x}{y} = \frac{AC}{BC} \quad \text{...(i)}$$

Now, in ΔARC and ΔAQB,

$\angle ACR = \angle ABQ$ [each 90°]

$\angle CAR = \angle BAQ$ [common angle]

$\Rightarrow$ $\Delta ARC \sim \Delta AQB$ [by AA similarity]

$$\therefore \quad \frac{RC}{QB} = \frac{AC}{AB}$$

$$\Rightarrow \quad \frac{z}{y} = \frac{AC}{AB} \quad \text{...(ii)}$$

$\therefore$ From Eq. (i), we get

$$BC = \frac{y}{x} AC \quad \text{...(iii)}$$

$\therefore$ From Eq. (ii), we get

$$AB = \frac{y}{z} AC \quad \text{...(iv)}$$

On adding Eqs. (iii) and (iv), we get

$$AB + BC = \left(\frac{y}{x} + \frac{y}{z}\right) AC$$

$$\Rightarrow \quad AC = y\left[\frac{1}{x} + \frac{1}{z}\right] AC$$

$$\Rightarrow \quad \frac{1}{y} = \frac{1}{x} + \frac{1}{z}$$

27. (a) In ΔOPS and ΔOAB,

$PS \parallel AB$

$\angle POS = \angle AOB$ [common angle]

$\angle OSP = \angle OBA$ [corresponding angle]

$\therefore \Delta OPS \sim \Delta OAB$ [by AA similarity criterion]

$$\text{Then, } \frac{PS}{AB} = \frac{OS}{OB} \quad \text{...(i)}$$

In ΔCQR and ΔCAB,

$QR \parallel PS \parallel AB$

$\angle QCR = \angle ACB$ [common angle]

$\angle CRQ = \angle CBA$ [corresponding angle]

$\therefore \Delta CQR \sim \Delta CAB$ [by AA similarity criterion]

$$\text{Then, } \frac{QR}{AB} = \frac{CR}{CB}$$

$$\Rightarrow \quad \frac{PS}{AB} = \frac{CR}{CB} \quad \text{...(ii)}$$

From Eqs. (i) and (ii), we get

$$\frac{OS}{OB} = \frac{CR}{CB} \text{ or } \frac{OB}{OS} = \frac{CB}{CR}$$

On subtracting 1 from both sides, we get

$$\frac{OB}{OS} - 1 = \frac{CB}{CR} - 1$$

$$\Rightarrow \frac{OB - OS}{OS} = \frac{CB - CR}{CR}$$

$$\Rightarrow \quad \frac{BS}{OS} = \frac{BR}{CR}$$

By converse of basic proportionality theorem, we get result

$OC \parallel SR$

28. (a) Given $ABCD$ is a trapezium Diagonals AC and BD intersect at O.

$\therefore PQ \parallel AB \parallel DC$

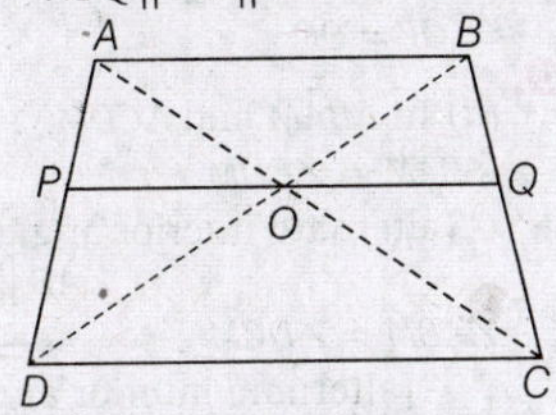

In ΔABD and ΔPOD

$PO \parallel AB$ [$\because PQ \parallel AB$]

$\angle ADB = \angle PDO$ [common angle]

$\angle ABD = \angle POD$ [Corresponding angles]

$\Delta ABD = \Delta POD$ [by AA similarity criterion]

$$\text{Then, } \frac{OP}{AB} = \frac{PD}{AD} \quad \text{...(i)}$$

In ΔABC and ΔOQC, $OQ \parallel AB$ [$\because PQ \parallel AB$]

$\angle ACB = \angle OCQ$ [common angles]

and $\angle BAC = \angle QOC$ [corresponding angles]

$\Delta ABC \sim \Delta OQC$ [by AA similarity]

$$\text{Then, } \frac{OQ}{AB} = \frac{QC}{BC} \quad \text{...(ii)}$$

Now, in ΔADC, $OP \parallel DC$

$$\frac{AP}{PD} = \frac{OA}{OC} \quad \text{...(iii)}$$

[by BPT]

In ΔABC, $OQ \parallel AB$

$$\frac{BQ}{QC} = \frac{OA}{OC} \quad \text{...(iv)}$$

[By BPT]

From Eqs. (iii) and (iv),

$$\frac{AP}{PD} = \frac{BQ}{QC}$$

On adding 1 to both sides, we get

$$\frac{AP}{PD} + 1 = \frac{BQ}{QC} + 1$$

$$\Rightarrow \frac{AP + PD}{PD} = \frac{BQ + QC}{QC}$$

$\Rightarrow \dfrac{AD}{PD} = \dfrac{BC}{QC}$

$\Rightarrow \dfrac{PD}{AD} = \dfrac{QC}{BC}$

[reciprocal the terms]

$\Rightarrow \dfrac{OP}{AB} = \dfrac{OQ}{AB}$

[from Eqs. (i) and (ii)]

$\Rightarrow OP = OQ$

29. (a) In ΔBAM and ΔCDM,

$\angle BAM = \angle CDM$

[alternate interior angles as $AB \parallel CD$]

$\angle ABM = \angle DCM$

[alternate interior angles]

and $\angle AMB = \angle DMC$

[vertically opposite angles]

$\therefore \Delta BAM \sim \Delta CDM$

[by AAA similarity criterion]

So, $\dfrac{AM}{DM} = \dfrac{BA}{CD} = \dfrac{BM}{CM}$

[Since, corresponding sides of similar triangles are proportional]

$\therefore \dfrac{AM}{4.5} = \dfrac{21}{5} = \dfrac{14.5}{CM}$

Now, consider $\dfrac{AM}{4.5} = \dfrac{21}{5}$

$\Rightarrow AM = \dfrac{21 \times 4.5}{5}$

$= 21 \times 0.9 = 18.9\text{ km}$

and consider $\dfrac{21}{5} = \dfrac{14.5}{CM}$

$CM = \dfrac{5 \times 14.5}{21} = 3.45\text{ km}$

There are four routes which Radhika may follow to reach friend's house are given below.

1st route

$R \rightarrow A \rightarrow M \rightarrow C \rightarrow F$

Total distance

$= RA + AM + MC + CF$

$= 10.5 + 18.9 + 3.45 + 2.5$

$= 35.35\text{ km}$

2nd route

$R \rightarrow B \rightarrow M \rightarrow D \rightarrow F$

Total distance

$= RB + BM + MD + DF$

$= 10.5 + 14.5 + 4.5 + 2.5$

$= 32\text{ km}$

3rd route

$R \rightarrow A \rightarrow M \rightarrow D \rightarrow F$

Total distance

$= RA + AM + MD + DF$

$= 10.5 + 18.9 + 4.5 + 2.5$

$= 36.4\text{ km}$

4th route

$R \rightarrow B \rightarrow M \rightarrow C \rightarrow F$

Total distance

$= RB + BM + MC + CF$

$= 10.5 + 14.5 + 3.45 + 2.5$

$= 30.95\text{ km}$

Hence, the shortest distance which Radhika has to travel is 30.95 km.

Chapter 7 : Coordinate Geometry

1. (d) If the coordinate points reflect over the line $y = -x$, the x-coordinate and y-coordinate change places and are negative.

$\therefore (x, y)$ changes to $(-y, -x)$.

2. (d) The translation $T_{(a,b)}$ of a point (x, y) will be $(x + a, y + b)$.

$\therefore T_{(2,3)}\ (5, 2) = (5 + 2, 2 + 3)$

$= (7, 5)$

3. (c) Reflection of the point (4, 6) in the line $x = 6$

$= (-4 + 2 \times 6, 6)$

$= (-4 + 12, 6) = (8, 6)$

Reflection of the point (8, 6) in the line $y = 4 = (8, -6 + 2 \times 4)$

$= (8, -6 + 8)$

$= (8, 2)$

4. (d) Now,

$D = \sqrt{(x_2 - x_1)^2 + (y_2 - y_1)^2}$

$\therefore PQ = \sqrt{(a + b - a + b)^2 + (a - b - a - b)^2}$

$= \sqrt{4b^2 + 4b^2} = 2b\sqrt{2}$

5. (d) Coordinates of origin, $O = (0, 0)$

Let the point be $P\left(\dfrac{11}{2}, \dfrac{7}{2}\right)$.

Using distance formula, we get

$PO = \sqrt{\left(\dfrac{11}{2} - 0\right)^2 + \left(\dfrac{7}{2} - 0\right)^2}$

$= \sqrt{\left(\dfrac{11}{2}\right)^2 + \left(\dfrac{7}{2}\right)^2}$

$= \dfrac{1}{2}\sqrt{121 + 49} = \dfrac{1}{2}\sqrt{170}$ units

6. (a) Let point on X-axis be $(x, 0)$. Then

$\sqrt{(x - 2)^2 + (0 - 4)^2}$

$= \sqrt{(-4 - x)^2 + (8 - 0)^2}$

$\Rightarrow (x - 2)^2 + (-4)^2 = (4 + x)^2 + 8^2$

$\Rightarrow x^2 + 4 - 4x + 16 = 16 + x^2 + 8x + 64$

$\Rightarrow \quad -60 = 12x \quad \Rightarrow \quad x = -5$

Hence, the point on X-axis is $(-5, 0)$.

7. (b)

$AB = \sqrt{(-a - a)^2 + (-a - a)^2}$

$= \sqrt{4a^2 + 4a^2}$

$= \sqrt{8a^2} = 2a\sqrt{2}$

$BC = \sqrt{(-\sqrt{3}a + a)^2 + (\sqrt{3}a + a)^2}$

$= \sqrt{3a^2 + a^2 - 2\sqrt{3}a^2 + 3a^2 + a^2 + 2\sqrt{3}a^2}$

$= \sqrt{8a^2} = 2a\sqrt{2}$.

and

$AC = \sqrt{(-\sqrt{3}a - a)^2 + (\sqrt{3}a - a)^2}$

$= \sqrt{3a^2 + a^2 + 2\sqrt{3}a^2 + 3a^2 + a^2 - 2\sqrt{3}a^2}$

$= \sqrt{8a^2} = 2a\sqrt{2}$

$\therefore \quad AB = BC = AC$

So, the triangle formed by points A, B and C is an equilateral triangle.

8. (d)

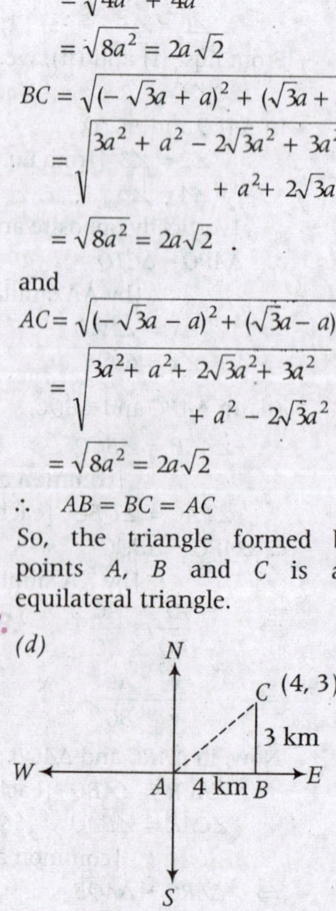

$AC = \sqrt{(x_2 - x_1)^2 + (y_2 - y_1)^2}$

$= \sqrt{(4 - 0)^2 + (3 - 0)^2}$

$= \sqrt{(4)^2 + (3)^2} = \sqrt{16+9}$

$= \sqrt{25} = 5$ km

9. (d) Given, $AP^2 = PB^2$

A (7, 1) —1— P (x, y) —1— B (−1, 7)

$(x-7)^2 + (y-1)^2 = (x+1)^2 + (y-7)^2$

$\Rightarrow x^2 + 49 - 14x + y^2 + 1 - 2y = x^2 + 1 + 2x + y^2 + 49 - 14y$

$\Rightarrow 12y = 16x \Rightarrow 3y = 4x$

10. (b) Let $P(x, y)$ be the circumcentre, then

$PA = PB = PC$

$\Rightarrow PA^2 = PB^2$

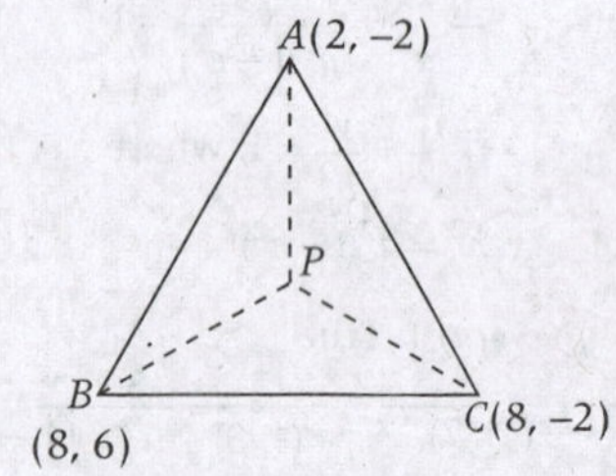

$\Rightarrow (x-2)^2 + (y+2)^2 = (x-8)^2 + (y-6)^2$

$\Rightarrow x^2 + 4 - 4x + y^2 + 4 - 4y = x^2 + 64 - 16x + y^2 + 36 - 12y$

$\Rightarrow 12x + 16y = 92$

$\Rightarrow 3x + 4y = 23$ ...(i)

and $PB^2 = PC^2$

$\Rightarrow (x-8)^2 + (y-6)^2 = (x-8)^2 + (y+2)^2$

$\Rightarrow y^2 + 36 - 12y = y^2 + 4 + 4y$

$\Rightarrow 16y = 32 \Rightarrow y = 2$

From Eq. (i)

$3x = 23 - 8$

$\Rightarrow 3x = 15 \Rightarrow x = 5$

$\therefore$ Coordinate of P is (5, 2).

Now, $PA = \sqrt{(5-2)^2 + (2+2)^2} = \sqrt{9+16} = 5$

11. (a) We have the points as follows:

$A(2, 3)$, $B(-2, 3)$ and $C(2, -3)$

Now, $AB = \sqrt{(2+2)^2 + (3-3)^2} = \sqrt{4^2 + 0^2} = 4$

$BC = \sqrt{(2+2)^2 + (-3-3)^2} = \sqrt{4^2 + 6^2} = \sqrt{16+36} = \sqrt{52}$

$AC = \sqrt{(2-2)^2 + (3+3)^2} = \sqrt{6^2} = 6$

$\therefore AB < AC < BC$

12. (d) Perimeter of the triangle so formed

$= AB + BC + AC$

$= 4 + \sqrt{52} + 6$

$= (10 + \sqrt{52})$ units

13. (a)

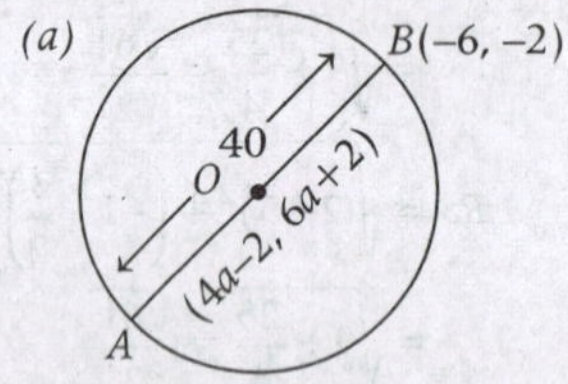

Given, AB = Diameter = 40

$\Rightarrow \frac{AB}{2}$ = Radius

$\Rightarrow \frac{40}{2}$ = Radius = OB

$\Rightarrow 20 = OB$

$\therefore 20 = \sqrt{(4a-2+6)^2 + (6a+2+2)^2}$

$\Rightarrow 20 = \sqrt{(4a+4)^2 + (6a+4)^2}$

$\Rightarrow 400 = 16a^2 + 16 + 32a + 36a^2 + 16 + 48a$

$\Rightarrow 100 = 4a^2 + 4 + 8a + 9a^2 + 4 + 12a$ [dividing by 4]

$\Rightarrow 13a^2 + 20a - 92 = 0$

$\therefore a = \frac{-20 \pm \sqrt{20^2 - 4 \times -92 \times 13}}{26}$

$= \frac{-20 \pm \sqrt{400 + 4784}}{26}$

$= \frac{-20 + 72}{26} = 2$

[−ve sign neglected]

14. (d) Let $A(-3, 0)$, $B(1, -3)$ and $C(x, y)$

Now, $AB = \sqrt{(1+3)^2 + (-3-0)^2}$

$= \sqrt{4^2 + (-3)^2}$

$= \sqrt{16+9} = \sqrt{25} = 5$ units

and $BC = \sqrt{(x-1)^2 + (y+3)^2}$

$\Rightarrow (5\sqrt{2})^2 = (x-1)^2 + (y+3)^2$

$\Rightarrow 50 = x^2 + 1 - 2x + y^2 + 9 + 6y$

$\Rightarrow 50 = x^2 + y^2 - 2x + 6y + 10$

$\Rightarrow x^2 + y^2 - 2x + 6y - 40 = 0$

$\therefore$ Data is insufficient.

15. (a) Let the ratio be $k : 1$.

Using section formula, we get

$8 = \frac{(9k+5)}{k+1}$

$\Rightarrow 8k + 8 = 9k + 5 \Rightarrow k = 3$

$\therefore AP : PB = 3 : 1$

$\Rightarrow \frac{AP}{PB} = \frac{3}{1} \Rightarrow AP = 3PB$

16. (d) Let it divides in the ratio $k : 1$.

$\therefore \left(\frac{4k-6}{k+1}, \frac{-3k+5}{k+1}\right)$

Since, it is divided by the line $x = 2$

$\therefore \frac{4k-6}{k+1} = 2$

$\Rightarrow 4k - 6 = 2k + 2$

$\Rightarrow 2k = 8 \Rightarrow k = 4$

$\therefore$ Ratio = 4 : 1

17. (d) Given, $M(-6, 4)$

(−6, 4) M —— (x, y) N —— (0, 0) O

Given, MN = NO

$\Rightarrow N$ divides MO equally.

Using mid-point formula, we get

$x = \frac{-6+0}{2}$ and $y = \frac{4+0}{2}$

$\Rightarrow x = -3$ and $y = 2$

$\therefore N(-3, 2)$

18. (a)

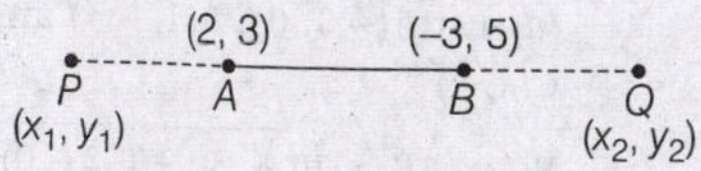

Let $P(x_1, y_1)$ and $Q(x_2, y_2)$ be the new end points

Now, $PA = AB = BQ$

$\therefore$ A is the mid-point of PB.

$\Rightarrow 2 = \frac{x_1 + (-3)}{2}$ and $3 = \frac{y_1 + 5}{2}$

$\Rightarrow 4 = x_1 - 3$ and $6 = y_1 + 5$

which gives $x_1 = 7$ and $y_1 = 1$

Thus, the coordinates of the point P is (7, 1), again B is the mid-point of AQ.

$\therefore \frac{2 + x_2}{2} = -3$ and $\frac{3 + y_2}{2} = 5$

$\Rightarrow 2 + x_2 = -6$

and $3 + y_2 = 10$

$\Rightarrow x_2 = -8$ and $y_2 = 7$

$\therefore$ Therefore, the coordinates of Q are (–8, 7).

Hence, the coordinates of the new ends are (7, 1) and (–8, 7).

19. (b) Length of diagonal, d

$= \sqrt{(9-1)^2 + (-9+3)^2}$

$= \sqrt{(8)^2 + (-6)^2} = \sqrt{64 + 36}$

$= \sqrt{100} = 10$

$\therefore$ Area of square

$= \frac{d^2}{2} = \frac{(10)^2}{2} = 50$ sq units

20. (c) P is the mid-point of AB.

$\therefore$ Coordinates of P are

$\left(\frac{-1-1}{2}, \frac{-1+4}{2}\right) = \left(-1, \frac{3}{2}\right)$

Q is the mid-point of BC

$\therefore$ Coordinates of Q is

$\left(\frac{-1+5}{2}, \frac{4+4}{2}\right) = (2, 4)$

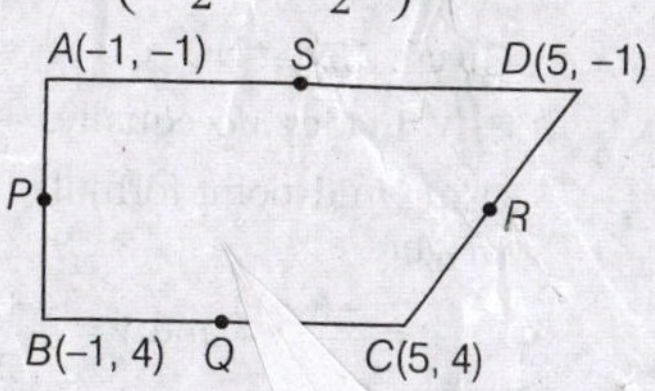

R is the mid- [illegible] of CD,

$\therefore$ Coordinate [illegible]

$\left(\frac{5+5}{2}, \frac{-1+4}{2}\right)$

S is the mid-point of DA

$\therefore$ Coordinates of S is

$\left(\frac{5-1}{2}, \frac{-1-1}{2}\right) = (2, -1)$

$\therefore P\left(-1, \frac{3}{2}\right), Q(2, 4), R\left(5, \frac{3}{2}\right)$ and $S(2, -1)$ are the mid-points of AB, BC, CD and DA respectively.

Now,

$PQ = \sqrt{(2+1)^2 + \left(4 - \frac{3}{2}\right)^2}$

$= \sqrt{9 + \frac{25}{4}} = \sqrt{\frac{61}{4}} = \frac{\sqrt{61}}{2}$

$QR = \sqrt{(5-2)^2 + \left(\frac{3}{2} - 4\right)^2}$

$= \sqrt{9 + \frac{25}{4}} = \frac{\sqrt{61}}{2}$

$RS = \sqrt{(2-5)^2 + \left(-1 - \frac{3}{2}\right)^2}$

$= \sqrt{9 + \frac{25}{4}} = \frac{\sqrt{61}}{2}$

$SP = \sqrt{(-1-2)^2 + \left(\frac{3}{2} + 1\right)^2}$

$= \sqrt{9 + \frac{25}{4}} = \frac{\sqrt{61}}{2}$

Also, diagonal

$PR = \sqrt{(5+1)^2 + \left(\frac{3}{2} - \frac{3}{2}\right)^2}$

$= \sqrt{36 + 0} = \sqrt{36} = 6$

and $SQ = \sqrt{(2-2)^2 + (4+1)^2}$

$= \sqrt{0 + (5)^2} = \sqrt{25} = 5$

$\therefore$ Diagonal $PR \neq$ Diagonal QS

So, $PQRS$ is a rhombus.

21. (c) Let $P(x, y)$ be the moving point such that the sum of its distances from $A(ae, 0)$ and $B(-ae, 0)$ is $2a$.

Then, $PA + PB = 2a$

$\Rightarrow \sqrt{(x - ae)^2 + (y - 0)^2}$

$+ \sqrt{(x + ae)^2 + (y - 0)^2} = 2a$

$\left[\because \text{distance} = \sqrt{(x_2 - x_1)^2 + (y_2 - y_1)^2}\right]$

$\Rightarrow \sqrt{(x - ae)^2 + y^2}$

$= 2a - \sqrt{(x + ae)^2 + y^2}$

$\Rightarrow (x - ae)^2 + y^2$

$= 4a^2 + (x + ae)^2 + y^2$

$-4a\sqrt{(x + ae)^2 + y^2}$

[squaring on both sides]

$\Rightarrow x^2 + a^2e^2 - 2xae$

$= 4a^2 + x^2 + a^2e^2 + 2xae$

$-4a\sqrt{(x + ae)^2 + y^2}$

$\Rightarrow -4aex - 4a^2$

$= -4a\sqrt{(x + ae)^2 + y^2}$

$\Rightarrow (ex + a) = \sqrt{(x + ae)^2 + y^2}$

$\Rightarrow (ex + a)^2 = (x + ae)^2 + y^2$

[again, squaring on both sides]

$\Rightarrow e^2x^2 + 2aex + a^2$

$= x^2 + a^2e^2 + 2aex + y^2$

$\Rightarrow x^2(1 - e^2) + y^2 = a^2(1 - e^2)$

$\Rightarrow \frac{x^2}{a^2} + \frac{y^2}{a^2(1 - e^2)} = 1$

$\therefore \frac{x^2}{a^2} + \frac{y^2}{b^2} = 1$, where

$b^2 = a^2(1 - e^2)$

22. (a) I. True

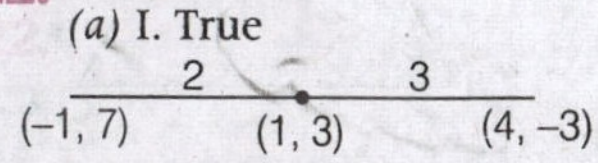

$\therefore x = \frac{2(4) + 3(-1)}{5}$

$\Rightarrow x = \frac{8 - 3}{5} = 1$

$\therefore y = \frac{2(-3) + 3(7)}{5} = \frac{15}{5} = 3$

$x = 1$ and $y = 3$

II. False

Distance

$= \sqrt{(5\sin 60° - 0)^2 + (0 - 5\cos 60°)^2}$

$= \sqrt{25\sin^2 60° + 25\cos^2 60°}$

$= \sqrt{25(\sin^2 60° + \cos^2 60°)}$

$= \sqrt{25} = 5$

III. False

The line is intersecting the X-axis at point (15, 0) and Y-axis at the point (0, 8).

$\therefore$ Distance or length of the intercept

$= \sqrt{(15 - 0)^2 + (0 - 8)^2}$

$= \sqrt{15^2 + 8^2} = \sqrt{225 + 64} = 17$

IV. False

Let $A(x, y)$ be equidistant from both the axes. Then

$$x = y$$

The distance between $A(x, y)$ and $O(0, 0)$ is

$$= \sqrt{(x-0)^2 + (y-0)^2}$$
$$= \sqrt{x^2 + y^2}$$
$$= \sqrt{x^2 + x^2} \text{ or } \sqrt{y^2 + y^2}$$
$$= x\sqrt{2} \text{ or } y\sqrt{2}$$

23. *(c)*

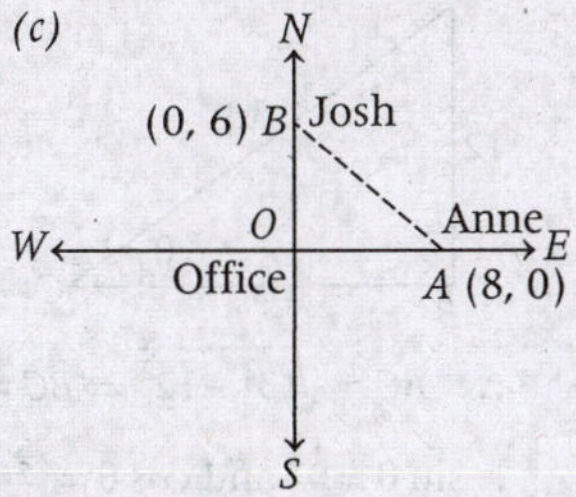

From figure, we find that the shortest distance is AB.

By using Pythagoras theorem, we get, $AB^2 = OA^2 + OB^2$

$$= [\sqrt{(8-0)^2 + (0-0)^2}]^2 + [\sqrt{(0-0)^2 + (6-0)^2}]^2$$
$$= (\sqrt{8^2})^2 + (\sqrt{6^2})^2 = 8^2 + 6^2$$
$$\Rightarrow AB^2 = 100 \Rightarrow AB = 10 \text{ km}$$

24. *(d)* Let $A = (-2, 3)$, $B = (2, -1)$, $C = (4, 0)$

Let the centre of the circumcircle of the ΔABC be $P = (\alpha, \beta)$

Then, $PA = PB = PC$

i.e. $PA^2 = PB^2 = PC^2$ ...(i)

$$(\alpha + 2)^2 + (\beta - 3)^2$$
$$= (\alpha - 2)^2 + (\beta + 1)^2$$
$$= (\alpha - 4)^2 + (\beta - 0)^2$$
$$\alpha^2 + \beta^2 + 4\alpha - 6\beta + 13$$
$$= \alpha^2 + \beta^2 - 4\alpha + 2\beta + 5$$
$$= \alpha^2 + \beta^2 - 8\alpha + 16$$

Subtracting $\alpha^2 + \beta^2$ from each,

$$4\alpha - 6\beta + 13 = -4\alpha + 2\beta + 5$$
$$= -8\alpha + 16$$

From the first two,

$$8\alpha - 8\beta + 8 = 0$$
$$\Rightarrow \alpha - \beta + 1 = 0 \quad \text{...(ii)}$$

From the last two,

$$4\alpha + 2\beta - 11 = 0 \quad \text{...(iii)}$$

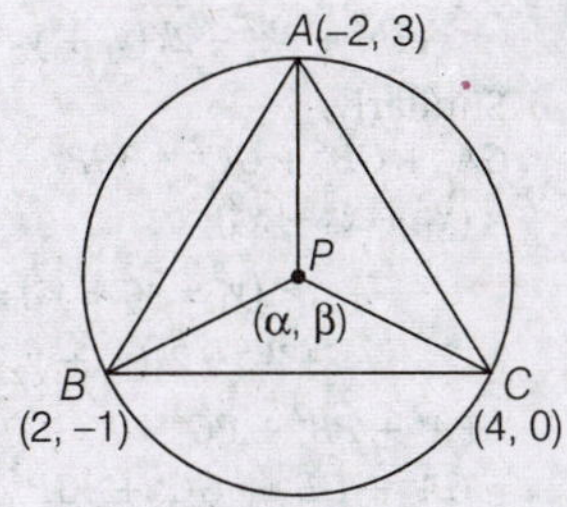

Solving Eqs. (ii) and (iii), we get $\alpha = \frac{3}{2}$ and $\beta = \frac{5}{2}$

$$\therefore (\alpha, \beta) = \left(\frac{3}{2}, \frac{5}{2}\right)$$
$$= \text{circumcentre}$$

Now, radius

$$= PC = \sqrt{\left(\frac{3}{2} - 4\right)^2 + \left(\frac{5}{2} - 0\right)^2}$$
$$= \sqrt{\left(\frac{-5}{2}\right)^2 + \left(\frac{5}{2}\right)^2}$$
$$= \sqrt{\frac{25}{4} + \frac{25}{4}} = \sqrt{\frac{50}{4}} = \frac{5\sqrt{2}}{2}$$

25. *(a)*

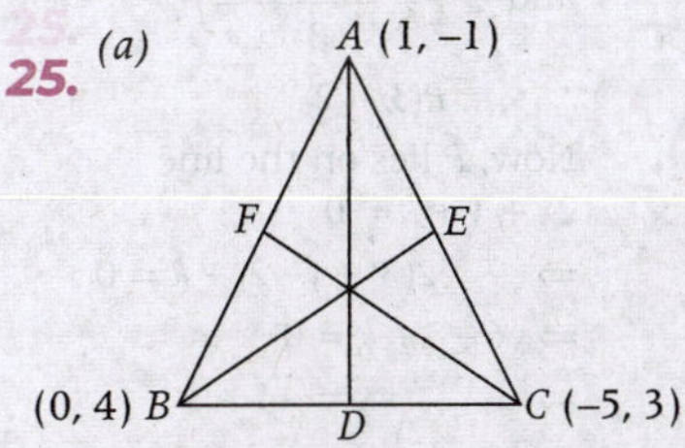

Now, D divides BC in the ratio 1 : 1.

$$\therefore D(x, y) = \left(\frac{0-5}{2}, \frac{4+3}{2}\right)$$
$$= \left(\frac{-5}{2}, \frac{7}{2}\right)$$

Similarly, E

$$= \left(\frac{-5+1}{2}, \frac{-1+3}{2}\right)$$
$$= \left(\frac{-4}{2}, \frac{2}{2}\right) = (-2, 1)$$
$$F = \left(\frac{0+1}{2}, \frac{4-1}{2}\right) = \left(\frac{1}{2}, \frac{3}{2}\right)$$

$\therefore$ Length of AD

$$= \sqrt{\left(1 + \frac{5}{2}\right)^2 + \left(-1 - \frac{7}{2}\right)^2}$$
$$= \frac{1}{2}\sqrt{(2+5)^2 + (2+7)^2}$$
$$= \frac{1}{2}\sqrt{7^2 + 9^2} = \frac{1}{2}\sqrt{49 + 81}$$
$$= \frac{1}{2}\sqrt{130} = \frac{\sqrt{130}}{2} \text{ units}$$

Length of BE

$$= \sqrt{(0+2)^2 + (4-1)^2}$$
$$= \sqrt{2^2 + 3^2} = \sqrt{4+9}$$
$$= \sqrt{13} \text{ units}$$

Length of CF

$$= \sqrt{\left(\frac{1}{2} + 5\right)^2 + \left(\frac{3}{2} - 3\right)^2}$$
$$= \sqrt{\left(\frac{1+10}{2}\right)^2 + \left(\frac{3-6}{2}\right)^2}$$
$$= \frac{1}{2}\sqrt{11^2 + (-3)^2}$$
$$= \frac{1}{2}\sqrt{121 + 9}$$
$$= \frac{\sqrt{130}}{2} \text{ units}$$

26. *(d)* Let the vertices of a triangle be $A(x_1, y_1)$, $B(x_2, y_2)$ and $C(x_3, y_3)$.

Again, let coordinates of P be (h, k).

Since, G is the centroid of a ΔABC.

$\therefore$ Coordinates of

$$G = \left(\frac{x_1 + x_2 + x_3}{3}, \frac{y_1 + y_2 + y_3}{3}\right)$$

Let $P(h, k)$ be a point in the plane.

Now, $PA^2 = (x_1 - h)^2 + (y_1 - k)^2$

$$\left[\because \text{distance} = \sqrt{(x_2 - x_1)^2 + (y_2 - y_1)^2}\right]$$
$$= x_1^2 + h^2 - 2x_1h + y_1^2 + k^2 - 2y_1k$$
$$PB^2 = (x_2 - h)^2 + (y_2 - k)^2$$
$$= x_2^2 + h^2 - 2x_2h + y_2^2 + k^2 - 2y_2k$$

and $PC^2 = (x_3 - h)^2 + (y_3 - k)^2$

$$= x_3^2 + h^2 - 2x_3h + y_3^2 + k^2 - 2y_3k$$

Now,

$$GA^2 = \left(x_1 - \frac{x_1 + x_2 + x_3}{3}\right)^2 + \left(y_1 - \frac{y_1 + y_2 + y_3}{3}\right)^2$$

$$= \left(\frac{2x_1 - x_2 - x_3}{3}\right)^2 + \left(\frac{2y_1 - y_2 - y_3}{3}\right)^2$$

$$= \frac{1}{9}\begin{bmatrix} 4x_1^2 + x_2^2 + x_3^2 - 4x_1x_2 \\ +2x_2x_3 - 4x_1x_3 + 4y_1^2 \\ +y_2^2 + y_3^2 - 4y_1y_2 \\ +2y_2y_3 - 4y_1y_3 \end{bmatrix}$$

$[\because (a + b + c)^2 = a^2 + b^2 + c^2 + 2ab + 2bc + 2ca]$

Similarly,

$$GB^2 = \frac{1}{9}\begin{bmatrix} x_1^2 + 4x_2^2 + x_3^2 - 4x_1x_2 \\ +2x_1x_3 - 4x_2x_3 + y_1^2 \\ +4y_2^2 + y_3^2 - 4y_1y_2 \\ +2y_1y_3 - 4y_2y_3 \end{bmatrix}$$

$$GC^2 = \frac{1}{9}\begin{bmatrix} x_1^2 + x_2^2 + 4x_3^2 \\ +2x_1x_2 - 4x_1x_3 \\ -4x_2x_3 + y_1^2 + y_2^2 \\ +4y_3^2 + 2y_1y_2 \\ -4y_2y_3 - 4y_1y_3 \end{bmatrix}$$

Also,

$$GP^2 = \left(h - \frac{x_1 + x_2 + x_3}{3}\right)^2 + \left(k - \frac{y_1 + y_2 + y_3}{3}\right)^2$$

$$= h^2 + \left(\frac{x_1 + x_2 + x_3}{3}\right)^2 - 2h\left(\frac{x_1 + x_2 + x_3}{3}\right) + k^2 + \left(\frac{y_1 + y_2 + y_3}{3}\right)^2 - 2k\left(\frac{y_1 + y_2 + y_3}{3}\right)$$

$$\Rightarrow 3GP^2 = 3h^2 + \frac{1}{3}(x_1 + x_2 + x_3)^2 - 2h(x_1 + x_2 + x_3) + 3k^2 + \frac{1}{3}(y_1 + y_2 + y_3)^2 - 2k(y_1 + y_2 + y_3)$$

$\Rightarrow$ Now, $PA^2 + PB^2 + PC^2$

$$= 3(x_1^2 + x_2^2 + x_3^2) + 3(y_1^2 + y_2^2 + y_3^2) - 2h(x_1 + x_2 + x_3) + 3h^2 + 3k^2 - 2k(y_1 + y_2 + y_3)$$

Similarly,

$GA^2 + GB^2 + GC^2 + 3GP^2$

$$= (x_1^2 + x_2^2 + x_3^2) + (y_1^3 + y_2^2 + y_3^2) + 3h^2 + 3k^2 - 2k(y_1 + y_2 + y_3)$$

$\therefore PA^2 + PB^2 + PC^2$

$= GA^2 + GB^2 + GC^2 + 3GP^2$

27. (b)

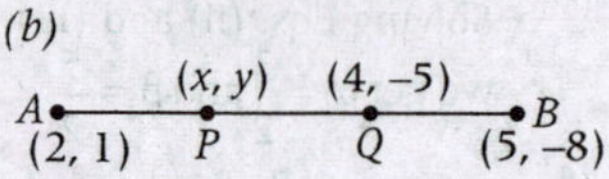

Given, $\frac{AP}{PB} = \frac{BQ}{QA}$; Let $\frac{AQ}{QB} = \frac{k'}{1}$

Using section formula, we get

$$4 = \frac{5k' + 2}{k' + 1}$$

$\Rightarrow \quad 4k' + 4 = 2 + 5k' \Rightarrow k' = 2$

$\therefore \quad \frac{AP}{PB} = \frac{1}{2}$

$\Rightarrow \quad x = \frac{1 \times 5 + 2 \times 2}{2 + 1} = \frac{9}{3}$

and $\quad y = \frac{-8 + 2}{3} = -2$

$\therefore \quad P(3, -2)$

Now, P lies on the line

$2x + y + k = 0$

$\Rightarrow \quad 2(3) + (-2) + k = 0$

$\Rightarrow \quad 6 - 2 + k = 0$

$\Rightarrow \quad k = -4$

Chapter 8 : Trigonometry

1. (a) Now, $\frac{m^2 + n^2}{n^2} = \frac{m^2}{n^2} + 1$

$$= 1 + \left(\frac{m}{n}\right)^2 = 1 + \left(\frac{\sin\theta}{\cos\theta}\right)^2$$

$$= 1 + \tan^2\theta$$

2. (d) Now, $\frac{3\sin\theta - 5\cos\theta}{3\sin\theta + 5\cos\theta}$

$$= \frac{\frac{3\sin\theta - 5\cos\theta}{\cos\theta}}{\frac{3\sin\theta + 5\cos\theta}{\cos\theta}}$$

$$= \frac{3\tan\theta - 5}{3\tan\theta + 5} = \frac{3 \times \frac{5}{3} - 5}{3 \times \frac{5}{3} + 5} = 0$$

3. (b) When $\theta = 45°$

The greatest value is

$\sin 45° + \cos 45°$

$$= \frac{1}{\sqrt{2}} + \frac{1}{\sqrt{2}} = \frac{2}{\sqrt{2}} = \sqrt{2} = 1.414$$

4. (c) Given, $\operatorname{cosec}\theta = \frac{13}{12}$

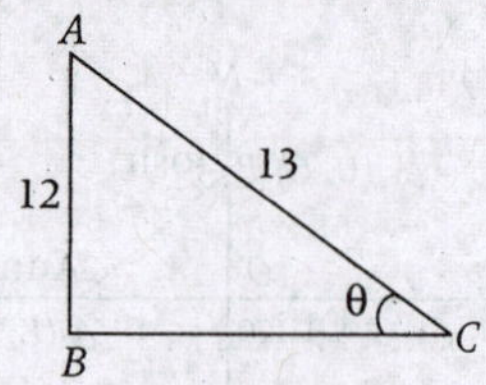

$\therefore \quad BC = \sqrt{13^2 - 12^2} \Rightarrow BC = 5$

$\therefore \sin\theta = \frac{12}{13}$ and $\cos\theta = \frac{5}{13}$

$\therefore \quad \frac{2\sin\theta - 3\cos\theta}{4\sin\theta - 9\cos\theta}$

$$= \frac{2 \times \frac{12}{13} - 3 \times \frac{5}{13}}{4 \times \frac{12}{13} - 9 \times \frac{5}{13}}$$

$$= \frac{24 - 15}{48 - 45} = \frac{9}{3} = 3$$

5. (c) $\therefore \left(\sin\theta + \frac{1}{\sin\theta}\right)^2 = \sin^2\theta + \frac{1}{\sin^2\theta} + 2$

$$\Rightarrow \sin^2\theta + \frac{1}{\sin^2\theta} = (4)^2 - 2$$

$$= 16 - 2 = 14$$

6. (c) Given,

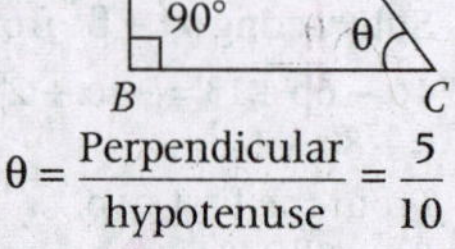

$$\sin\theta = \frac{\text{Perpendicular}}{\text{hypotenuse}} = \frac{5}{10} = \frac{1}{2}$$

$\sin\theta = \sin 30° \Rightarrow \angle C = \theta = 30°$

7.

(c) On squaring given equations, we get

$$\left(\frac{x}{a}\right)^2\cos^2\theta+\left(\frac{y}{b}\right)^2\sin^2\theta+\frac{2xy}{ab}\cos\theta\tan\theta=1 \quad \ldots(i)$$

and $$\frac{x^2}{a^2}\sin^2\theta+\frac{y^2}{b^2}\cos^2\theta-\frac{2xy}{ab}\sin\theta\cos\theta=1 \quad \ldots(ii)$$

On adding Eqs. (i) and (ii), we get

$$\frac{x^2}{a^2}(\sin^2\theta+\cos^2\theta)+\frac{y^2}{b^2}(\sin^2\theta+\cos^2\theta)=2$$

$$\Rightarrow \frac{x^2}{a^2}+\frac{y^2}{b^2}=2$$

8.

(b) Given, $\frac{1+\sin\alpha}{1-\sin\alpha}=\frac{m^2}{n^2}$

By componendo and dividendo,

$$\frac{1+\sin\alpha+1-\sin\alpha}{1+\sin\alpha-1+\sin\alpha}=\frac{m^2+n^2}{m^2-n^2}$$

$$\Rightarrow \frac{2}{2\sin\alpha}=\frac{m^2+n^2}{m^2-n^2}$$

$$\Rightarrow \sin\alpha=\frac{m^2-n^2}{m^2+n^2}$$

9.

(c) Since, BC is diameter, then ΔABC is right angled triangle at A.

Then, by Pythagoras theorem,

$$BC^2=AB^2+AC^2$$

$$\Rightarrow BC^2=12^2+5^2$$

$$\Rightarrow BC^2=144+25$$

$$\Rightarrow BC^2=169\Rightarrow BC=13 \text{ units}$$

Now, $\sin^2\theta+\cos^2\theta-1$

$$=\left(\frac{P}{H}\right)^2+\left(\frac{B}{H}\right)^2-1$$

$$=\frac{5^2}{13^2}+\frac{12^2}{13^2}-1=\frac{25+144}{13^2}-1$$

$$=\frac{13^2}{13^2}-1=0$$

10.

(c) On squaring given equations, we get

$$(x\cos\theta-y\sin\theta)^2=z^2$$

$$\Rightarrow x^2\cos^2\theta+y^2\sin^2\theta-2xy\cos\theta\sin\theta=z^2$$

$$\Rightarrow 2xy\cos\theta\sin\theta=x^2\cos^2\theta+y^2\sin^2\theta-z^2 \quad \ldots(i)$$

and

$$(x\sin\theta+y\cos\theta)^2=x^2\sin^2\theta+y^2\cos^2\theta+2xy\cos\theta\sin\theta \ldots(ii)$$

From Eqs. (i) and (ii), we get

$$x^2(\sin^2\theta+\cos^2\theta)+y^2(\cos^2\theta+\sin^2\theta)-z^2$$

$$=x^2+y^2-z^2$$

$$[\because \sin^2\theta+\cos^2\theta=1]$$

$$\Rightarrow (x\sin\theta+y\cos\theta)=\pm\sqrt{x^2+y^2-z^2}$$

11.

(a) $$E=\frac{(\sqrt{3})^2+8\times\left(\frac{1}{\sqrt{2}}\right)^2+\frac{3}{2}\times\left(\frac{2}{\sqrt{3}}\right)^2+2\times 0}{2\times 2+3\times 2-\frac{7}{3}\times(\sqrt{3})^2}$$

$$=\frac{3+4+2+0}{4+6-7}=\frac{9}{3}=3$$

12.

(a) $$\frac{2\cos^2 60^\circ+3\sec^2 30^\circ-2\tan^2 45^\circ}{\sin^2 30^\circ+\cos^2 45^\circ}$$

$$=\frac{2\times\frac{1}{4}+3\times\frac{4}{3}-2\times 1}{\frac{1}{4}+\frac{1}{2}}$$

$$=\frac{\frac{1}{2}+4-2}{\frac{3}{4}}=\frac{5}{2}\times\frac{4}{3}=\frac{10}{3}$$

Also, $4(\sin^2 30^\circ+\cos^4 60^\circ)-3(\cos^2 45^\circ-\sin^2 90^\circ)$

$$=4\left(\frac{1}{4}+\frac{1}{16}\right)-3\left(\frac{1}{2}-1\right)$$

$$=4\times\frac{5}{16}+3\times\frac{1}{2}=\frac{11}{4}$$

Now, $[4(\sin^2 30^\circ+\cos^4 60^\circ)-3(\cos^2 45^\circ-\sin^2 90^\circ)]\times\frac{2\cos^2 60^\circ\ 3\sec^2 30^\circ-2\tan^2 45^\circ}{\sin^2 30^\circ+\cos^2 45^\circ}$

$$=\frac{11}{4}\times\frac{10}{3}=\frac{55}{6}$$

13.

(c) $$\frac{\cot\theta+\operatorname{cosec}\theta-1}{\cot\theta-\operatorname{cosec}\theta+1}$$

$$=\frac{(\cot\theta+\operatorname{cosec}\theta)-(\operatorname{cosec}^2\theta-\cot^2\theta)}{\cot\theta-\operatorname{cosec}\theta+1}$$

$$=\frac{(\cot\theta+\operatorname{cosec}\theta)-(\operatorname{cosec}\theta+\cot\theta)(\operatorname{cosec}\theta-\cot\theta)}{\cot\theta-\operatorname{cosec}\theta+1}$$

$$=\frac{(\cot\theta+\operatorname{cosec}\theta)(1-\operatorname{cosec}\theta+\cot\theta)}{(\cot\theta-\operatorname{cosec}\theta+1)}$$

$$=\cot\theta+\operatorname{cosec}\theta$$

$$=\frac{\cos\theta}{\sin\theta}+\frac{1}{\sin\theta}=\frac{1+\cos\theta}{\sin\theta}$$

14.

(a) (a) $$\frac{(\sin\theta+\cos\theta)(\sin^2+\cos^2\theta-\sin\theta\cos\theta)}{\sin\theta+\cos\theta}+\sin\theta\cos\theta$$

$$=(1-\sin\theta\cos\theta)+\sin\theta\cos\theta=1$$

(b) Now,

$$\frac{\cos^2 45^\circ}{\tan^2 45^\circ}=\frac{(1/\sqrt{2})^2}{(1)^2}=\frac{1}{2}$$

(c) $$\frac{1}{[(\sin^2\theta)^2-(\cos^2\theta)^2+1]\operatorname{cosec}^2\theta}$$

$$=\frac{1}{[(\sin^2\theta-\cos^2\theta)(\sin^2\theta+\cos^2\theta)+1]\operatorname{cosec}^2\theta}$$

$$=\frac{1}{(\sin^2\theta-\cos^2\theta+1)\operatorname{cosec}^2\theta}$$

$$=\frac{1}{(\sin^2\theta-1+\sin^2\theta+1)\operatorname{cosec}^2\theta}$$

$$[\because \cos^2\theta=1-\sin^2\theta]$$

$$=\frac{1}{2\sin^2\theta\times\frac{1}{\sin^2\theta}}=\frac{1}{2}$$

(d) Now,

$$(1/2)(\cos^2 25^\circ+\sin^2 25^\circ)=\frac{1}{2}$$

$\therefore$ The value of option (a) is odd one here.

15. (a) $\tan\theta = -1$

$\tan\theta = \frac{\sin\theta}{\cos\theta} = -1, \sin\theta = -\cos\theta$

Now, $\frac{\sec\theta + \text{cosec}\theta}{\cos\theta - \sin\theta}$

$= \frac{\frac{1}{\cos\theta} + \frac{1}{\sin\theta}}{\cos\theta - \sin\theta} = \frac{\frac{\sin\theta + \cos\theta}{\cos\theta \sin\theta}}{\cos\theta - \sin\theta}$

$= \frac{-\cos\theta + \cos\theta}{\sin\theta \times \cos\theta\,(\cos\theta - \sin\theta)}$

$= \frac{0}{\sin\theta \times \cos\theta\,(\cos\theta - \sin\theta)} = 0$

16. (d) (a) $\frac{\sin^2\theta - \cos^2\theta}{\cos\theta\tan\theta + \sin\theta\cot\theta}$

$= \frac{\sin^2\theta - \cos^2\theta}{\cos\theta \cdot \frac{\sin\theta}{\cos\theta} + \sin\theta \cdot \frac{\cos\theta}{\sin\theta}}$

$= \frac{(\sin\theta + \cos\theta)(\sin\theta - \cos\theta)}{(\sin\theta + \cos\theta)}$

$= \sin\theta - \cos\theta$

(b) $\frac{\sin^2\theta - \cos^2\theta}{\cos\theta\tan\theta - \sin\theta\cot\theta}$

$= \frac{(\sin\theta + \cos\theta)(\sin\theta - \cos\theta)}{\cos\theta \cdot \frac{\sin\theta}{\cos\theta} - \sin\theta \cdot \frac{\cos\theta}{\sin\theta}}$

$= \frac{(\sin\theta + \cos\theta)(\sin\theta - \cos\theta)}{(\sin\theta - \cos\theta)}$

$= \sin\theta + \cos\theta$

$\therefore$ None of the above is correctly matched.

17. (d)

(cosec $A - \sin A$) ($\sec A - \cos A$) ($\tan A + \cot A$)

$= \left(\frac{1}{\sin A} - \sin A\right)\left(\frac{1}{\cos A} - \cos A\right)(\tan A + \cot A)$

$= \left(\frac{1 - \sin^2 A}{\sin A}\right)\left(\frac{1 - \cos^2 A}{\cos A}\right)(\tan A + \cot A)$

$= \left(\frac{\cos^2 A}{\sin A} . \frac{\sin^2 A}{\cos A}\right)(\tan A + \cot A)$

$= (\cos A \sin A)\left(\frac{\sin A}{\cos A} + \frac{\cos A}{\sin A}\right)$

$= \frac{\sin^2 A + \cos^2 A}{(\sin A \cos A)}(\sin A \cos A)$

$= \sin^2 A + \cos^2 A = 1$

18. (c)

$\frac{\sin\theta + \cos\theta}{\sin\theta - \cos\theta} + \frac{\sin\theta - \cos\theta}{\sin\theta + \cos\theta}$

$= \frac{\begin{bmatrix}\sin^2\theta + \cos^2\theta + 2\sin\theta\cos\theta \\ + \sin^2\theta + \cos^2\theta - 2\sin\theta\cos\theta\end{bmatrix}}{\sin^2\theta - \cos^2\theta}$

$= \frac{1+1}{\sin^2\theta + \sin^2\theta - 1} = \frac{2}{2\sin^2\theta - 1}$

$[\because \sin^2\theta + \cos^2\theta = 1]$

$= \frac{2}{1 - \cos^2\theta - \cos^2\theta}$

$= \frac{2}{1 - 2\cos^2\theta}$

$\therefore$ Both (a) and (b) are correct.

19. (c) We have, $m = \text{cosec}\theta - \sin\theta$

$= \frac{1}{\sin\theta} - \sin\theta = \frac{1 - \sin^2\theta}{\sin\theta}$

$= \frac{\cos^2\theta}{\sin\theta}$

and $n = \sec\theta - \cos\theta$

$= \frac{1}{\cos\theta} - \cos\theta = \frac{1 - \cos^2\theta}{\cos\theta}$

$= \frac{\sin^2\theta}{\cos\theta}$

Now, $(m^2 n)^{2/3} + (mn^2)^{2/3}$

$= \left(\frac{\cos^4\theta}{\sin^2\theta} \times \frac{\sin^2\theta}{\cos\theta}\right)^{2/3} + \left(\frac{\cos^2\theta}{\sin\theta} \times \frac{\sin^4\theta}{\cos^2\theta}\right)^{2/3}$

$= (\cos^3\theta)^{2/3} + (\sin^3\theta)^{2/3}$

$= \cos^2\theta + \sin^2\theta$

$= 1$

20. (a) We have,

$P_n = \cos^n x + \sin^n x$

$\therefore 2P_6 - 3P_4 + 1$

$= 2(\cos^6 x + \sin^6 x) - 3(\sin^4 x + \cos^4 x) + 1$

$= 2[(\cos^2 x + \sin^2 x)^3 - 3\sin^2 x \cos^2 x(\sin^2 x + \cos^2 x)] - 3[(\cos^2 x + \sin^2 x)^2 - 2\sin^2 x \cos^2 x] + 1$

$= 2[1 - 3\sin^2 x \cos^2 x] - 3[1 - 2\sin^2 x \cos^2 x] + 1$

$[\because \sin^2 x + \cos^2 x = 1]$

$= 2 - 6\sin^2 x \cos^2 x - 3 + 6\sin^2 x \cos^2 x + 1$

$= 2 - 3 + 1 = 0$

21. (b) We have,

$\text{cosec}\,\theta - \sin\theta = x^3$

$\frac{1}{\sin\theta} - \sin\theta = x^3$

$\frac{1 - \sin^2\theta}{\sin\theta} = x^3$

$\Rightarrow \frac{\cos^2\theta}{\sin\theta} = x^3$ ...(i)

and $\sec\theta - \cos\theta = y^3$ ...(ii)

$\frac{1 - \cos^2\theta}{\cos\theta} = y^3$

$\Rightarrow \frac{\sin^2\theta}{\cos\theta} = y^3$ ...(iii)

From Eqs. (i) and (ii), we get

$\frac{y^3}{x^3} = \frac{\sin^2\theta / \cos\theta}{\cos^2\theta / \sin\theta}$

$\Rightarrow \frac{y^3}{x^3} = \frac{\sin^3\theta}{\cos^3\theta}$

$\Rightarrow \tan^3\theta = \frac{y^3}{x^3} \Rightarrow \tan\theta = \frac{y}{x}$

$\sin\theta = \frac{y}{\sqrt{x^2 + y^2}}$ and

$\cos\theta = \frac{x}{\sqrt{x^2 + y^2}}$

$\left[\therefore \sin\theta = \frac{\tan\theta}{\sqrt{1 + \tan^2\theta}} \text{ and } \cos\theta = \frac{1}{\sqrt{1 + \tan^2\theta}}\right]$

Now, putting the values of $\sin\theta$ and $\cos\theta$ in Eq. (i), we get

$x^3 = \frac{\frac{x^2}{(\sqrt{x^2 + y^2})^2}}{\frac{y}{\sqrt{x^2 + y^2}}}$

$\Rightarrow x^3 y\sqrt{x^2 + y^2} = x^2$

$\Rightarrow xy\sqrt{x^2 + y^2} = 1$

$\Rightarrow x^2 y^2 (x^2 + y^2) = 1$

[$\because$ squaring both sides]

22. (b) $\tan(\theta_1 + \theta_2) = \sqrt{3}$ [given]

$\Rightarrow \quad \theta_1 + \theta_2 = 60°$ ...(i)

Also, $\sec(\theta_1 - \theta_2) = \dfrac{2}{\sqrt{3}}$

$\Rightarrow \quad \theta_1 - \theta_2 = 30°$ ....(ii)

On adding Eqs. (i) and (ii), we get

$2\theta_1 = 90°$

$\Rightarrow \quad \theta_1 = 45° \Rightarrow \theta_2 = 15°$

$\therefore \sin 2\theta_1 + \tan 3\theta_2$

$= \sin 90° + \tan 45°$

$= 1 + 1 = 2$

23. (a) I. $\dfrac{\cos A}{1-\sin A} + \dfrac{\sin A}{1-\cos A} + 1$

$$= \frac{\begin{bmatrix}(1-\cos A)\cos A + (1-\sin A)\sin A \\ + (1-\sin A)(1-\cos A)\end{bmatrix}}{(1-\sin A)(1-\cos A)}$$

$$= \frac{\begin{bmatrix}\cos A - \cos^2 A + \sin A - \sin^2 A \\ + 1 - \sin A - \cos A + \cos A \sin A\end{bmatrix}}{(1-\sin A)(1-\cos A)}$$

$$= \frac{\cos A \sin A}{(1-\sin A)(1-\cos A)}$$

II. $\dfrac{(1+\cot A + \tan A)(\sin A - \cos A)}{\sec^3 A - \operatorname{cosec}^3 A}$

$$= \frac{\left(1 + \dfrac{\cos A}{\sin A} + \dfrac{\sin A}{\cos A}\right)(\sin A - \cos A)}{\dfrac{1}{\cos^3 A} - \dfrac{1}{\sin^3 A}}$$

$$= \frac{\left[\left(\dfrac{\sin A \cos A + \cos^2 A + \sin^2 A}{\sin A \cos A}\right)(\sin A - \cos A)\right]}{\dfrac{\sin^3 A - \cos^3 A}{\sin^3 A \cos^3 A}}$$

$$= \frac{\dfrac{\sin^3 A - \cos^3 A}{\sin A \cos A}}{\dfrac{\sin^3 A - \cos^3 A}{\sin^3 A \cos^3 A}} = \sin^2 A \cos^2 A$$

24. (d) (i) Given, $\sin A = \dfrac{1}{2}$

$\Rightarrow \quad A = 30°$ and $\tan B = \sqrt{3}$

Then, $A + B = 30° + 60° = 90°$

$\therefore \cot 90° = 0$ [false]

(ii) Given, $2\sin A = 1$

$\Rightarrow \sin A = \dfrac{1}{2} \Rightarrow A = 30°$

$\therefore \quad 3A = 90°$ [true]

(iii) Given, $1 - \cos^2\theta = \dfrac{3}{4}$

$\Rightarrow \cos^2\theta = 1 - \dfrac{3}{4} = \dfrac{1}{4}$

$\Rightarrow \cos\theta = \dfrac{1}{2} \Rightarrow \theta = 60°$

Then, $\sin 60° = \dfrac{\sqrt{3}}{2}$ [false]

(iv) Given, $\sin\theta = \dfrac{a}{b}$

$\therefore \quad \cos\theta = \sqrt{1 - \sin^2\theta}$

$= \sqrt{1 - \dfrac{a^2}{b^2}} = \sqrt{\dfrac{b^2 - a^2}{b}}$

[true]

$\therefore$ Final result

$= (-\text{False} + \text{True} - \text{False} + \text{True})$

$= -1 + 1 - 1 + 1 = 0$

25. (b) A. Given, $\sec A = \dfrac{17}{8}$

$= \dfrac{\text{Hypotenuse (H)}}{\text{Base (B)}}$

Perpendicular $= \sqrt{H^2 - B^2}$

$= \sqrt{17^2 - 8^2} = \sqrt{289 - 64}$

$= \sqrt{225} = 15$

$$\text{LHS} = \frac{3 - 4\sin^2 A}{4\cos^2 A - 3}$$

$$= \frac{3 - 4 \times \dfrac{15^2}{17^2}}{4 \times \dfrac{8^2}{17^2} - 3}$$

$$= \frac{867 - 900}{4 \times 64 - 3 \times 289}$$

$$= \frac{-33}{-611} = \frac{33}{611}$$

$$\text{RHS} = \frac{3 - \tan^2 A}{1 - 3\tan^2 A}$$

$$= \frac{3 - \left(\dfrac{15}{8}\right)^2}{1 - 3 \times \left(\dfrac{15}{8}\right)^2}$$

$$= \frac{3 - \dfrac{225}{64}}{1 - \dfrac{675}{64}}$$

$$= \frac{-33}{-611} = \frac{33}{611}$$

B. Given, $\tan\theta = \dfrac{20}{21} = \dfrac{P}{B}$

$\therefore \sin\theta = \dfrac{P}{H} = \dfrac{20}{\sqrt{(21)^2 + (20)^2}}$

$= \dfrac{20}{29}$

and $\cos\theta = \dfrac{B}{H} = \dfrac{21}{29}$

Now, $\dfrac{1 - \sin\theta + \cos\theta}{1 + \sin\theta + \cos\theta}$

$$= \frac{1 - \dfrac{20}{29} + \dfrac{21}{29}}{1 + \dfrac{20}{29} + \dfrac{21}{29}} = \frac{30}{70} = \frac{3}{7}$$

C. Given, $\sin\theta = \dfrac{12}{13}$

$\therefore \cos\theta = \dfrac{5}{13}$ and $\tan\theta = \dfrac{12}{5}$

Now, $\dfrac{\sin^2\theta - \cos^2\theta}{2\sin\theta\cos\theta} \times \dfrac{1}{\tan^2\theta}$

$$= \frac{\left(\dfrac{12}{13}\right)^2 - \left(\dfrac{5}{13}\right)^2}{2 \times \dfrac{12}{13} \times \dfrac{5}{13}} \times \left(\frac{5}{12}\right)^2$$

$$= \frac{144 - 25}{2 \times 12 \times 5} \times \left(\frac{5}{12}\right)^2$$

$$= \frac{119}{120} \times \frac{25}{144}$$

$$= \frac{119}{24} \times \frac{5}{144} = \frac{595}{3456}$$

26. (b) Given,

$x\sin^3\theta + y\cos^3\theta = \sin\theta\cos\theta$ ...(i)

and $\quad x\sin\theta = y\cos\theta$

$\Rightarrow \quad \sin\theta = \dfrac{y}{x}\cos\theta$

On putting the value of $\sin\theta$ in Eq. (i), we get

$x\left(\dfrac{y}{x}\right)^3 \cos^3\theta + y\cos^3\theta$

$= \dfrac{y}{x}\cos\theta\cos\theta$

$\Rightarrow y\left(\dfrac{y^2}{x^2}\cos^3\theta + \cos^3\theta\right)$

$= \dfrac{y}{x}\cos^2\theta$

$$\Rightarrow y\cos^3\theta\left(\frac{y^2+x^2}{x^2}\right)=\frac{y}{x}\cos^2\theta$$

$$\Rightarrow \cos\theta\,(x^2+y^2)=x \quad \text{...(ii)}$$

Similarly, for $\cos\theta=\frac{x}{y}\sin\theta$,

$$y=\sin\theta\,(x^2+y^2) \quad \text{...(iii)}$$

On squaring Eqs. (ii) and (iii) and then adding, we get

$$x^2+y^2=(\cos^2\theta+\sin^2\theta)\,(x^2+y^2)^2$$

$$\Rightarrow x^2+y^2=1$$

Hence, the statement is in correct.

27. (a) By angle subtended by an arc at the center,

we get, $\theta=\frac{60}{2}=30°$

$$\therefore \quad \sin\theta+\cos^2\theta=\frac{x^2+1}{x^2}$$

$$\Rightarrow \sin 30°+\cos^2 30°=\frac{x^2+1}{x^2}$$

$$\Rightarrow \quad \frac{1}{2}+\left(\frac{\sqrt{3}}{2}\right)^2=\frac{x^2+1}{x^2}$$

$$\Rightarrow \quad \frac{1}{2}+\frac{3}{4}=\frac{x^2+1}{x^2}$$

$$\Rightarrow \frac{2+3}{4}=\frac{x^2+1}{x^2}\Rightarrow\frac{5}{4}=\frac{x^2+1}{x^2}$$

$$\Rightarrow \quad 5x^2=4x^2+4$$

$$\Rightarrow \quad 5x^2-4x^2=4\Rightarrow x^2=4$$

$$\Rightarrow \quad x=\sqrt{4}=2$$

Chapter 9 : Applications of Trigonometry

1. (a) The angle of depression = Angle of elevation from bottom = 60°.

2. (c) $\because \tan\theta=\frac{P}{B}=\frac{20\sqrt{3}}{20}=\sqrt{3}$

$$\therefore \quad \theta=60°$$

3. (b) By definition

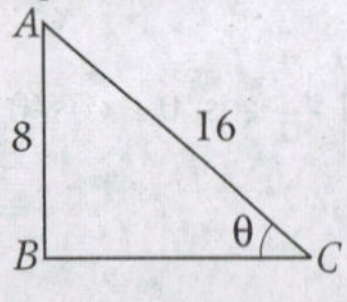

$$\sin\theta=\frac{P}{H}=\frac{AB}{AC}=\frac{8}{16}$$

$$\Rightarrow \quad \sin\theta=1/2\Rightarrow\theta=30°$$

4. (b) In ΔABC, we have, $AB\perp BC$

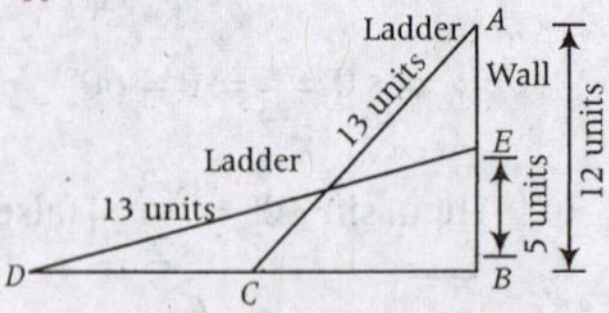

By Pythagoras theorem,

$$AC^2=AB^2+BC^2$$

$$\Rightarrow \quad 13^2=12^2+BC^2$$

$$\Rightarrow \quad 169-144=BC^2$$

$$\Rightarrow \quad BC=5\text{ units}$$

Now, in ΔEBD, by Pythagoras theorem,

$$ED^2=EB^2+BD^2$$

$$\Rightarrow \quad 13^2=5^2+BD^2$$

$$\Rightarrow 13^2-5^2=BD^2\Rightarrow BD=12$$

$$\therefore CD=BD-BC=12-5=7\text{ units}$$

5. (c)

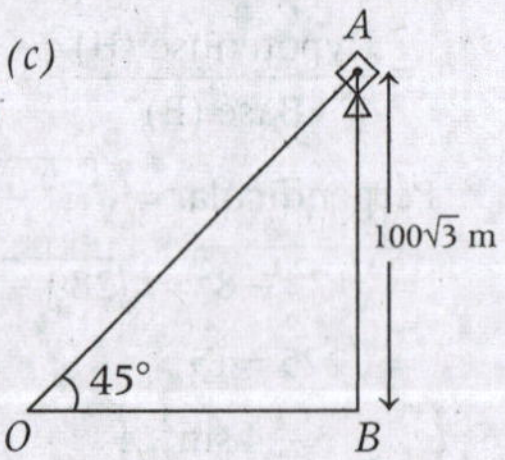

Let the length of the string be $OA=l$ m

$$\therefore \sin 45°=\frac{100\sqrt{3}}{OA}$$

$$\Rightarrow \quad \frac{1}{\sqrt{2}}=\frac{100\sqrt{3}}{l}$$

$$\Rightarrow \quad l=\frac{100\sqrt{3}}{\frac{1}{\sqrt{2}}}$$

$$=100\sqrt{3}\times\sqrt{2}=100\sqrt{6}\text{ m}$$

6. (a)

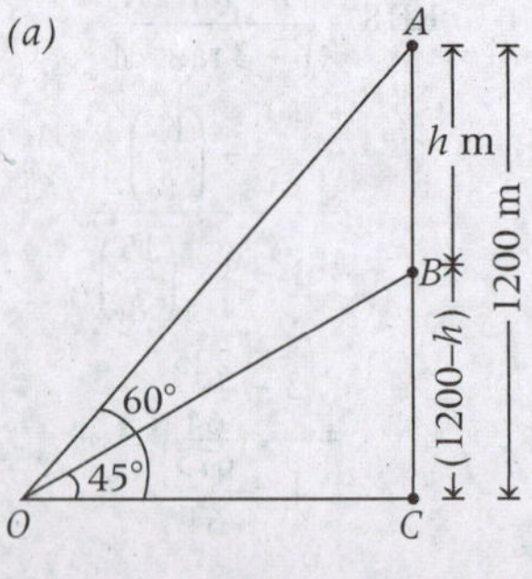

Let the first eagle's height above the second eagle be h m.

$\therefore$ In ΔAOC,

$$\tan 60°=\frac{AC}{OC}\Rightarrow\sqrt{3}=\frac{1200}{OC}$$

$$\Rightarrow OC=\frac{1200}{\sqrt{3}}\times\frac{\sqrt{3}}{\sqrt{3}}$$

$$=\frac{1200\sqrt{3}}{3}$$

$$OC=400\sqrt{3}\text{ m}$$

Again in ΔOBC,

$$\tan 45°=\frac{BC}{OC}=\frac{1200-h}{400\sqrt{3}}$$

$$\therefore \quad 1=\frac{1200-h}{400\sqrt{3}}$$

$$\Rightarrow 1200-h=400\sqrt{3}$$

$$h=1200-400\sqrt{3}$$

$$h=1200-69282$$

$$=507.20\text{ m}$$

7. (a) Let the height of the tree before breaking $=h$ m

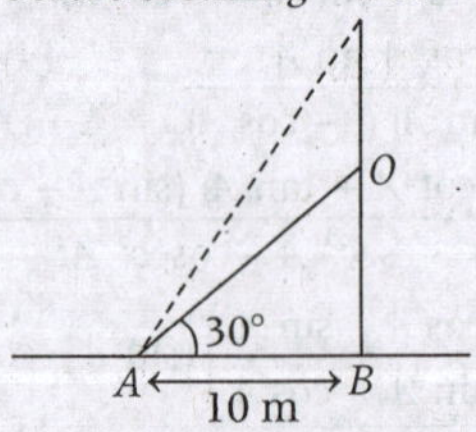

i.e. $\quad h=(OB+OA)$

$$\therefore \quad \cos 30°=\frac{AB}{OA}=\frac{10}{OA}$$

$$\Rightarrow \quad \frac{\sqrt{3}}{2}=\frac{10}{OA}\Rightarrow OA=\left(\frac{20}{\sqrt{3}}\right)$$

$$\therefore \quad \sin 30°=\frac{OB}{OA}=\frac{OB}{\left(\frac{20}{\sqrt{3}}\right)}$$

$$\Rightarrow \quad \frac{1}{2}=\frac{\sqrt{3}\,OB}{20}$$

$$\Rightarrow \quad OB=\left(\frac{10}{\sqrt{3}}\right)\text{m}$$

$$\therefore \quad AB=(OA+OB)$$

$$=\left(\frac{20}{\sqrt{3}}+\frac{10}{\sqrt{3}}\right)$$

$$=\frac{30}{\sqrt{3}}\times\frac{\sqrt{3}}{\sqrt{3}}$$

$$=10\sqrt{3}\text{ m}$$

8. *(b)*

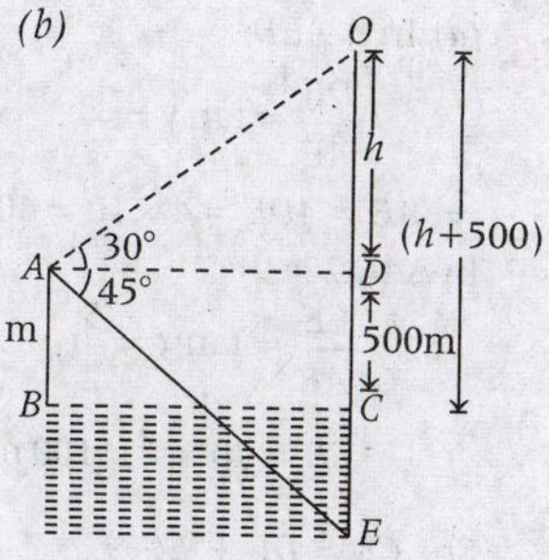

Let the height of the object $OC = (h + 500)$

$\therefore \quad CE = OC = (h + 500)$

In ΔADO,

$$\tan 30° = \frac{OD}{AD} = \frac{h}{AD}$$

$$\Rightarrow \quad \frac{1}{\sqrt{3}} = \frac{h}{AD}$$

$$\therefore \quad AD = \sqrt{3}h \qquad \ldots(i)$$

and $\tan 45° = \dfrac{DE}{AD}$

$$\Rightarrow \quad 1 = \left(\frac{h + 500 + 500}{AD}\right)$$

$$\Rightarrow \quad AD = (h + 1000) \qquad \ldots(ii)$$

$$\therefore \quad \sqrt{3}h = h + 1000$$

$$\Rightarrow \quad h(\sqrt{3} - 1) = 1000$$

$$\Rightarrow \quad h = \frac{1000}{\sqrt{3} - 1} \times \frac{\sqrt{3} + 1}{\sqrt{3} + 1}$$

$$= 500(\sqrt{3} + 1) \text{ m}$$

$$\therefore \quad OC = \{500(\sqrt{3} + 1) + 500\}$$

$$= 500(\sqrt{3} + 2) \text{ m}$$

9. *(a)* Let the height of pole first $= AB = h$

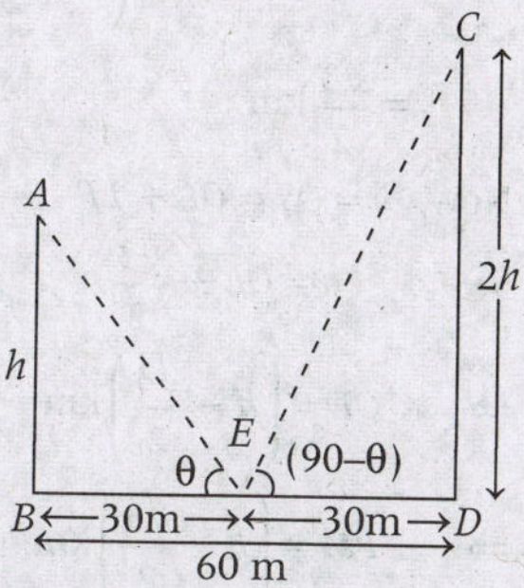

$\therefore$ Height of 2nd pole

$$DC = (2 \times h)$$

In ΔABE, $\tan\theta = \dfrac{h}{30} \qquad \ldots(i)$

and ΔEDC,

$$\tan(90° - \theta) = \frac{2h}{30} = \frac{h}{15}$$

$$\Rightarrow \quad \cot\theta = \frac{h}{15}$$

$$\Rightarrow \quad \tan\theta = \left(\frac{15}{h}\right) \qquad \ldots(ii)$$

$$\Rightarrow \quad \frac{h}{30} = \frac{15}{h} \Rightarrow h^2 = 450$$

$$\therefore \quad h = \sqrt{450} = 21.21 \text{ m}$$

and height of the second pole

$$= 2h$$

$$= 2 \times 21.21 = 42.42 \text{ m}$$

10. *(c)* Let AB be the height of tower and $CB = a$ and $BD = b$

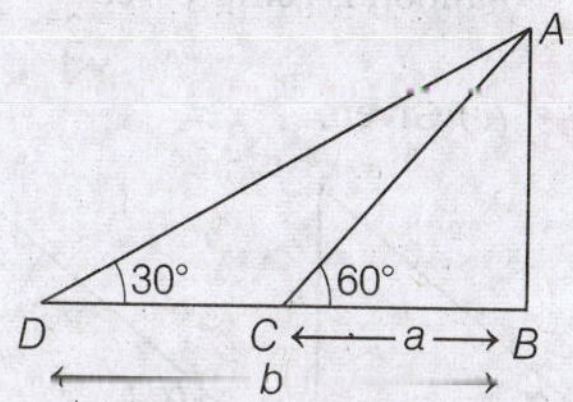

In ΔABC, $\tan 60° = \dfrac{AB}{BC} = \dfrac{AB}{a}$

$$\Rightarrow \quad AB = a\sqrt{3} \qquad \ldots(i)$$

In ΔABD, $\tan 30° = \dfrac{AB}{BD}$

$$\Rightarrow \quad \frac{1}{\sqrt{3}} = \frac{AB}{b}$$

$$\Rightarrow \quad AB = \frac{b}{\sqrt{3}} \qquad \ldots(ii)$$

On multiplying Eqs. (i) and (ii), we get

$$AB^2 = ab \quad \Rightarrow AB = \sqrt{ab}$$

11. *(b)* Let the height of the building $CD = h$

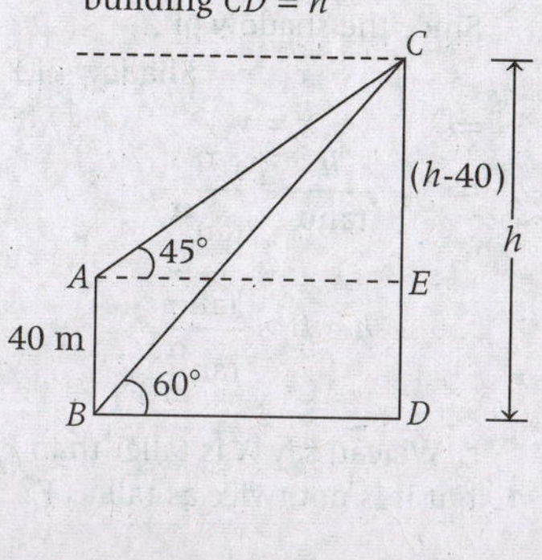

$$\therefore \quad \tan 45° = \frac{CE}{AE}$$

and $\tan 60° = \dfrac{CD}{BD}$

$$\Rightarrow \quad 1 = \frac{h - 40}{AE} \text{ and } \sqrt{3} = \frac{h}{AE}$$

$$\Rightarrow \quad AE = h - 40$$

and $AE = \left(\dfrac{h}{\sqrt{3}}\right)$

$$\therefore \quad h - 40 = \frac{h}{\sqrt{3}}$$

$$\Rightarrow \quad \sqrt{3}h - 40\sqrt{3} = h$$

$$\Rightarrow \quad h(\sqrt{3} - 1) = 40\sqrt{3}$$

$$\Rightarrow h = \frac{40\sqrt{3}}{\sqrt{3} - 1} \times \frac{\sqrt{3} + 1}{\sqrt{3} + 1}$$

$$\Rightarrow \quad h = \frac{40}{2}(\sqrt{3})(\sqrt{3} + 1)$$

$$= 20(\sqrt{3} + 3)$$

$$= 60 + 20 \times 1.73$$

$$= 60 + 34.6 = 94.6 \text{ m}$$

12. *(b)* Given,

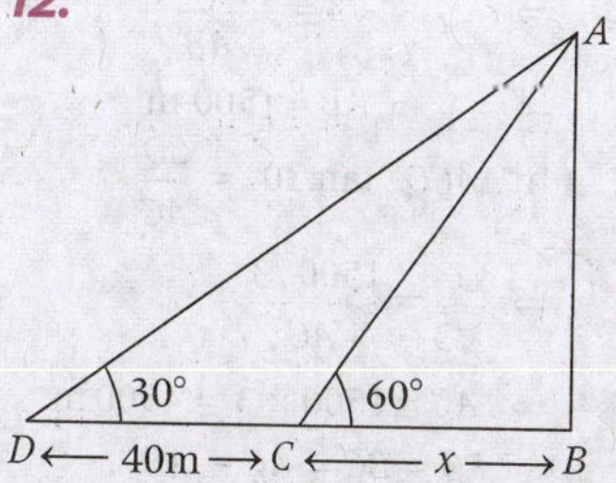

Let the width of the river be BC $= x$ m.

$\therefore$ In ΔADB,

$$\tan 30° = \frac{AB}{40 + x}$$

$$\frac{1}{\sqrt{3}} = \frac{AB}{40 + x}$$

$$\Rightarrow \quad AB = \frac{40 + x}{\sqrt{3}} \text{ m} \qquad \ldots(i)$$

In ΔACB,

$$\tan 60° = \frac{AB}{x}$$

$$\sqrt{3} = \frac{AB}{x}$$

$$\Rightarrow \quad AB = \sqrt{3}\, x \text{ m} \qquad \ldots(ii)$$

From Eqs. (i) and (ii),

$$\frac{40+x}{\sqrt{3}} = \sqrt{3}x$$

$$\Rightarrow \quad 40 + x = \sqrt{3}\times\sqrt{3}\,x$$

$$\Rightarrow \quad 40 + x = 3x$$

$$\Rightarrow \quad 2x = 40$$

$$\Rightarrow \quad x = \frac{40}{2} = 20 \text{ m}$$

13. (a)

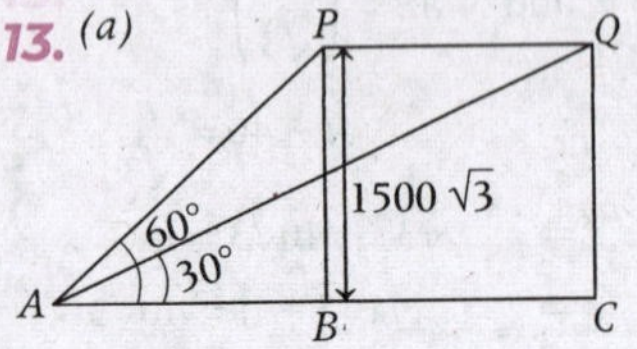

P and Q are the positions of the plane.

$\angle PAB = 60°$, $\angle QAB = 30°$

$PB = 1500\sqrt{3}$ m

In ΔABP,

$$\tan 60° = \frac{BP}{AB}$$

$$\Rightarrow \quad \sqrt{3} = \frac{1500\sqrt{3}}{AB}$$

$$\Rightarrow \quad AB = 1500 \text{ m}$$

In ΔACQ, $\tan 30° = \frac{CQ}{AC}$

$$\Rightarrow \quad \frac{1}{\sqrt{3}} = \frac{1500\sqrt{3}}{AC}$$

$$\Rightarrow \quad AC = 1500 \times 3 = 4500 \text{ m}$$

$$PQ = BC = AC - AB$$

$$= 4500 - 1500$$

$$= 3000 \text{ m}$$

$$\therefore \text{Speed of plane} = \frac{3000}{15}$$

$$= 200 \text{ m/s}$$

14. (a) Given,

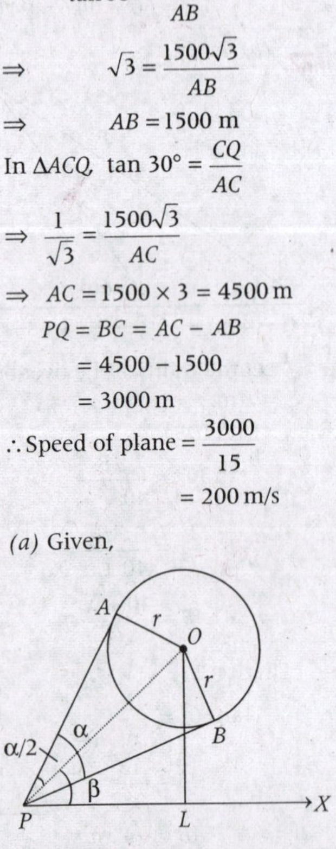

Let O be the centre of the circle with radius r and P be the ... Also PA and PB be tangents from P to the balloon such that $\angle APB = \alpha$.

In ΔOAP,

$$\sin\frac{\alpha}{2} = \frac{OA}{OP}$$

$$\Rightarrow \quad \sin\frac{\alpha}{2} = \frac{r}{OP}$$

$$\Rightarrow \quad OP = r \operatorname{cosec}\frac{\alpha}{2} \quad \ldots\text{(i)}$$

In ΔOPL,

we have $\sin\beta = \dfrac{OL}{OP}$

$$\Rightarrow \quad OL = OP\sin\beta$$

$$= r \operatorname{cosec}\frac{\alpha}{2}\sin\beta$$

[from Eq. (i)]

$\therefore$ Height of the centre of the balloon is $r\sin\beta \operatorname{cosec}\dfrac{\alpha}{2}$.

15. (c) Given,

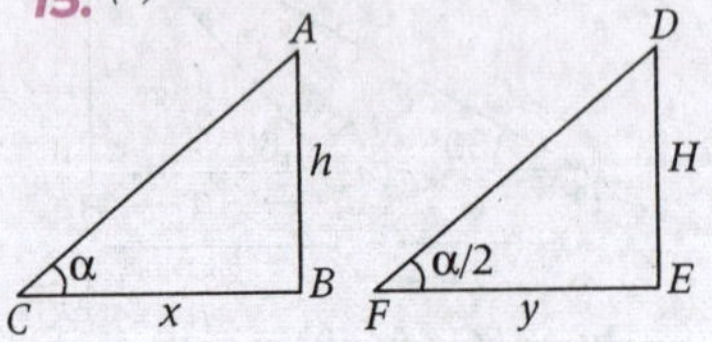

Let the length of the shadow of person X and person Y be x m and y m respectively.

$\therefore$ In ΔABC,

$$\frac{h}{x} = \tan\alpha$$

$$\Rightarrow \quad x = \frac{h}{\tan\alpha} \quad \ldots\text{(i)}$$

and ΔEFD, $\dfrac{H}{y} = \tan\dfrac{\alpha}{2}$

$$\Rightarrow \quad y = \frac{H}{\tan\frac{\alpha}{2}} \quad \ldots\text{(ii)}$$

Since the shadow of X = Shadow of Y

$$\Rightarrow \quad x = y$$

$$\Rightarrow \quad \frac{h}{\tan\alpha} = \frac{H}{\tan\frac{\alpha}{2}}$$

$$\therefore \quad h = H \times \frac{\tan\alpha}{\tan\frac{\alpha}{2}}$$

$\therefore$ We can say X is taller than Y but it is not twice as tall as Y.

16. (d) In ΔAED,

$$\frac{DE}{AE} = \tan y = \frac{1}{4}$$

$$\Rightarrow AE = 4DE = 4 \times 10 = 40 \text{ m}$$

In ΔAEC,

$$\frac{CE}{AE} = \tan x = \frac{5}{2}$$

$$CE = 40 \times \frac{5}{2} = 100 \text{ m}$$

So, $CD = DE + EC$

$$= 10 + 100 = 110 \text{ m}.$$

Therefore, the height of the tower CD is 110 m.

17. (c)

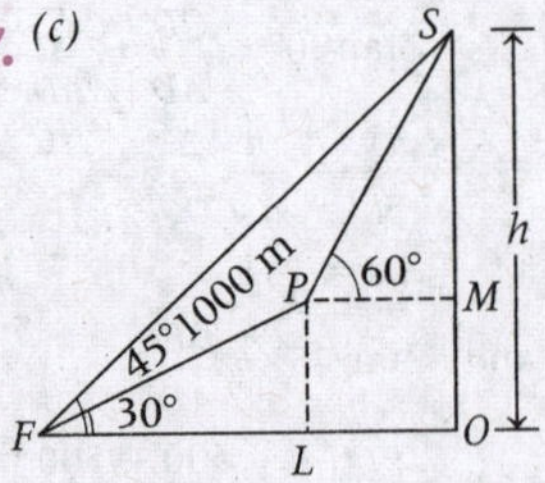

In ΔFPL, $\sin 30° = \dfrac{PL}{PF}$

$$\Rightarrow PL = PF \sin 30°$$

$$= \left(1 \times \frac{1}{2}\right)\text{km} = \frac{1}{2}\text{ km}$$

$$\therefore OM = PL = \frac{1}{2}\text{ km}$$

$$\Rightarrow MS = OS - OM = \left(h - \frac{1}{2}\right)\text{km}$$

Also, $\cos 30° = \dfrac{FL}{PF}$

$$\Rightarrow FL = PF \cos 30° = \left(1 \times \frac{\sqrt{3}}{2}\right)$$

$$= \frac{\sqrt{3}}{2}\text{ km}$$

Now, $h = OS = OL + LF$

$$\Rightarrow \quad h = OL + \frac{\sqrt{3}}{2}$$

$$\Rightarrow \quad OL = \left(h - \frac{\sqrt{3}}{2}\right)\text{km}$$

$$\Rightarrow \quad PM = \left(h - \frac{\sqrt{3}}{2}\right)\text{km}$$

In ΔSPM, $\tan 60° = \dfrac{SM}{PM}$

$$\Rightarrow \quad SM = PM \tan 60°$$

$\Rightarrow \quad \left(h-\frac{1}{2}\right)=\left(h-\frac{\sqrt{3}}{2}\right)\sqrt{3}$

$\Rightarrow \quad \left(h-\frac{1}{2}\right)=\left(\sqrt{3}h-\frac{3}{2}\right)$

$\Rightarrow \quad (\sqrt{3}\,h-h)=\frac{3}{2}-\frac{1}{2}$

$\Rightarrow \quad h(\sqrt{3}-1)=1$

$\Rightarrow \quad h=\frac{1}{\sqrt{3}-1}$

Both the statements are required.

18. *(b)*

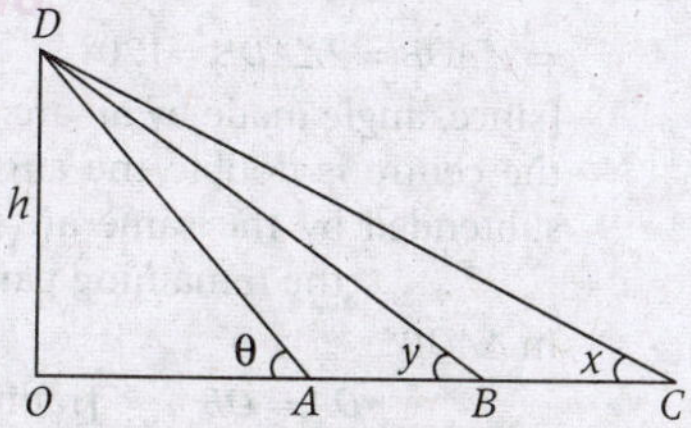

Let $OD = h$ and $OA = l$

$\therefore \tan\theta=\frac{h}{l}$ and $\cot\theta=\frac{l}{h}$

$\tan\alpha=\frac{h}{l+a}$ and $\cot\alpha=\frac{l}{h}+\frac{a}{h}$

$\Rightarrow \cot\alpha=\cot\theta+\frac{a}{h}$ ...(i)

and $\cot\beta=\cot\theta+\frac{b}{h}$ ...(ii)

Multiply Eq. (i) by b and multiply Eq. (ii) by a, and then subtract;

$b\cot x-a\cot y=(b-a)\cot\theta$

$\therefore \quad \cot\theta=\frac{b\cot x-a\cot y}{(b-a)}$

19. *(a)* **A.** In ΔABC,

$\sin\beta=\frac{P}{H}$

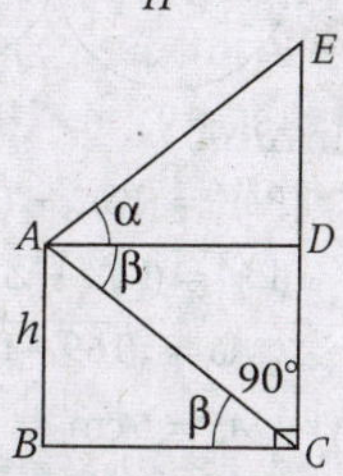

$\Rightarrow \quad \sin\beta=\frac{AB}{AC}$

$\Rightarrow \quad \sin\beta=\frac{h}{AC}\Rightarrow AC=\frac{h}{\sin\beta}$

B. In ΔEDA,

$\frac{DE}{AD}=\tan\alpha$

$\Rightarrow \quad DE=AD\tan\alpha$ ...(i)

In ΔABC,

$\frac{AB}{BC}=\tan\beta\Rightarrow\frac{h}{BC}=\tan\beta$

$\Rightarrow h\cot\beta=BC=AD$ ...(ii)

From Eqs. (i) and (ii), we get

$DE=h\tan\alpha\cot\beta$

C. $EC=DE+DC$

$=h\tan\alpha\cot\beta+h$ $[\because DC=AB]$

$=h(1+\tan\alpha\cot\beta)$

D. Distance between the two buildings

$=BC=h\cot\beta$ [from Eq. (ii)]

Chapter 10 : Circles

1. *(a)* Since, ΔOPQ is right angled triangle at Q. Then

$OP^2=OQ^2+PQ^2$

$\Rightarrow \quad 13^2=5^2+PQ^2$

$\Rightarrow 169-25=PQ^2$

$\therefore \quad PQ=12\,\text{cm}$

2. *(c)* We know that, the angle made by a chord with the tangent is equal to the angle made by the same chord in the alternate segment.

$\angle a=60°$

3. *(b)* Given, ΔABC with a circle inscribe. in it such that sides of ΔABC are tangent to the circle.

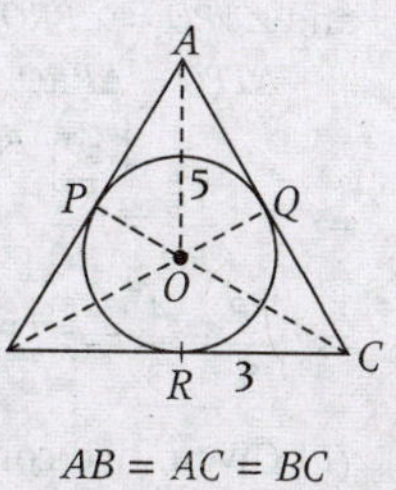

Now, $\quad AB=AC=BC$

$\Rightarrow \quad \frac{1}{2}AB=\frac{1}{2}AC=\frac{1}{2}BC$

$\Rightarrow \quad AP=RC=3\,\text{cm}$

In ΔOPA,

$OA^2=OP^2+AP^2$

[since, radius is perpendicular to the tangent at point of the contact]

$\Rightarrow \quad 5^2=OP^2+3^2$

$\Rightarrow 25-9=OP^2\Rightarrow 16=OP^2$

$\Rightarrow \quad OP=4\text{ units}=r$

$\therefore$ Diameter $=2r=8$ units

4. *(c)* Since, the direct common tangent divides the line joining the centre of two circles externally in the ratio of their radii.

$\therefore$ Required ratio $=5:11$ [externally]

5. *(a)* In the given figure,

$\angle OBP=90°$ and $\angle OBC=30°$

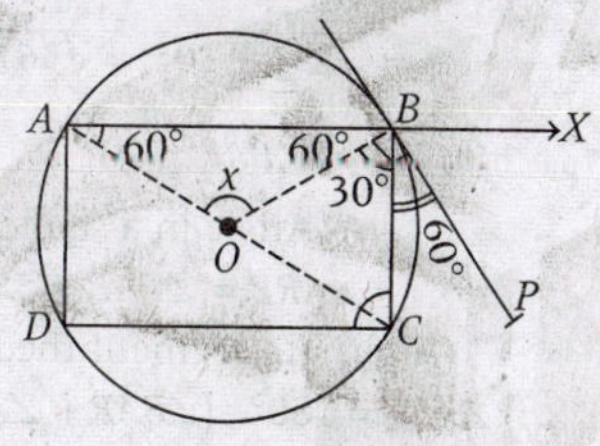

$\therefore \quad \angle CBP=90°-30°=60°$

$\Rightarrow \quad \angle CAB=60°$

[$\because \angle CAB=\angle CBP$, alternate segment of chord]

In ΔOAB, $OA=OB$

$\Rightarrow \angle OAB=\angle OBA=60°$

In ΔOAB,

$\angle OAB+\angle OBA+\angle AOB=180°$

$\Rightarrow \quad 60°+60°+\angle AOB=180°$

$\therefore \angle AOB=180°-120°=60°$

6. *(c)* In the given figure,

$OR=OS$ [radii]

In ΔORS,

$\angle ORS=\angle OSR=y$

Also, $\quad \angle ORT=90°$

[radius of a circle is perpendicular to the tangent at the point of contact]

In ΔPRS,

$\angle SPR+\angle PSR+\angle PRS=180°$

$\Rightarrow \angle x+\angle y+90°+\angle y=180°$

$\therefore \quad \angle x+2\angle y=90°$

7. (c) In ΔBDO and ΔBEA,

$\angle DBO = \angle EBA$ (Common)

$\frac{BD}{BE} = \frac{BO}{BA}$

(O is the centre of the circle and OD bisects BE)

$\Delta BDO \sim \Delta BEA$

$AE = 2DO = 2(8\text{ cm}) = 16\text{ cm}$

$BD = \sqrt{BO^2 - DO^2} = \sqrt{13^2 - 8^2}$

$= \sqrt{169 - 64} = \sqrt{105}\text{ cm}$

$DE = BD = \sqrt{105}\text{ cm}$

$\angle AED = \angle ODB = 90°$

(since $\Delta BDO \sim \Delta BEA$)

In ΔDAE,

$AD = \sqrt{AE^2 + DE^2}$

$= \sqrt{16^2 + 105}$

$= \sqrt{256 + 105} = \sqrt{361}\text{ cm}$

8. (b) Here, $\angle BAR = 90°$

(Angle in a semicircle)

$\angle ARB = \angle PAB = 58°$

(Alternate segment theorem)

$\angle ABQ = 180° - (\angle BAR + \angle ARB)$

(Angle sum property of a triangle)

$= 180° - (90° + 58°)$

$= 180° - 148° = 32°$

$\angle QAR = \angle ABR = 32°$

and

$\angle AQB = 180° - (\angle ABQ + \angle BAQ)$

$= 180° - (32° + 90° + 32°)$

$= 180° - 154° = 26°$

9. (a) Given, $\angle TRQ = 30°$

At point R, $OR \perp RQ$.

So, $\angle ORQ = 90°$

$\Rightarrow \angle TRQ + \angle ORT = 90°$

$\Rightarrow \angle ORT = 90° - 30° = 60°$

It's seen that, ST is diameter,

So, $\angle SRT = 90°$

[$\because$ Angle in semicircle = 90°]

Then, $\angle ORT + \angle SRO = 90°$

$\angle SRO + \angle PRS = 90°$

$\therefore \angle PRS = 90° - 30° = 60°$

10. (a) Let C_1 and C_2 be the two circles having same centre O.

And, AC is a chord which touches the C_1 at point D

Let's join OD

So, $OD \perp AC$,

$AD = DC = 4\text{ cm}$

[perpendicular line OD bisects the chord]

Thus, in right angled ΔAOD,

$OA^2 = AD^2 + DO^2$

[By Pythagoras theorem]

$DO^2 = 5^2 - 4^2 = 25 - 16 = 9$

$\Rightarrow DO = 3\text{ cm}$

11. (b)

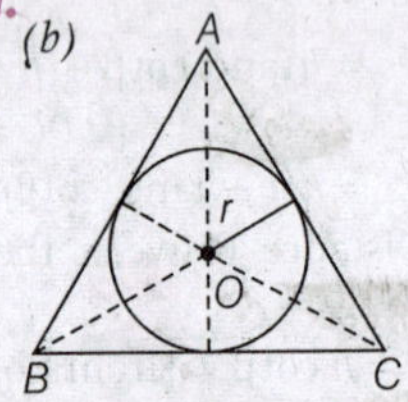

Area of ΔABC = Area of ΔOBA + Area of ΔOBC + Area of ΔOAC

$= \frac{1}{2} \times r \times AB + \frac{1}{2} \times r \times BC + \frac{1}{2} \times r \times AC$

$= \frac{1}{2} \times r\,(AB + BC + CA)$

$\Rightarrow \Delta = \frac{1}{2} \times r \times 2s \Rightarrow r = \frac{\Delta}{s}$

12. (b) Since, $OR \perp PQ$

So, OR bisects PQ.

$\Rightarrow PR = RQ = 4\text{ cm}$

In ΔPOR,

$OP^2 = OR^2 + PR^2$

$\Rightarrow 5^2 = OR^2 + 4^2 \Rightarrow OR = 3\text{ cm}$

In ΔTPO and ΔPRO,

$\angle TOP = \angle ROP$ [common]

and $\angle TPO = \angle PRO$ [each 90°]

$\therefore \Delta TPO \sim \Delta PRO$

[by AA similarity]

$\Rightarrow \frac{TP}{PO} = \frac{RP}{RO}$ [by BPT]

$\Rightarrow \frac{TP}{5} = \frac{4}{3} \Rightarrow TP = \frac{20}{3}\text{ cm}$

13. (b) Given, two concentric circles with radius O. Now, PQ, QR and PR are sides of equilateral ΔPQR.

We have,

$PQ = QR = PR$

$\Rightarrow \angle QPR = 60°$

$\therefore \angle QOR = 120°$

[angle subtended by an arc at the centre is twice the angle subtended by the same arc in the remaining part]

Also, in smaller circle,

$\angle BAC = \frac{1}{2}\angle BOC = \frac{1}{2}\angle QOR$

$\therefore \angle BAC = 60°$

14. (b) Given, $\angle ADB = 60°$

$\Rightarrow \angle AOB = 2\angle ADB = 120°$

[since, angle made by an arc at the centre is double the angle subtended by the same arc in the remaining part]

In ΔAOB,

$OA = OB$ [radii]

$\therefore \angle OAB = \angle OBA$

So, we have

$\angle OAB = \angle OBA = 30°$

[since, $\angle OAB + \angle OBA + \angle AOB = 180°$

$\Rightarrow 2\angle OAB = 2\angle OBA = 60°$

$\Rightarrow \angle OAB = \angle OBA = 30°$]

$\Rightarrow \angle PAB = \angle PAO - \angle OAB$

$= 90° - 30°$

$= 60°$

Similarly, $\angle PBA = 60°$

$\Rightarrow \angle APB = 60°$

$\therefore \Delta PAB$ is equilateral triangle.

15. (c)

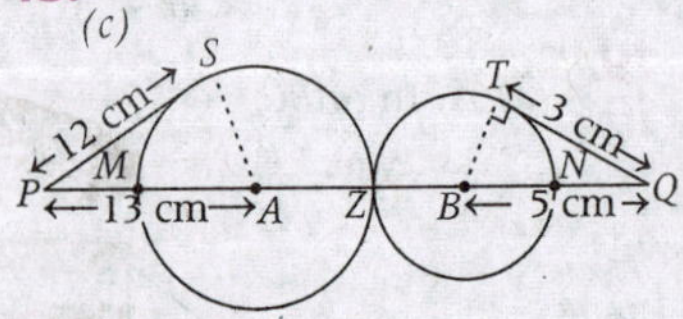

In ΔPSA,

$(PA)^2 = (PS)^2 + (AS)^2$

$(13)^2 = (12)^2 + AS^2$

$AS = \sqrt{169 - 144}$

$AS = 5\text{ cm}$

$AS = AM$ (radii)

In ΔQTB,

$(QB)^2 = (QT)^2 + (TB)^2$

$(5)^2 = (3)^2 + (TB)^2$

$TB = \sqrt{25-9}$

$TB = 4\text{ cm}$

$TB = BN$

So, Length of PQ

$= PA + AZ + ZB + BQ$

$= 13 + 5 + 4 + 5 = 27\text{ cm}$

16. (*b*) Since, AP and AR are the tangents to the circle,

$AP = AR$

Similarly, $CR = CQ$ and $BQ = BP$

OP and OQ are radii of the circle

$OP \perp AB$ and $OQ \perp BC$ and $\angle B = 90°$ (given)

Hence, $BPOQ$ is a square

Thus, $BP = BQ = r$ (sides of a square are equal)

So,

$AR = AP = AB - PB = 8 - r$

and $CR = CQ = BC - BQ = 6 - r$

But $AC^2 = AB^2 + BC^2$

(By Phythagoras Theorem)

$= (8)^2 + (6)^2 = 64 + 36$

$= 100 = (10)^2$

So, $AC = 10\text{ cm}$

$\Rightarrow AR + CR = 10$

$\Rightarrow 8 - r + 6 - r = 10$

$\Rightarrow 2r = 14 - 10 \Rightarrow r = 2\text{cm}$

17. (*d*) Let $AD = x$

As AP and AS are the tangents to the circle. Then

$AP = AS$

Similarly,

$BP = BQ$

$CQ = CR$

and $DR = DS$

So, In $ABCD$

$AB + CD = AD + BC$

[Property of a cyclic quadrilateral]

$\Rightarrow 6 + 4 = 7 + x$

$\Rightarrow x = 10 - 7 = 3$

Therefore, $AD = 3\text{cm}$.

18. (*c*) Perimeter of ΔAPQ,

$= AP + AQ + PQ$

$= AP + AQ + (PX + QX)$

We know that,

The two tangents drawn from external point to the circle are equal in length from point A.

So, $AB = AC = 5\text{cm}$

From point P, $PX = PB$

From point Q, $QX = QC$

Thus, Perimeter (P)

$= AP + AQ + (PB + QC)$

$= (AP + PB) + (AQ + QC)$

$= AB + AC = 5 + 5 = 10\text{ cm}$

19. (*b*) As we know, $OS = OQ = OR$

[radii of same circle]

$\angle OSQ = \angle OQS = 90° - 50°$

$= 40°$

$\angle RSO = \angle SRO = 90° - 60° = 30°$

Therefore,

$\angle QSR = 40° + 30° = 70°$

20. (*a*) Tangents drawn from an external point are equal.

Therefore,

$QR - QP$

$\Rightarrow \angle QPR = \angle QRP = 55°$

[angles opposite to the equal sides of a triangle]

$\angle OPQ = 90°$ $[OP \perp PQ]$

$\angle OPR = \angle OPQ - QPR$

$= 90° - 55° = 35°$

In ΔOPS,

$OP = OS$ (Radii),

Hence, $\angle OPS = \angle OSP = x$ (let)

$\because \angle OPS + \angle OSP + \angle POS = 180°$

(Angle sum property)

$\therefore x + x + 120° = 180°$

$\Rightarrow x = 30°$

Now, $\angle SPR = \angle SPR + \angle OPR$

$= 30° + 35° = 65°$

21. (*d*) $\therefore$ In ΔABD,

$\angle DAB + \angle ABD + \angle ADB = 180°$

$\Rightarrow \angle ADB = 180° - 40° = 40°$

In ΔODC, $OD = OC$ = (radii of same circle)

$\angle OCD = \angle CDO = 40°$

[$\therefore$ angles opposite to equal sides are equal]

$\angle DOC + \angle OCD + \angle CDO = 180°$

[$\because$ sum of angles in a triangle is 180°]

$\Rightarrow \angle DOC = 100°$

Since, AD is a straight line.

$\therefore \angle DOC + \angle COA = 180°$

$\Rightarrow \angle COA = 80°$

22. (*b*) Since, $\angle OPA = 90°$

[Tangent at any point of a circle is perpendicular to the radius through the point of contact]

$OA^2 = OP^2 + PA^2$

[by Pythagoras Theorem]

$(13)^2 = 5^2 + PA^2$

$\Rightarrow PA^2 = 144 = 12^2$

$\Rightarrow PA = 12\text{cm}$

Now, perimeter of

$\Delta ABC = AB + BC + CA$

$= (AB + BR) + (RC + CA)$

$= AB + BP + CQ + CA$

[$BR = BP$, $RC = CQ$ tangents from internal point to a circle are equal]

$= AP + AQ = 2AP$

$= 2x(12) = 24\text{ cm}$

[$AP = AQ$ tangent from internal point to a circle are equal]

Therefore, the perimeter of $\Delta ABC = 24\text{ cm}$.

23. (*a*) (A) Given, $\angle EDC = \theta$

$\Rightarrow \angle ODC = \theta$

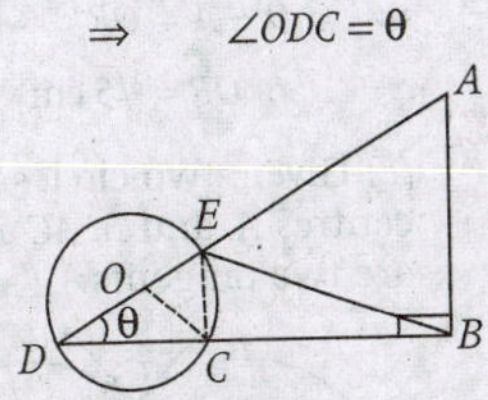

Now, $OD = OC$ [radii]

$\Rightarrow \angle OCD = \angle ODC = \theta$

In ΔABD,

$\angle ABD + \angle BDA + \angle DAB = 180°$

$\Rightarrow 90° + \theta + \angle DAB = 180°$

$\Rightarrow \angle DAB = 90° - \theta$

(B) In ΔECD,

$\angle ECD + \angle CDE + \angle DEC = 180°$

$\Rightarrow 90° + \theta + \angle DEC = 180°$

[$\angle ECD = 90°$, angle in a semi-circle]

$\Rightarrow \angle DEC = 90° - q$

Also, $OE \perp EB$

[Since, EB is tangent and OE is radius.]

$\Rightarrow \angle CEB = 90° - (90° - \theta) = \theta$

(C) In ΔDOC,

$\angle DOC + \angle ODC + \angle OCD = 180°$

$\Rightarrow \angle DOC + \theta + \theta = 180°$

$\Rightarrow \angle DOC = 180° - 2\theta$

$= 2(90° - \theta)$

$= 2\angle DEC$

24. (b) Here, $OA \perp AP$ and $OR \perp AB$

In ΔOAP, $OA^2 + AP^2 = OP^2$

$\Rightarrow 3^2 + AP^2 = 5^2$

$\Rightarrow AP^2 = 16$

$\Rightarrow AP = 4$ cm

Now, in ΔAPB,

$\angle APB = \angle ABP = 30°$

$\Rightarrow AP = AB = 4$ cm

$\Rightarrow AB = 4$ cm

Now, AB is chord to smaller circle with $OR \perp AB$.

So, OR bisects AB.

[perpendicular from the centre to the chord, bisects the chord]

$\Rightarrow AR = RB = 2$ cm

Now, in ΔORA,

$OA^2 = OR^2 + AR^2$

$\Rightarrow 3^2 = OR^2 + 2^2$

$\Rightarrow 9 - 4 = OR^2$

$\therefore OR = \sqrt{5}$ cm

25. (c) Given, two circles with centres A and B, AC and BC are two tangents.

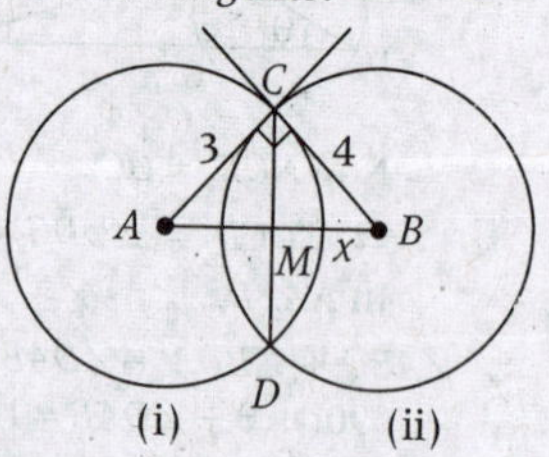

$\therefore$ Radius of circle (i) $= AC = 3$ cm and radius of circle (ii) $= BC = 4$ cm

In ΔACB,

$AC \perp BC$

Since, AC is radius and BC is tangent.

$\therefore AC^2 + BC^2 = AB^2$

$\Rightarrow 3^2 + 4^2 = AB^2$

$\Rightarrow AB = 5$ cm

$\therefore$ In ΔBMC,

$BM \perp CM$

$\therefore BC^2 = CM^2 + BM^2$

$\Rightarrow 4^2 = CM^2 + x^2$

$\Rightarrow 4^2 - x^2 = CM^2$

$\Rightarrow \sqrt{16 - x^2} = CM$

Also, in ΔACM,

$AC^2 = CM^2 + AM^2$

$\Rightarrow 3^2 = (16 - x^2) + (5 - x)^2$

$\Rightarrow 3^2 = 16 - x^2 + 25 + x^2 - 10x$

$\Rightarrow 9 = 16 + 25 - 10x$

$\Rightarrow -32 = -10x \Rightarrow x = 3.2$

In ΔCMB,

$CM = \sqrt{16 - (3.2)^2} = 2.4$ cm

$CD = 2CM = 4.8$ cm

Hence, both statements are required.

Chapter 11 : Areas Related to Circle

1. (d) Given, area of square $= 196 \text{ cm}^2$

$\Rightarrow \text{Side}^2 = 196 \text{ cm}^2$

$\Rightarrow \text{Side} = 14$ cm

Now, radius of circle $= \frac{1}{2}$ side of the square

$= 7$ cm

$\therefore$ Area of circle $= \pi r^2$

$= \frac{22}{7} \times 7 \times 7 = 154 \text{ cm}^2$

2. (d) Since, ΔABC is a right angled at A.

Given, area of $\Delta ABC = 6$ cm

$\Rightarrow \frac{1}{2} \times AB \times AC = 6$

$\Rightarrow \frac{1}{2} \times 3 \times AC = 6$

$\therefore AC = 4$ cm

$\therefore$ Diameter of circle

= Hypotenuse of ΔABC

$= \sqrt{4^2 + 3^2} = 5$ cm

$\therefore$ Area of circle $= \pi r^2$

$= \frac{22}{7} \times \frac{5}{2} \times \frac{5}{2}$

$= \frac{275}{14} \text{ cm}^2 = 19\frac{9}{14} \text{ cm}^2$

3. (c) Area of shaded portion

$= \pi r_1^2 - 4\pi r_2^2$

$= \pi(6^2 - 4 \times 2^2) = \pi(36 - 16)$

$= \frac{22}{7} \times 20 = 62.8 \text{ cm}^2$

4. (a) Radius of the wheel = 28 cm

Circumference of the wheel

$= 2\pi r = 2 \times \frac{22}{7} \times 28$

Also, speed of the car = 66 km/h

$\therefore$ Distance travelled in 10 min

$= \frac{66}{60} \times 10 = 11$ km

$= 11 \times 1000 \times 100$ cm

$\therefore$ Number of revolutions

$= \frac{\text{Distance covered in 10 min}}{\text{Circumference of the wheel}}$

$= \frac{11 \times 1000 \times 100}{2 \times \frac{22}{7} \times 28}$

$= \frac{11 \times 1000 \times 100}{2 \times 22 \times 4} = 6250$

5. (a) Area of shaded region

= Area of semi-circle APD + Area of semicircle $BRC - 2 \times$ Area of semi-circle AQB

$= \frac{1}{2}\pi(7)^2 + \frac{1}{2}\pi\left(\frac{7}{2}\right)^2 - 2 \times \frac{1}{2}\pi\left(\frac{7}{4}\right)^2$

$= \frac{\pi}{2}\left[49 + \frac{49}{4} - \frac{49}{8}\right]$

$= \frac{1}{2} \times \frac{22}{7} \times \left(\frac{392 + 98 - 49}{8}\right)$

$= \frac{11}{7} \times \frac{441}{8}$

$= \frac{693}{8} \text{ cm}^2$

$= 86.625 \text{ cm}^2$

6. (b) ∵ Length of wire

$= \text{Circumference of circle}$

$\Rightarrow \quad 44 = 2\pi r$

$\Rightarrow \quad 2 \times \frac{22}{7} \times r = 44$

$\Rightarrow \quad r = 7 \text{ cm}$

$\therefore$ Area of the circle $= \pi r^2$

$= \frac{22}{7} \times 7 \times 7 = 154 \text{ cm}^2$

Again, length of wire = perimeter of the rectangle of length 12 cm

$\Rightarrow \quad 44 = 2(l + b)$

$\Rightarrow \quad 12 + b = 22$

$\Rightarrow \quad b = 10 \text{ cm}$

And area of rectangle

$= l \times b$

$= 12 \times 10 = 120 \text{ cm}$

$\therefore \frac{\text{Area of the circle}}{\text{Area of rectangle}} = \frac{154}{120} = \frac{77}{60}$

7. (c) Notice that there are 4 half small circles and one full small circle.

This makes them 3 small circles altogether perimeter of small circle $= 2\pi r$

$= 2 \times \pi \times 2 = 4\pi$

Perimeter of 3 small circles

$= 12\pi$

There are two big half circles which makes 1 full circle.

Circumference of one full circle

$= 2\pi \times 4 = 8\pi$

Hence, the perimeter of the total figure $= 12\pi + 8\pi = 20\pi$

8. (c) Let r be the radius of the semi-circle APB, i.e. $OB = OA = r$, then $r/2$ is the radius of the semi-circle AQO.

Given, Perimeter of the figure is 40 cm.

$\therefore$ Length of arc APB + length of arc AQO + $OB = 40$

$\Rightarrow \quad \pi r + \pi \frac{r}{2} + r = 40$

$\frac{22}{7} \times r + \frac{22}{7} \times \frac{r}{2} + r = 40$

$\Rightarrow \frac{80}{14} r = 40 \Rightarrow r = \frac{40 \times 14}{80}$

$= 7 \text{ cm}$

Now, area of shaded portion

= area of semi-circle APB + area of semi-circle AQO

$= \frac{1}{2} \pi r^2 + \frac{1}{2} \pi \left(\frac{r}{2}\right)^2$

$= \frac{1}{2} \pi \left(r^2 + \left(\frac{r}{4}\right)^2 \right)$

$= \frac{1}{2} \pi \left(49 + \frac{49}{4} \right)$

$= \frac{1}{2} \times \frac{22}{7} \times \frac{245}{4} = 96.25 \text{ cm}^2$

9. (b) ∵ Area of the circle $= \pi r^2$

and angle of the circle $= 360°$

$\therefore$ Area of sector of angle 60°

$= \frac{\pi r^2 \times 60°}{360°}$

$= \frac{\pi r^2}{6} = \frac{1}{6}$ area of circle

10. (a) $\therefore$ Required area

$= \pi r_1^2 \times \frac{45°}{360°} - \pi r_2^2 \frac{45°}{360°}$

[where, $r_1 = 4$ ft, $r_2 = 2$ ft]

$= \frac{\pi}{8} (4^2 - 2^2) = \frac{\pi}{8} \times 12 = 4.7$ sq ft

11. (c) Let the radii of the two circles be r_1 cm and r_2 cm (where $r_1 > r_2$)

Distance between the centres of the circles i.e., $C_1 C_2 = 12$ cm (given)

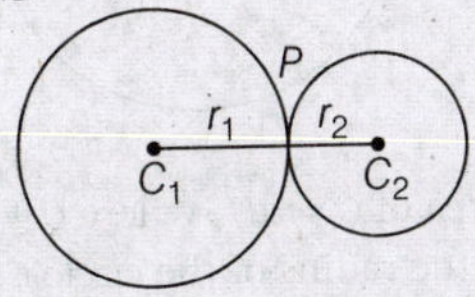

$\Rightarrow r_1 + r_2 = 12 \quad \ldots\text{(i)}$

Given, sum of the areas of the two circles $= 90\pi \text{ cm}^2$

$\Rightarrow \pi r_1^2 + \pi r_2^2 = 90\pi$

$\Rightarrow r_1^2 + r_2^2 = 90 \quad \ldots\text{(ii)}$

We know,

$(r_1 + r_2)^2 + (r_1 - r_2)^2 = 2(r_1^2 + r_2^2)$

$\Rightarrow (12)^2 + (r_1 - r_2)^2 = 2 \times 90$

$\Rightarrow \quad 144 + (r_1 - r_2)^2 = 180$

$\Rightarrow \quad (r_1 - r_2) = 180 - 144 = 36$

$\Rightarrow \quad r_1 - r_2 = 6 \quad \ldots\text{(iii)}$

Adding Eqs. (i) and (iii), we get

$2r_1 = 18 \Rightarrow r_1 = 9$

From Eq. (i), $9 + r_2 = 12$

$\Rightarrow \quad r_2 = 3$

Hence, the radii of two circles are 9 cm and 3 cm.

12. (a)

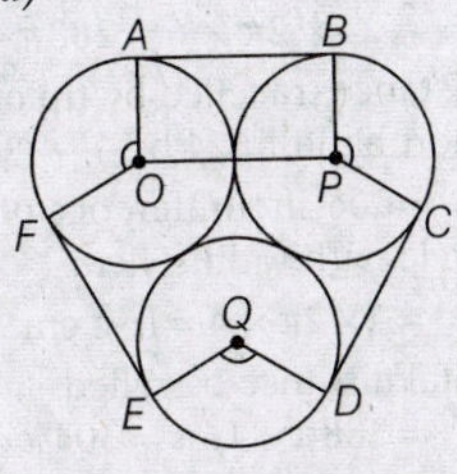

$AB = CD = EF$ = Distance between two radii = 4 m

$\angle AOF = \angle BPC = \angle DQE = 120°$

$\therefore$ Perimeter of the circumscribing figure

$= AB + CD + EF$ + circumference of sectors ($FOA + BPC + DQE$)

Since, three equal sectors of $120° = 1$ full circle of same radius

$\therefore$ Perimeter of the circumscribing figure

$= 2\pi \times 2 + 4 + 4 + 4$

$= (4\pi + 12)$ m

If R is the radius of the circumscribing circle, then,

$2\pi R = 4\pi + 12$

$= (4 \times 3.14 + 12) = 24.56$ m

$\Rightarrow R = \frac{24.56}{2 \times 3.14} = 4$ m

$\therefore$ Area of circumscribing circle

$= \pi R^2 = (3.14 \times 16) = 50.24 \text{ m}^2$

13. (d) Let $AB = h$ cm

$\therefore$ Area of the trapezium

$= \frac{1}{2} (AD + BC) \times AB$

$\Rightarrow \quad 24.5 = \frac{1}{2} (10 + 4) \times h$

$\Rightarrow \quad h = \frac{24.5}{7} = 3.5 \text{ cm}$

Now, area of quadrant ABE

$= \frac{90°}{360°} \times \pi (3.5)^2 \text{ cm}^2$

$= \frac{1}{4} \times \frac{22}{7} \times (3.5)^2 \text{ cm}^2$

$= 9.625 \text{ cm}^2$

$\therefore$ Area of shaded region
$= 24.5 - 9.625 = 14.875\,\text{cm}^2$

14. (*a*) Distance covered by the tip of long hand in 24 h
$= 24 \times$ Circumference of the circle with radius 6 cm
$= 24 \times 2\pi \times 6 = 288\pi$
Distance travelled by tip of short hand in 24 h.
$= 2 \times$ Circumference of the circle with radius 4 cm
$= 2 \times 2\pi \times 4 = 16\pi$ cm
Total distance travelled
$= 288\pi + 16\pi = 304\pi$ cm
$= (304 \times 3.14)$ cm
$= 954.56$ cm

15. (*c*) Area of minor segment
$APBQ = \theta / 360° \times \pi r^2 - \frac{1}{2} r^2$
$= \frac{3.14}{4} \times 100 - 100 \times \frac{1}{2}$
$= (78.5 - 50)\,\text{cm}^2$
$= 28.5\,\text{cm}^2$
Area of major segment
$ALBQA = \pi r^2$ − area of minor segment
$= 3.14 \times (10)^2 - 28.5$
$= (314 - 28.5)\,\text{cm}^2 = 285.5\,\text{cm}^2$

16. (*b*) Let r be the radius of the circle. Then, increased circumference
$= 2\pi r + 2\pi r \times \frac{10}{100} = \frac{11\pi r}{5}$
If R is the radius of the increased circle, then
$2\pi R = \frac{11\pi r}{5} \Rightarrow R = \frac{11r}{2 \times 5}$
$\therefore$ Radius of increased circle
$= \frac{11r}{10}$
$\therefore$ Increased area
$= \pi\left(\frac{11r}{10}\right)^2 - \pi r^2$
$= \frac{121\pi r^2}{100} - \pi r^2 = \frac{21\pi r^2}{100}$
$\therefore$ Percentage increase in area
$= \frac{\frac{21\pi r^2}{100}}{\pi r^2} \times 100\% = 21\%$

17. (*a*) $\because$ Length of each rope
$= 35$ cm

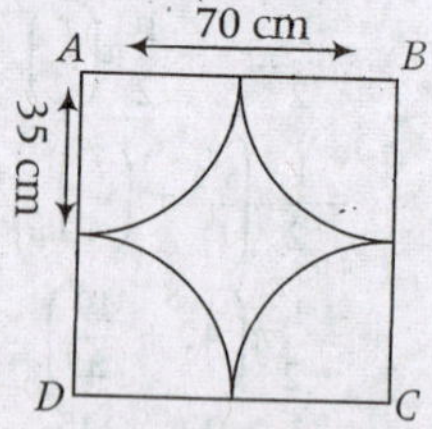

$\therefore$ Area grazed by each horse
$= \frac{1}{4}\pi r^2$
$= \frac{22}{7} \times \frac{35 \times 35}{4} = \frac{3850}{4}\,\text{m}^2$
$\therefore$ Area grazed by 4 horses
$= 4 \times \frac{3850}{4} = 3850\,\text{m}^2$
Now, total area of the field
$= 70 \times 70 = 4900\,\text{m}^2$
$\therefore$ Area left by the horses
= Total area of the field − Area grazed by 4 horses
$= 4900 - 3850 = 1050\,\text{m}^2$

18. (*d*)

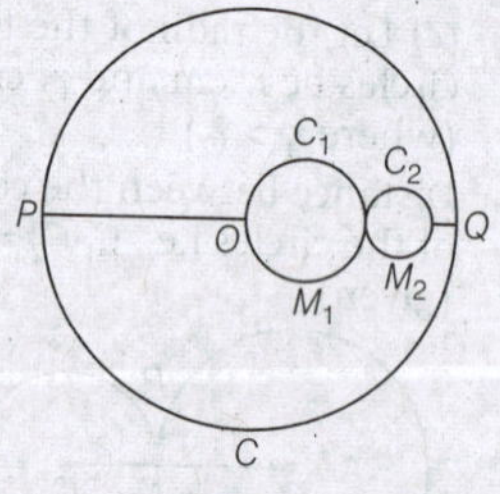

Area of $C = \pi r^2$, where $OQ = r$ is the radius of the circle C.
Then, radius of circle $C_1 = r/4$
radius of circle $C_2 = r/8$ and so on
$\therefore$ Area of shaded region = Area of C_1 + Area of C_2 + ...
$= \pi(r/4)^2 + \pi(r/8)^2 + \ldots\ldots$
$= \frac{\pi r^2}{16} + \frac{\pi r^2}{64} + \ldots\ldots\ldots$
$= \pi r^2\left[\frac{1}{16} + \frac{1}{64} + \ldots\ldots\ldots\right]$
$= \pi r^2\left[\frac{1/16}{1 - \frac{1}{4}}\right]$ $\left[\because \text{Infinite GP with } a = \frac{1}{16}, r = \frac{1}{4}\right]$
$= \pi r^2 \times \frac{1}{16} \times \frac{4}{3} = \frac{\pi r^2}{12}$
$\therefore$ Required ratio
$= \frac{\text{Area of unshaded region}}{\text{Area of original circle}}$
$= \frac{\pi r^2 - \frac{\pi r^2}{12}}{\pi r^2} = \frac{11}{12} = 11:12$

19. (*b*) Angle make by the hours hand of the clock in 35 min is $= 17.5°$ (angle of sector)
Area swept by hour hand in 35 min
= Area of a sector of angle 17.5° in a circle of radius 6 cm
$= \frac{17.5}{360} \times \frac{22}{7} \times (6)^2\,\text{cm}^2 = 5.5\,\text{cm}^2$

20. (*d*) Diagonal of a rhombus are perpendicular bisector of each other.
$\therefore$ Each diagonal is diameter of the circle.

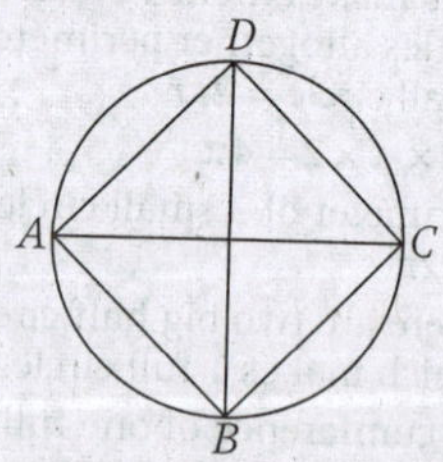

Now, area of circle $= 1256\,\text{cm}^2$
$\Rightarrow \pi r^2 = 1256 \Rightarrow r^2 = \frac{1256}{\pi}$
$\Rightarrow \quad r^2 = \frac{1256}{3.14} = 400$
$\Rightarrow \quad r = 20$ cm
$\therefore$ Diameter of the circle = 40 cm
= Each diagonal of the rhombus
$\therefore$ Area of rhombus
$= \frac{1}{2}(d_1 \times d_2)$
$= \frac{1}{2} \times 40 \times 40 = 800\,\text{cm}^2$

21. (*b*) In 1 day, i.e. 24h, short (hour) hand of the clock make 2 revolutions and long (minute) hand make 24 revolutions.

In 1 revolution, distance travelled by tip of hour hand = Circumference of circle of radius 6 cm $= 2\times\frac{22}{7}\times 6$

In 1 revolution distance travelled by tip of minute hand = circumference of circle of radius 8 cm $= 2\times\frac{22}{7}\times 8$

$\therefore$ Sum of distance travelled by tips of both hand in 1 day

$= 2\times 2\times\frac{22}{7}\times 6 + 24\times 2\times\frac{22}{7}\times 8$

$= 2\times\frac{22}{7}(12+192) = 2\times\frac{22}{7}\times 204$

$= 128229$ cm (approx)

22. (a) Region where red colour is to be painted = Area of square – Area of quadrant *BGDC*

$= 10\times 10 - \frac{1}{4}\times\pi\times 10\times 10$

$= 100 - \frac{1}{4}\times 3.14\times 100$

$= 100 - \frac{314}{4} = 100 - 78.5$

$= 21.5$ units

$\therefore$ Ratio of region of red colour area to blue colour $= \frac{21.5}{78.5} = \frac{43}{157}$

23. (a) Circumference of the given circle $= 2\pi r$

= Perimeter of a square with side 11 cm

$\Rightarrow 2\pi r = 4(11) \Rightarrow 2\pi r = 44$

$r = \frac{22}{\pi}$ cm

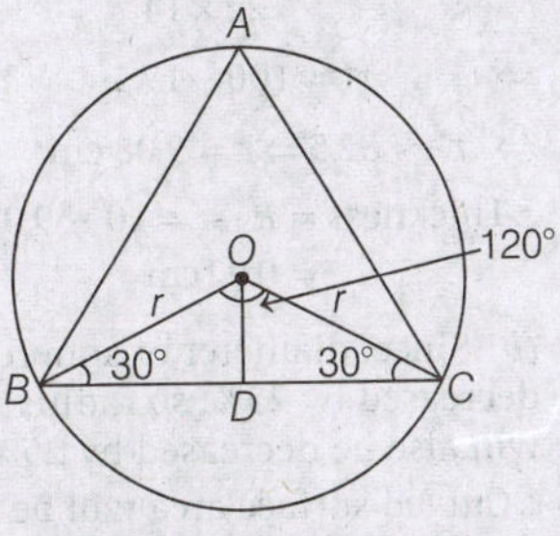

Now,

In ΔODC

$\cos 30° = \frac{DC}{OC} = \frac{DC}{22}\times\pi$

$\Rightarrow \frac{\sqrt{3}}{2}\times\frac{22}{\pi} = DC$

$\Rightarrow DC = \frac{7}{2}\sqrt{3}\text{ cm} = 3.5\sqrt{3}$ cm

Now, sides of the ΔABC

$= BC = 2\times DC$

$= 2\times 3.5\sqrt{3} = 7\sqrt{3}$ cm

24. (a) We have,

Angle described by the minute hand in one minute = 6°

Angle described by the minute hand in 35 min $= (6\times 35) = 210°$

Area swept by the minute hand in 35 min.

= Area of a sector of angle 210° in a circle of radius 40 cm

$= \left\{\frac{210°}{360°}\times\frac{22}{7}\times(40)^2\right\}\text{ cm}^2$

$= 2933.3\text{ cm}^2$

25. (d) Let r_1 and r_2 be the radii of circles *A* and *B* respectively.

$\therefore \frac{2\pi r_1\times 105°}{360°} = \frac{2\pi r_2 45°}{360°}$

$\Rightarrow \frac{r_1}{r_2} = \frac{45°}{105°} = \frac{3}{7}$

$\therefore$ Ratio of areas $= \frac{\pi r_1^2}{\pi r_2^2} = \left(\frac{r_1}{r_2}\right)^2$

$= \left(\frac{3}{7}\right)^2 = \frac{9}{49}$

$\therefore$ Ratio = 9 : 49

26. (c) Given, length of arc $AB = 10\pi$ cm

Let $\angle AOB = \theta$

We know that, $l = \frac{\theta}{360°}\times 2\pi r$

$\Rightarrow 10\pi = \frac{\theta}{180°}\times\pi r \Rightarrow \frac{1800°}{r} = \theta$

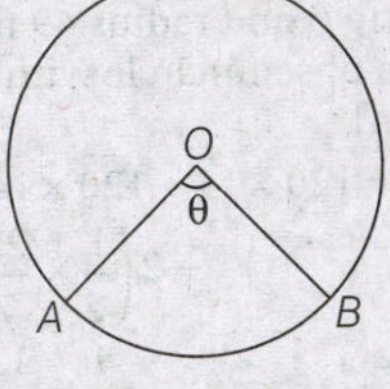

Now, area of sector

$= \frac{\theta}{360°}\times\pi r^2$

$\Rightarrow 40\pi = \frac{1800°}{r(360°)}\times\pi r^2$

$\Rightarrow 8 = r \Rightarrow r = 8$

27. (d) Given, chord *AB* substends an angle 60° at the centre.

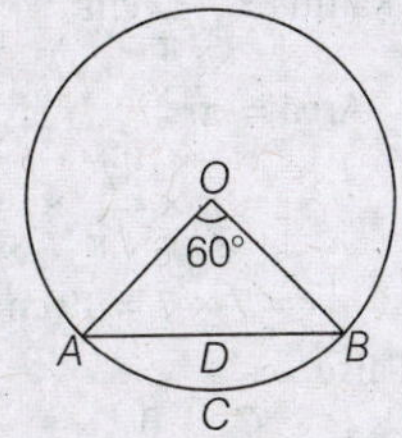

$\therefore \angle AOB = 60°$ and $OA = OB$ [radii of circle]

$\angle OBA = \angle OAB = x$ [say]

[$\because$ angle opposite to equal sides and also equal]

In ΔAOB,

$\angle AOB + \angle OBA + \angle OAB = 180°$ [by angle sum property of triangle]

$\Rightarrow 60° + x + x = 180°$

$\Rightarrow 2x = 180° - 60°$

$\Rightarrow x = \frac{120°}{2} = 60°$

$\Rightarrow \angle OBA = \angle OAB = 60° = \angle AOB$

$\therefore \Delta AOB$ is an equilateral triangle.

Now, area of $\Delta AOB = \frac{\sqrt{3}}{4}\times(15)^2$

[$\because$ area of equilateral triangle $= \frac{\sqrt{3}}{4}(\text{side})^2$]

$= 56.25\times 1.73 = 97.3125\text{ cm}^2$

$\therefore$ Area of sector *OACBO*

$= \frac{\theta}{360°}\times\pi r^2$

$= \frac{60}{360}\times 3.14\times(15)^2$

$= \frac{3.14\times 225}{6} = \frac{706.5}{6} = 117.75\text{ cm}^2$

$\therefore$ Area of minor segment *ACBDA*

= Area of sector *OACBO* – Area of ΔAOB

$= 117.75 - 97.3125 = 20.4375\text{ cm}^2$

Now, area of major segment

= Area of circle – Area of minor segement

$= \pi(15)^2 - 20.4375$

$= 3.14\times 225 - 20.4375$

$= 706.5 - 20.4375$

$= 686.0625\text{ cm}^2$

28. *(a)* I. True

$\because$ Radius $= \dfrac{7}{\sqrt{\pi}}$ cm

$\therefore$ Area $= \pi r^2$

$$= \pi \times \frac{7}{\sqrt{\pi}} \times \frac{7}{\sqrt{\pi}}$$

$$= 7 \times 7 = 49\text{ cm}^2$$

II. False

Given, $\dfrac{C_1}{C_2} = \dfrac{3}{5}$

$$\Rightarrow \frac{2\pi r_1}{2\pi r_2} = \frac{3}{5} \Rightarrow \frac{r_1}{r_2} = \frac{3}{5}$$

$$\therefore \frac{\text{Area }(A_1)}{\text{Area }(A_2)} = \frac{\pi r_1^2}{\pi r_2^2}$$

$$= \left(\frac{r_1}{r_2}\right)^2 = \left(\frac{3}{5}\right)^2 = \frac{9}{25}$$

III. False

Given, area $= A$, radius $= r$ and circumference $= C$

$\therefore$ $C = 2\pi r \Rightarrow A = \pi r^2$

Now, $\dfrac{C}{A} = \dfrac{2\pi r}{\pi r^2} = \dfrac{2}{r}$

IV. False

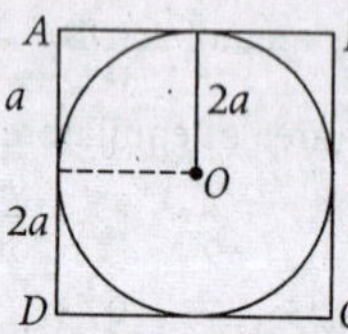

Given, radius of circle $= 2a$

$\therefore$ Side of square $= 2 \times 2a = 4a$

$\therefore$ Perimeter of square $= 4 \times 4a$

$= 16a$

29. *(d)* (A) Radius of bigger semi-circle $= 14$ cm

Area of bigger semi-circle

$$= \frac{1}{2}\pi r^2 = \frac{1}{2} \times \frac{22}{7} \times 14 \times 14$$

$= 308\text{ cm}^2$

Now, radius of each of the smaller semi-circle $= 7$ cm

$\therefore$ Area of two smaller semi-circles

$$= 2\left(\frac{1}{2} \times \frac{22}{7} \times 7^2\right) = 154\text{ cm}^2$$

$\therefore$ Required area $= 308 + 154$

$= 462\text{ cm}^2$

(B) Radius of the smaller circle $= 21$ cm

Radius of the bigger circle

$= (21 + 3.5)$ cm $= 24.5$ cm

$\therefore$ Area of the path

$$= [\pi(24.5)^2 - \pi(21)^2]$$

$$= [\pi(24.5)^2 - \pi(21)^2]$$

$$= \pi\,(24.5 + 21)\,(24.5 - 21)$$

$$[\because a^2 - b^2 = (a+b)(a-b)]$$

$$= \frac{22}{7} \times 45.5 \times 3.5$$

$$= 500.5\text{ cm}^2$$

(C) Required area

= Area of sector of angle 30° with radius 7 cm – Area of sector of angle 30° with radius 3.5 cm

$$= \left(\frac{30°}{360°} \times \frac{22}{7} \times 7^2\right) - \left(\frac{30°}{360°} \times \frac{22}{7} \times (3.5)^2\right)$$

$$= \left(\frac{77}{6} - \frac{77}{24}\right) = \frac{77}{24} \times 3$$

$$= \frac{77}{8} = 9.625\text{ cm}^2$$

Sol. (Q. Nos. 30 and 31)

Here, $AD = FG = 120$ m

Now, $OA = O'D$

$= (35 + 14)$ m

$= 49$ m

30. *(a)* Area of the region (boundary)

= Area of rectangle $ABCD$ + Area of rectangle $EFGH$ + 2{area of semi-circle with centre O and radius 49 m – Area of semi-circle with radius 35 m}

$$= 120 \times 14 + 120 \times 14 + 2\left(\frac{1}{2} \times \frac{22}{7} \times 49^2 - \frac{1}{2} \times \frac{22}{7} \times 35^2\right)$$

$$= \left[1680 + 1680 + \frac{22}{7}(49^2 - 35^2)\right]$$

$$= \left[3360 + \frac{22}{7}\,(49 + 35)\,(49 - 35)\right]$$

$$= 3360 + 3696 = 7056\text{ m}^2$$

31. *(a)* Cost of flooring per sq metre $= ₹\ 50$

Cost of flooring 7056 m^2

$= 7056 \times 50 = ₹\ 352800$

Chapter 12 : Surface Area and Volume

1. *(b)* $l = 6 + 6 + 6 = 18$ cm

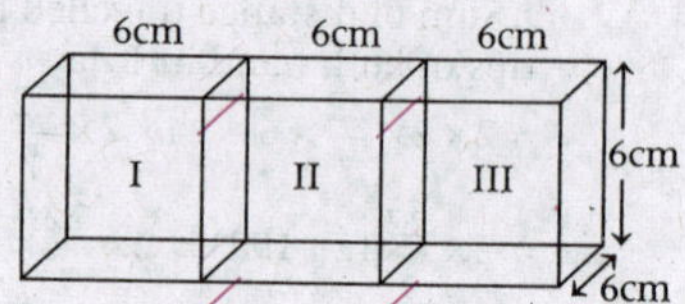

$b = 6$ cm and $h = 6$ cm

$\therefore$ Surface area of resulting solid

= Surface area of new solid

$= 2(lb + bh + hl)$

$= 2(18 \times 6 + 6 \times 6 + 6 \times 18)$

$= 2(108 + 36 + 108) = 504\text{ cm}^2$

2. *(a)* $r = \dfrac{1.4}{2} = 0.7$ m, and $h = 3$ m

Area covered = Curved Surface Area × number of revolutions

$= 2\pi rh \times 6 = 12\,\pi rh$

$$= 12\left(\frac{22}{7}\right)(0.7)\,(3) = 79.2\text{ m}^2$$

3. *(c)* Volume of metal = volume of outer cylinder – volume of inner cylinder

$$770 = \pi h(R^2 - r^2)$$

$$770 = \frac{22}{7} \times 14[(10)^2 - r^2]$$

$$(10)^2 - r^2 = \frac{770 \times 7}{22 \times 14}$$

$$\Rightarrow r^2 = 100 - 17.5$$

$$\Rightarrow r^2 = 82.5 \Rightarrow r = 9.08\text{ cm}$$

$\therefore$ Thickness $= R - r = 10 - 9.08$

$= 0.92$ cm

4. *(b)* Since, diameter of sphere is decreased by 25%, so radius will also be decreased by 25%.

$\therefore$ Curved surface area will be decreased by

$$4\pi r^2 - 4\pi\left(\frac{75r}{100}\right)^2$$

$$= 4\pi r^2\left(1 - \frac{9}{16}\right) = 4\pi r^2\left(\frac{7}{16}\right)$$

$= \frac{7\pi r^2}{4}$

$\therefore$ Required percentage

$= \frac{\frac{7\pi r^2}{4}}{4\pi r^2} \times 100$

$= 43\frac{3}{4}\%$

$= \frac{175}{4}\%$

5. (b) Let S be the edge of the cube.

$\therefore$ Radius of sphere $= S/2$

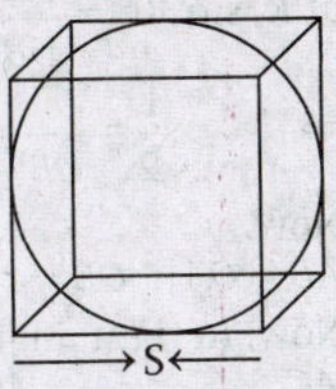

Volume of cube $= S^3$

Volume of the sphere $= \frac{4}{3}\pi(S/2)^3$

$\therefore$ Ratio $= S^3 : \frac{4}{3}\pi\frac{S^3}{8} = 6 : \pi$

6. (a) Curved surface area of hemisphere,

$S_1 = 2\pi r^2 = 2 \times \frac{22}{7} \times \frac{7}{2} \times \frac{7}{2}$

$= 77\text{cm}^2$

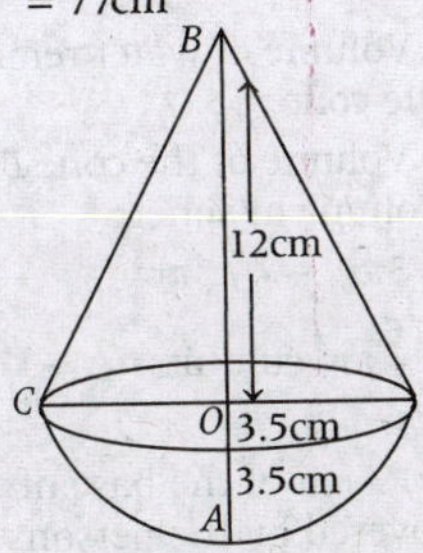

Slant height of cone,

$l = \sqrt{r^2 + h^2} = \sqrt{(3.5)^2 + (12)^2}$

$= \sqrt{1225 + 144}$

$= \sqrt{156.25} = 12.5\,\text{cm}$

Curved surface area of cone,

$S_2 = \pi rl = \frac{22}{7} \times \frac{7}{2} \times 12.5$

$= 137.5\,\text{cm}^2$

$\therefore$ Total surface area of toy

$= S_1 + S_2 = 77 + 137.5 = 214.5\,\text{cm}^2$

7. (b)

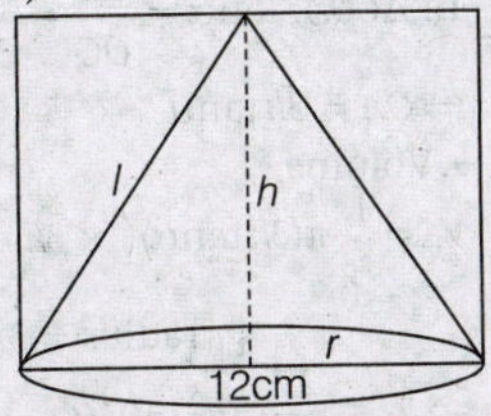

Let the diameter of cone be the edge of the cube.

$\therefore\ d = 12\,\text{cm},\ h = 12\,\text{cm}$

$r = 6$ cm

Volume of a cone $= 1/3\ \pi r^2 h$

$V = 1/3\ \pi(6)^2 \times 12$

$= \frac{1}{3}\pi\,(36) \times 12$

$= 36 \times 4\pi = 144\,\pi$

8. (b) Here, height of cylinder

$= 104 - 14 = 90$ cm

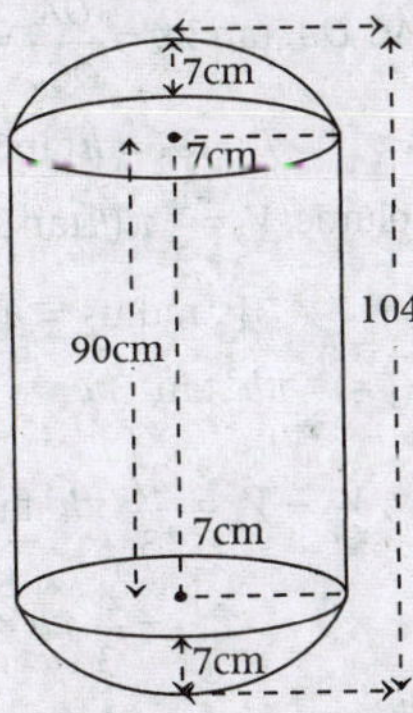

$\therefore$ Total surface area of the solid $= 2\times$ Curved surface area of a hemisphere + Curved surface area of cylindrical part

$= 2[2\pi r^2] + 2\pi rh$

$= 2 \times [2\pi\,(7)^2] + 2\pi\,(7)\,(90)$

$= 2 \times \left[2 \times \frac{22}{7} \times (7)^2\right] + 2 \times \frac{22}{7} \times (7)\,(90)$

$= 4 \times 22 \times 7 + 2 \times 22 \times 90$

$= 22[28 + 180] = 4576\,\text{cm}^2$

Then, the cost of polishing at the rate of ₹ 3 per dm^2

$= ₹\ \frac{4576 \times 3}{100}$ $[\because 1\,\text{dm}^2 = 100\,\text{cm}^2]$

$= ₹\,137.28$

9. (d) Let the radius and height of the given cone be R and H.

$\therefore$ Height of upper part $= \frac{H}{2}$

Radius of upper part $= \frac{R}{2}$

$[\because \Delta VO'B' \sim \Delta VOB]$

Volume of the given cone

$= \frac{1}{3}\pi R^2 H$

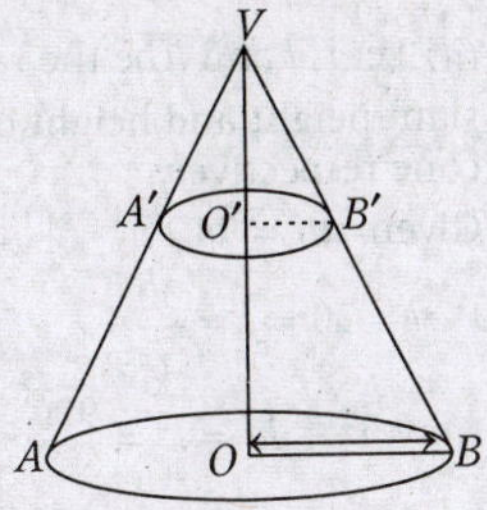

Volume of upper part

$= \frac{1}{3}\pi\left(\frac{R}{2}\right)^2 \cdot \frac{H}{2} = \frac{1}{3 \times 8}\pi R^2 H$

$\therefore$ Required ratio

$= \frac{1}{3 \times 8}\pi R^2 H : \frac{1}{3}\pi R^2 H = 1:8$

10. (c)

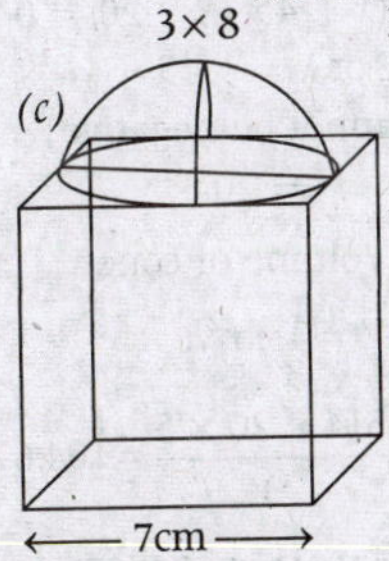

Edge of cube = 7 cm

$\therefore$ Radius of hemi-sphere

$= \frac{7}{2}$ cm

Now, required surface area of solid

= Total surface Area of the cube + Curved surface area of hemi-sphere – Area of circular base of hemi-sphere.

$= 6 \times (\text{Edge})^2 + 2\pi r^2 - \pi r^2$

$= 6 \times (\text{Edge})^2 + \pi r^2$

$= 6 \times (7)^2 + \frac{22}{7} \times \frac{7}{2} \times \frac{7}{2}$

$= 294 + \frac{11 \times 7}{2} = 294 + \frac{77}{2}$

$= 294 + 38.5 = 332.5\,\text{cm}^2$

11. (c) Number of balls

$$= \frac{\text{Volume of lead}}{\text{Volume of a ball}} = \frac{(\text{Edge})^3}{\frac{4}{3}\pi r^3}$$

$$= \frac{44 \times 44 \times 44}{\frac{4}{3} \times \frac{22}{7} \times (1)^3}$$

$$= \frac{44 \times 44 \times 44}{4 \times 22} \times 21 = 20328$$

12. (d) Let r, l and h be the radius, slant height and height of the cone respectively.

Given, $\pi rl = 94.2 \text{ m}^2$

$$rl = 30 \Rightarrow l = \frac{30}{r}$$

Now, $r^2 + h^2 = l^2 = \frac{900}{r^2}$

Let $r^2 = x$, then $x + h^2 = \frac{900}{x}$

$\Rightarrow \quad x^2 + 25x - 900 = 0$

$\Rightarrow x^2 + 45x - 20x - 900 = 0$

$\Rightarrow x(x + 45) - 20(x + 45) = 0$

$\Rightarrow \quad (x + 45)(x - 20) = 0$

$x = 20$ or $x = -45$

[$\therefore x$ cannot be negative]

$\therefore \quad r^2 = 20$

Now, Volume of cone

$$= V = \frac{1}{3}\pi r^2 h$$

$$= \frac{3.14 \times 20 \times 5}{3} = 104.67 \text{ m}^3$$

13. (b) Let V_1, V_2 and V_3 be the volumes of the cones CAB, C_1AB and C_2AB, respectively.

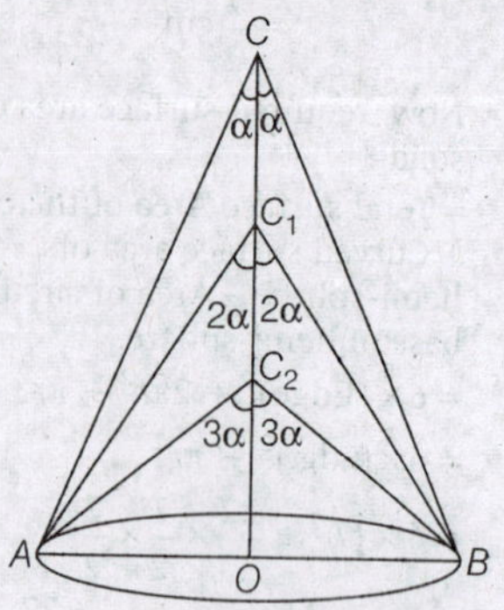

For cone CAB, we have $CO = 3h$

In ΔCOA, $\tan\alpha = \frac{OA}{OC} = \frac{OA}{3h}$

$\Rightarrow OA = 3h\tan\alpha$

$\therefore$ Volume,

$$V_1 = \frac{1}{3}\pi(3h\tan\alpha)^2 \times 3h$$

[$\because$ radius $= 3h\tan\alpha$]

$$\Rightarrow V_1 = \frac{27}{3}\pi h^3 \tan^2\alpha$$

For cone C_1AB, we have $C_1O = 2h$

In ΔC_1AO, $\tan 2\alpha = \frac{OA}{OC_1} = \frac{OA}{2h}$

$\Rightarrow \quad OA = 2h\tan 2\alpha$

$\therefore$ Volume,

$$V_2 = \frac{1}{3}\pi(2h\tan 2\alpha)^2 \times 2h$$

[$\because$ radius $= 2h\tan 2\alpha$]

$$\Rightarrow V_2 = \frac{8}{3}\pi h^3 \tan^2 2\alpha$$

For cone C_2AB, we have $C_2O = h$

In ΔC_2OA, $\tan 3\alpha = \frac{OA}{OC_2} = \frac{OA}{h}$

$\Rightarrow \quad OA = h\tan 3\alpha$

$\therefore$ Volume, $V_3 = \frac{1}{3}\pi(h\tan 3\alpha)^2 \times h$

[$\because$ radius $= h\tan 3\alpha$]

$$\Rightarrow V_3 = \frac{1}{3}\pi h^3 \tan^2 3\alpha$$

Now, $V_1 - V_2 = \frac{27}{3}\pi h^3 \tan^2\alpha - \frac{8}{3}\pi h^3 \tan^2 2\alpha$

$$= \frac{\pi h^3}{3}(27\tan^2\alpha - 8\tan^2 2\alpha)$$

and $V_2 - V_3 = \frac{8}{3}\pi h^3 \tan^2 2\alpha - \frac{1}{3}\pi h^3 \tan^2 3\alpha$

$$= \frac{\pi h^3}{3}(8\tan^2 2\alpha - \tan^2 3\alpha)$$

$\therefore$ Required ratio

$= (V_1 - V_2) : (V_2 - V_3)$

$= (27\tan^2\alpha - 8\tan^2 2\alpha) : (8\tan^2 2\alpha - \tan^2 3\alpha)$

14. (b) Let radius of sphere be r, i.e., $OK = OA = r$

Then, the centre O of sphere will be centroid of the ΔBCD.

$$OA = \frac{1}{3}AB \Rightarrow AB = 3(OA)$$

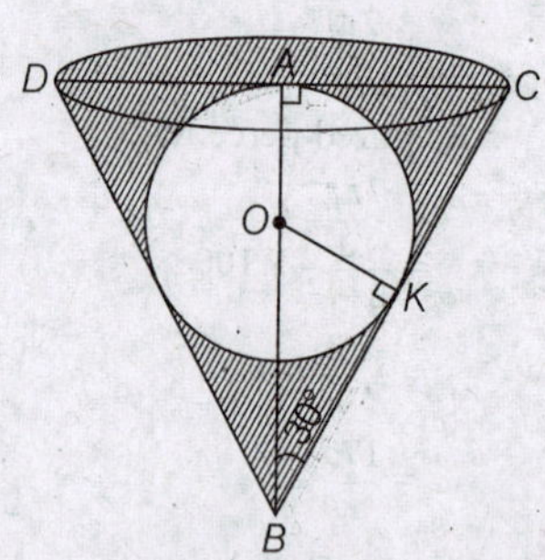

In ΔOKB, which is right angled at K, $\sin 30° = \frac{OK}{OB} = \frac{r}{OB}$

$$\Rightarrow \quad \frac{1}{2} = \frac{r}{OB} \Rightarrow OB = 2r$$

Now,

$AB = OA + OB = r + 2r = 3r$

Now, in right angled ΔBAC,

$$\frac{AC}{AB} = \tan 30° \Rightarrow \frac{AC}{AB} = \frac{1}{\sqrt{3}}$$

$$\therefore AC = \frac{AB}{\sqrt{3}} = \sqrt{3}r \text{ units}$$

Now, volume of a cone

$$BCD = \frac{1}{3}\pi(AC)^2 \times AB$$

$$= \frac{1}{3}\pi(\sqrt{3}r)^2 \times 3r = 3\pi r^3$$

and volume of a sphere

$= 4/3\ \pi r^3$

$\therefore$ Volume of water remaining in the cone

= Volume of the cone BCD – Volume of sphere

$= 3\pi r^3 - 4/3\pi r^3$

$$= \frac{5}{3}\pi r^3 \text{ cu units}$$

15. (c) Area of the base of the cone covered by the persons

$= 180 \times 5$

$\Rightarrow \quad \pi r^2 = 900$

$$\Rightarrow \quad r^2 = \frac{900}{\frac{22}{7}} = \frac{6300}{22}$$

Volume of air required by 180 persons $= 180 \times 30$

$$\therefore \quad \frac{1}{3}\pi r^2 h = 180 \times 30$$

$$\Rightarrow \frac{1}{3} \times \frac{22}{7} \times \frac{6300}{22} \times h = 180 \times 30$$

$$\Rightarrow h = \frac{180 \times 30 \times 7 \times 22 \times 3}{22 \times 6300} = 18 \text{ m}$$

16. *(b)* Suppose, the level of the water in the tank will rise by 9 cm in x h.

The length of the water flow in x h $= 10x$ km $= 10000x$ m

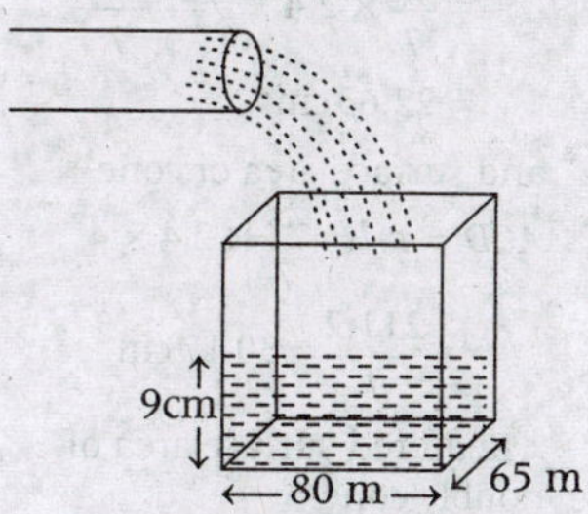

Radius of cylindrical pipe,

$$r = \frac{28}{2} = 14 \text{ cm} = \frac{14}{100} \text{ m}$$

Volume of the water flowing through the cylindrical pipe in x h, $V_1 = \pi r^2 h$

$$= \frac{22}{7} \times \left(\frac{14}{100}\right)^2 \times 10000\, x \text{ m}$$

$$= 616\, x \text{ m}^3$$

Also, volume of the water that falls into the tank in x h,

$V_2 = l \times b \times h$

$$80 \times 65 \times \frac{9}{100} = 468 \text{ m}^3$$

$\because \quad V_1 = V_2 \Rightarrow 616x = 468$

$$x = \frac{468}{616} = 0.76 \text{ h}$$

$$= 0.76 \times 60 \text{ min} = 45.6 \text{ min}$$

17. *(a)* ΔOAB and ΔODC are similar because $\angle ODC = \angle OAB = 90°$ and $\angle O$ is the common angle.

$$\therefore \quad \frac{OC}{OB} = \frac{CD}{BA}$$

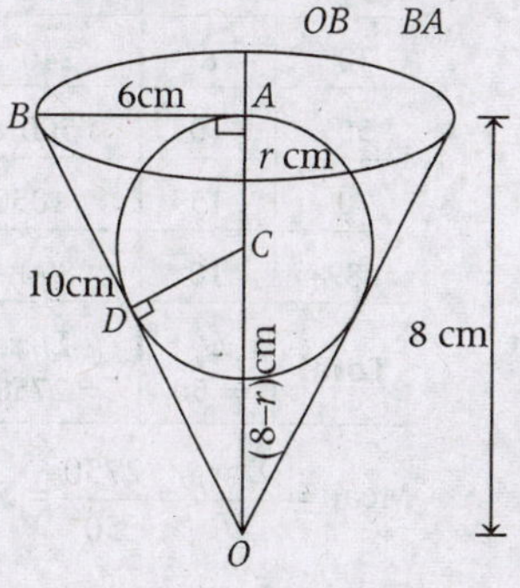

From the similarity of triangles, $\frac{8-r}{10} = \frac{r}{6}$

$48 - 6r = 10r$

$r = 3$

Fraction of water overflows

$$= \frac{\text{volume of sphere}}{\text{volume of cone}}$$

$$= \frac{\frac{4}{3}\pi(3)^3}{\frac{1}{3}\pi(6)^2(8)} = \frac{3}{8}$$

18. *(c)* Solid generated is a right circular cylinder of height $h = 16$ cm and radius $r = 3.5$ cm

Volume, $V = \pi r^2 h$

$$= \frac{22}{7} \times 3.5 \times 3.5 \times 16$$

$$= 616 \text{ cm}^3$$

Area of whole surface

$= 2\pi rh + 2\pi r^2 = 2\pi r(h + r)$

$= 2 \times \frac{22}{7} \times 3.5\,(16 + 3.5)$

$= 44 \times 0.5 \times 19.5 = 429 \text{ cm}^2$

19. *(a)* Let the initial depth of water in the can be x cm.

Now, volume of initial water + Volume of the sphere = Volume of the cylinder up to the height of water level.

$$\therefore \quad \pi r^2 h + \frac{4}{3}\pi r^3 = \pi r^2 H$$

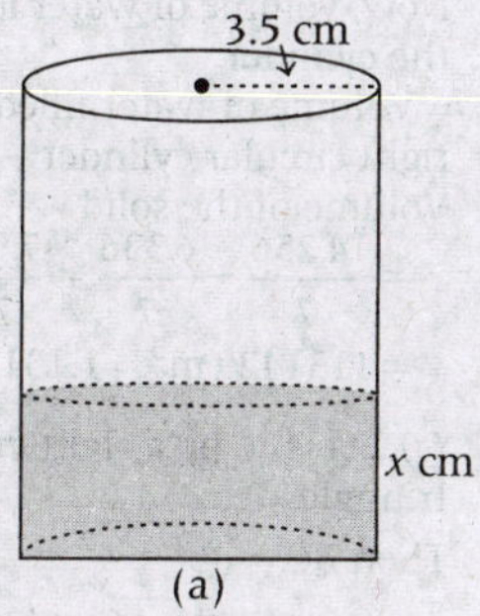

(a)

$$\Rightarrow \pi \times (3.5)^2 \times x + \frac{4}{3}\pi \times (3.5)^3 = \pi\left(\frac{7}{2}\right)^2 \times 7$$

$$\Rightarrow x + \frac{4}{3} \times 3.5 = 7 \Rightarrow x + \frac{14}{3} = 7$$

$$\Rightarrow x = 7 - \frac{14}{3} = \frac{7}{3} = 2.3 \text{ cm}$$

20. *(b)* (A) Volume of cylinder

$= \pi r^2 h = \pi \times 3.5 \times 3.5 \times 10$

$= 122.5\,\pi$

(B) Total surface Area = Curved surface area of cylinder + 2 × Curved surface area of hemi-sphere

$= 2\pi rh + 2 \times 2\pi r^2$

$= 2 \times \frac{22}{7} \times 3.5 \times 10 + 4 \times \frac{22}{7} \times 3.5 \times 3.5$

$= 220 + 154 = 374$

(C) Volume of scoops

$= 2 \times$ volume of hemi-sphere

$= 2 \times \frac{2}{3}\pi r^3$

$= \frac{4}{3}\pi \times 3.5 \times 3.5 \times 3.5 = \frac{171.5}{3}\pi$

(D) Volume of the article = Volume of cylinder – Volume of scoops

$= 122.5\pi - \frac{171.5}{3}\pi = \frac{196}{3}\pi$

21. *(b)* Radius of wall, $r = \frac{20}{2} = 10$ m

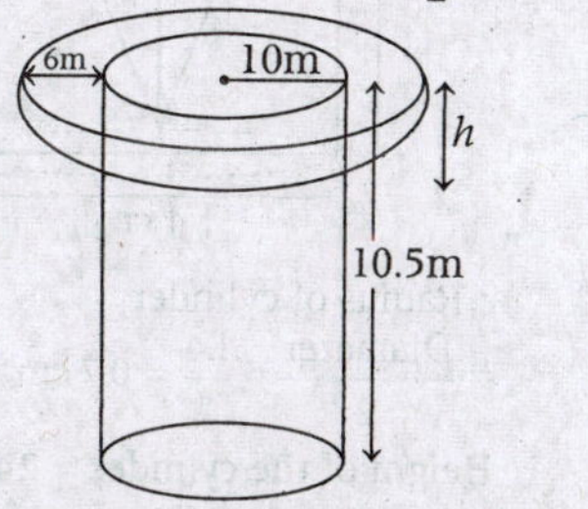

Volume of earth taken out on digging the wall

$= \pi r^2 h = \pi(10)^2 \times 10.5 = 1050\pi \text{ m}^3$

Since, embankment is in the form of cylindrical shell, so area of embankment

$= \pi(R^2 - r^2)$

$= \pi[(16)^2 - (10)^2] = 156\pi \text{ m}^2$

$\therefore$ Volume of embankment = Volume of earth taken out on digging the wall

$\Rightarrow$ Area of embankment × Height of embankment

= Volume of earth dugout

$\Rightarrow$ Height of embankment

$$= \frac{1050\pi}{156\pi} = 6.73 \text{ m}$$

22. (b) Speed of flow of water
$= 20\text{ km/h} = 20000\text{ m/h}$
Length of water flow in 45 min
$= \frac{45}{60} \times 20000 = 15000\text{ m}$
Volume of water flowing in 45 min = Volume of cuboid of length 15000 m, width 8 m and depth 1.2 m.
$= 15000 \times 8 \times 1.2 = 144000\text{ m}^3$
The required area covered for irrigation with 10 cm or $\frac{10}{100}$ m of standing water $= \frac{144000}{10} \times 100$
$= 1440000\text{ m}^2$
$= \frac{1440000}{10000}\text{ hec} = 144\text{ hec.}$

23. (d)

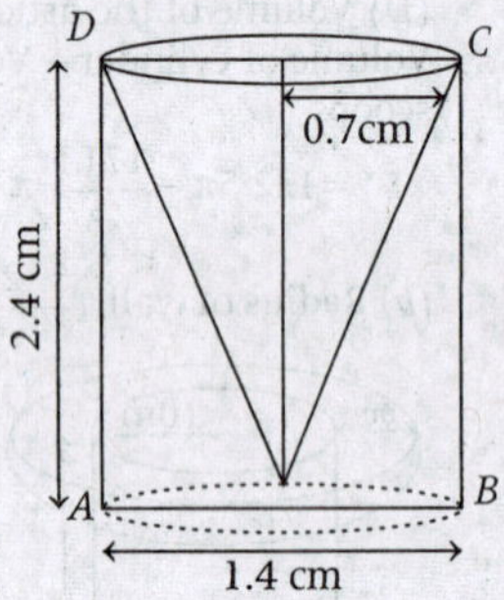

∴ Radius of cylinder
$= \frac{\text{Diameter}}{2} = \frac{1.4}{2} = 0.7\text{ cm}$
Height of the cylinder = 24 cm
∴ Slant height of the conical cavity,
$l = \sqrt{h^2 + r^2} = \sqrt{(24)^2 + (0.7)^2}$
$= \sqrt{5.76 + 0.49}$
$= \sqrt{6.25} = 2.5\text{ cm}$
Now, Total surface area of remaining solid
= Curved surface area of conical cavity + Curved surface area of cylinder + Area of the base of the cylinder
$= \pi rl + 2\pi rh + \pi r^2$
$= \pi r(l + 2h + r)$
$= \frac{22}{7} \times 0.7 \times (25 + 2 \times 24 + 0.7)$
$= 22 \times 0.1 \times (25 + 4.8 + 0.7)$
$= 22 \times 8 = 17.6 \approx 18\text{ cm}^2$

24. (b)

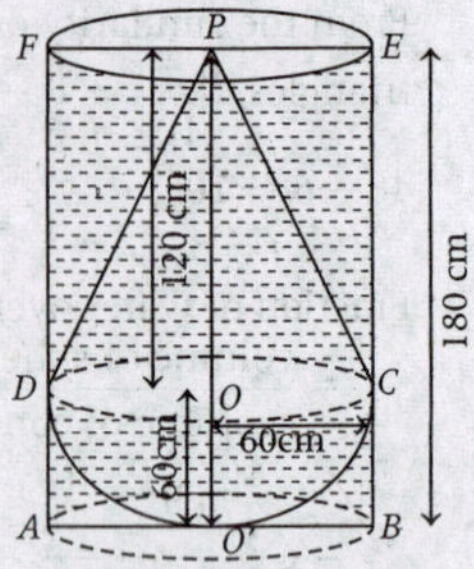

∴ Volume of water filled in a right circular cylinder $= \pi r^2 h$
$= \frac{22}{7} \times 0.6 \times 0.6 \times 1.8$
$= \frac{14.256}{7}\text{ m}^3$
∴ Volume of the solid
= Volume of the cone + Volume of the hemi-sphere
$= \frac{1}{3} \times \pi r_1^2 h_1 + \frac{2}{3}\pi r_2^3$
$= \frac{1}{3} \times \frac{22}{7} \times (0.6)^2 \times (1.2) + \frac{2}{3} \times \frac{22}{7} \times (0.6)^3$
$= \frac{22}{21} \times (0.6)^2\,[1.2 + 2 \times 0.6]$
$= \frac{22}{21} \times 0.36\,(1.2 + 1.2)$
$= \frac{22}{21} \times 0.36 \times 24 = \frac{19.008}{21}$
$= \frac{6.336}{7}\text{ m}^3$
Now, volume of water left in the cylinder
= Volume of water filled in a right circular cylinder – Volume of the solid
$= \frac{14.256}{7} - \frac{6.336}{7} = \frac{7.92}{7}$
$= 1.131429\text{ m}^3 \approx 1.131\text{ m}^3$

25. (c) Let ABC be a right circulur triangle.
Then $BC = \sqrt{3^2 + 4^2}$
$= \sqrt{9 + 16} = \sqrt{25} = 5\text{ cm}$

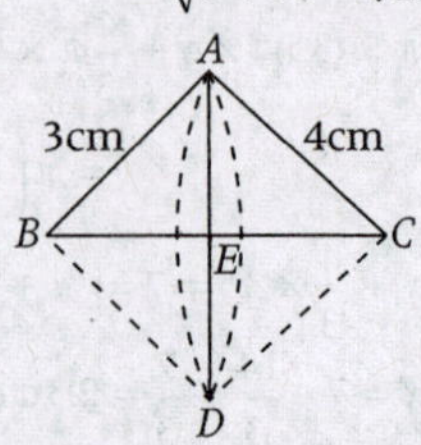

As ΔABC revolves about the hypotenuse BC. It forms two cones ABD and ACD.
So, radius of the base of each cone = AE = 24 cm
Now, surface area of cone ABD $= \pi rl$
$= \frac{22}{7} \times 2.4 \times 3 = \frac{158.4}{7}$
$= 22.63\text{ cm}^2$
and surface area of cone ACD $= \pi rl = \frac{22}{7} \times 2.4 \times 4$
$= \frac{211.2}{7} = 30.17\text{ cm}^2$
∴ Required surface area of double cone
$= 22.63 + 30.17 = 52.8\text{ cm}^2$

Chapter 13 : Statistics

1. (a) ∵ Mean $= \frac{x_1 + x_2 + \ldots + x_n}{n}$
$\therefore \frac{6 + 6 + 2x + 5 + 8 + 3x}{4} = 20$ [∵ mean = 20]
$\Rightarrow 25 + 5x = 80$
$\Rightarrow 5x = 80 - 25$
$\Rightarrow 5x = 55 \Rightarrow x = 11$

2. (c) ∴ Total number of marks
$= 40 \times 100 = 4000$
The correct sum of observations
$= 4000 + 53 - 83$
$= 4000 - 30 = 3970$
∴ Correct mean $= \frac{3970}{100} = 39.7$

3. (b)

x_i	f_i	$f_i x_I$
10	7	70
30	8	240
50	10	500
70	15	1050
89	10	890
Total	$\Sigma f_i = 50$	$\Sigma f_i x_i = 2750$

$\therefore$ Mean $= \frac{\Sigma f_i x_i}{\Sigma f_i} = \frac{2750}{50} = 55$

4. (*d*) So, new observation

$$= 19.3 \times 20 - 21 \times (19.3 - 0.5)$$
$$= 386 - 21 \times 18.8$$
$$= 386 - 394.8 = 8.8$$

5. (*b*) Given, $x_1 - 50 + x_2 - 50 + \ldots + x_n - 50 = -10$

$$\Rightarrow (x_1 + x_2 + \ldots + x_n) - 50n = -10$$
$$\Rightarrow (x_1 + x_2 + \ldots + x_n) = -10 + 50n \quad \ldots(i)$$

Also given that,

$$x_1 - 46 + x_2 - 46 + \ldots + x_n - 46 = 70$$
$$\Rightarrow x_1 + x_2 + \ldots + x_n - 46n = 70$$
$$\Rightarrow x_1 + x_2 + \ldots + x_n = 70 + 46n \quad \ldots(ii)$$

[From Eqs. (i) and (ii)]

$$0 = -80 + 4n \Rightarrow 4n = 80$$
$$\Rightarrow n = 20 \quad \text{[From Eq. (i)]}$$
$$\Rightarrow x_1 + x_2 + \ldots + x_n = 990$$
$$\therefore \text{ Mean} = \frac{x_1 + x_2 + \ldots + x_n}{n} = \frac{990}{20} = 49.5$$

6. (*a*)

x_i	f_i	f_ix_i
110	6	660
115	8	920
x_1	14	$14x_1$
120	f_1	$120f_1$
121	4	484
125	3	375
Total	$\Sigma f_i = 35 + f_1$	$\Sigma f_ix_i = 2439 + 14x_1 + 120f_1$

Now, $\Sigma f_i = 50$ [given]

$$\Rightarrow 35 + f_1 = 50 \Rightarrow f_1 = 15$$

We know that, $\bar{x} = \dfrac{\Sigma x_i f_i}{\Sigma f_i}$

$$\Rightarrow 117.8 = \frac{2439 + 14x_1 + 120f_1}{50}$$
$$\Rightarrow 5890 = 2439 + 14x_1 + 120 \times 15 \quad [\because f_1 = 15]$$
$$\Rightarrow 5890 - 4239 = 14x_1 \Rightarrow 1651 = 14x_1$$
$$\therefore x_1 = 117.93 \approx 118$$

7. (*b*) Let $a > b > c$ then

$$\frac{a+b+c}{3} = c + 10 = a - 15 = k \text{ (say)}$$
$$a = k + 15, b = 5 \text{ and } c = k - 10; a + b + c = 3k$$
$$k + 15 + 5 + k - 10 = 3k$$
$$2k + 10 = 3k \Rightarrow k = 10$$
$$a = 25, b = 5, c = 0$$
$$\therefore \text{Mean} = \frac{25^2 + 5^2 + 0^2}{3} = \frac{650}{3} = 216\frac{2}{3}$$

8. (*b*) Arrange the given observations in ascending order

21, 24, 27, 30, 32, 34, 35, 38, 48

Here, number of observations = 9 [odd]

$$\therefore \text{Median} = \left(\frac{9+1}{2}\right)\text{th observation}$$
$$= 5\text{th observation} = 32$$

9. (*d*) Arrange the given variables in ascending order

$$x - \frac{7}{2}, x - \frac{5}{2}, x - 3, x - 2, x - \frac{1}{2}, x + \frac{1}{2}, x + 4, x + 5$$

Here, number of observations = 8 [even]

$\therefore$ Median

$$= \frac{\frac{8}{2}\text{th observation} + \left(\frac{8}{2} + 1\right)\text{th observation}}{2}$$
$$= \frac{4\text{th observation} + 5\text{th observation}}{2}$$
$$= \frac{x - 2 + x - \frac{1}{2}}{2} = \frac{2x - \frac{5}{2}}{2} = x - \frac{5}{4}$$

10. (*b*) Given, numbers are 1, 2, 3, 4, *y*, 8, 9, 10, 12 and *x*.

$$\because \text{Mean} = \frac{\Sigma x_i}{N}$$
$$\Rightarrow 10 = \frac{1 + 2 + 3 + 4 + y + 8 + 9 + 10 + 12 + x}{10}$$
$$\Rightarrow 100 = 49 + x + y$$
$$\Rightarrow x + y = 51 \quad \ldots(i)$$

and median

$$= \frac{\left(\frac{10}{2}\right)\text{th observation} + \left(\frac{10}{2} + 1\right)\text{th observation}}{2}$$
$$\Rightarrow 10 = \frac{y + 8}{2}$$
$$\Rightarrow 20 = y + 8$$
$$\Rightarrow y = 12$$
$$\therefore x = 51 - 12 \quad \text{[from Eq. (i)]}$$
$$= 39$$

11. (b)

Marks	Number of students
0-10	5
10-30	f_1
30-60	30
60-80	f_2
80-90	2

$\because \quad \Sigma f = 60$ [given]

$\therefore \quad 5 + f_1 + 30 + f_2 + 2 = 60$

$\Rightarrow \quad 37 + f_1 + f_2 = 60$

$\Rightarrow \quad f_1 + f_2 = 23$ ...(i)

Now, $N = 60 \Rightarrow \dfrac{N}{2} = 30$ and median = 40

So, 30-60 is the median class.

Here, $l = 30, h = 30, f = 30, cf = 5 + f_1, n = 60$

$$\therefore \quad \text{Median} = l + \frac{\frac{n}{2} - cf}{f} \times h$$

$$\Rightarrow \quad 40 = 30 + \frac{30 - 5 - f_1}{30} \times 30$$

$$\Rightarrow \quad 40 = 30 + \frac{25 - f_1}{30} \times 30$$

$$\Rightarrow \quad 40 = 30 + 25 - f_1$$

$$\Rightarrow \quad 40 = 55 - f_1$$

$$\Rightarrow \quad f_1 = 15$$

and $\quad f_2 = 23 - 15$ [from Eq. (i)]

$= 8$

12. (d)

Class Interval (in cm)	Number of girls (f_i)	cf
Below 140	4	4
140-145	7	11
145-150	18	29 Median class
150-155	11	40
155-160	6	46
160-165	5	51
	$N = \Sigma f_i = 51$	

Here, $N = 51$,

So, $\dfrac{N}{2} = \dfrac{51}{2} = 25.5$, then median class 145-150

Here, $h = 5, l = 145, cf = 11, f = 18$

$$\text{Median} = l + \left\{\frac{\frac{N}{2} - cf}{f}\right\} \times h$$

$$= 145 + \left(\frac{25.5 - 11}{18}\right) \times 5 = 149.03$$

$\therefore$ Mean height of the girls is 149.03 cm

13. (b) Banana is bought in the highest (maximum) quantity.

14. (b) Mode = 3 Median − 2 Mean

$= 3 \times 12 - 2 \times 8 = 36 - 16 = 20$

15. (a) Change the class-intervals in inclusive form.

Age (in yr)	Number of cases
4.5-14.5	6
14.5-24.5	11
24.5-34.5	21
34.5-44.5	23
44.5-54.5	14
54.5-64.5	5

Since, the class 34.5-44.5 has maximum frequency.

$\therefore l = 34.5, h = 10, f_1 = 23, f_0 = 21$ and $f_2 = 14$

$$\therefore \text{Mode} = l + \frac{f_1 - f_0}{2f_1 - f_0 - f_2} \times h$$

$$= 34.5 + \frac{23 - 21}{46 - 21 - 14} \times 10$$

$$= 34.5 + \frac{2}{11} \times 10 = 36.31$$

16. (b) Here, the classes are not in inclusive form. So, we first convert them in inclusive form by subtracting 0.5 from the lower limit and adding 0.5 to the upper limit

Class	Frequency
149.5-152.5	15
152.5-155.5	118
155.5-158.5	142
158.5-161.5	127
161.5-164.5	18

142 is maximum frequency.

$\therefore$ 155.5-158.5 is modal class.

Here, $l = 155.5, f_1 = 142, f_0 = 118, f_2 = 127, h = 3$

$\therefore$ Mode $= l + \dfrac{f_1 - f_0}{2f_1 - f_0 - f_2} \times h = 155.5 + \dfrac{142-118}{284-118-127} \times 3 = 155.5 + \dfrac{24}{39} \times 3 = 157.35$

17. (c) We have, the frequency table as

Class interval	f_i	cf
60-63	5	5
63-66	18	23
66-69	42	65
69-72	27	92
72-75	8	100

For median, $\dfrac{N}{2} = \dfrac{100}{2} = 50$

$\therefore$ Median $= 66 + \dfrac{50-23}{42} \times 3$ $\left[\because \text{Median} = l + \dfrac{\frac{N}{2} - cf}{f} \times h\right]$

$= 66 + \dfrac{81}{42} = 66 + 1.93 = 67.93$

18. (c) The mode class is 66-69 because the frequency of this class is maximum.

19. (a) $\because$ Time spent in sleeping $= 25\% = \dfrac{25}{100} \times 24 = 6$ h

and time spent in sport $= 14\% = \dfrac{14}{100} \times 24 = \dfrac{336}{100}$ h

$\therefore$ Average time spent $= \dfrac{6 + \frac{336}{100}}{2} = 4.68$ h

20. (a) Here, 40% of time is being spent in studying.

21. (b) Here, $a = 70$ and $h = 20$

Class Interval	Class mark (x_i)	$u_i = \dfrac{x_i - a}{h}$	f_i	$f_i u_i$
0-20	10	−3	5	−15
20-40	30	−2	p	$-2p$
40-60	50	−1	10	−10
60-80	[70]	0	q	0
80-100	90	1	7	7
100-120	110	2	8	16
Total			$\Sigma f_i = 30 + p + q$	$\Sigma f_i u_i = -2p - 2$

Since, the sum of frequencies $= 50$ [given]

$\Rightarrow 30 + p + q = 50$

$\Rightarrow p + q = 20 \dots \text{(i)}$

$\therefore$ Mean $= a + h \times \dfrac{\Sigma f_i u_i}{\Sigma f_i}$

$\Rightarrow 62.8 = 70 + 20 \times \dfrac{-2p - 2}{50}$

$\Rightarrow \dfrac{2}{5}(2p + 2) = 70 - 62.8$

$\Rightarrow 2p + 2 = \dfrac{36}{2}$

$\Rightarrow p + 1 = 9 \Rightarrow p = 8$

From Eq. (i), we get

$8 + q = 20 \Rightarrow q = 20 - 8 = 12$

22. (b) I. $\bar{x} = \dfrac{1 + 2 + 3 + \dots + x}{x}$

$= \dfrac{\frac{x}{2}(x + 1)}{x} = \dfrac{x + 1}{2}$

$\left[\because 1 + 2 + 3 \dots + n = \dfrac{n(n+1)}{2}\right]$

II. Since, first 6 multiples of 3 are 3, 6, 9, 12, 15 and 18.

Sum of multiples $= \dfrac{6}{2}(3 + 18) = 63$

$\therefore$ Mean, $\bar{x} = \dfrac{63}{6} = 10.5$

III. Let the mean of $x_1, x_2, \dots, x_n$ be $\bar{x}$.

i.e. $\dfrac{x_1 + x_2 + \dots + x_n}{n} = \bar{x}$ ...(i)

Now, the new observations are, $ax_1, ax_2, \dots, ax_n$.

$\therefore \bar{x}_1 = \dfrac{a(x_1 + x_2 + \dots + x_n)}{n}$

$= \dfrac{a(x_1 + x_2 + \dots + x_n)}{n}$

$= a\bar{x}$ [from Eq. (i)]

IV. Given, $\mu_i = \dfrac{x_i - 25}{10}$

Here, $A = 25, h = 10$

$\therefore$ Mean $= A + h \times \dfrac{\Sigma f_i u_i}{\Sigma f_i}$

$= 25 + \dfrac{10 \times 20}{100} = 27$

$\left[\text{given, } \Sigma f_i u_i = 20 \text{ and } \Sigma f_i = 100\right]$

Chapter 14 : Probability

1. (c) Sample space = 1, 2, 3, 4, 5, 6

Event $(E) = 2, 4, 6$

$\therefore P(E) = \dfrac{3}{6} = \dfrac{1}{2}$

2. (d) $P(\bar{E}) = 1 - P(E)$

$= 1 - 0.7 = 0.3$

3. (b) Probability of getting a red ball $= P(E)$

$\Rightarrow P(E) = \dfrac{7}{12}$

$\therefore$ Probability of not getting a red ball

$= 1 - P(E) = 1 - \dfrac{7}{12} = \dfrac{5}{12}$

4. (d) $\because$ Total outcomes = GGG, BBB, GGB, BBG

[$\because$B = Boy, G = Girl]

and E = Atleast one boy = BBB, BBG, GGB

$\therefore P(E) = \dfrac{3}{4}$

5. (b) Probability of green marbles = 3/5

$\therefore$ Out of 40, the number of marbles, which are green

$= \dfrac{40 \times 3}{5} = 24$

6. (a) Number of favourable outcomes = 10

$\therefore$ Required probability

$= \dfrac{10}{52} = \dfrac{5}{26}$

7. (c) $\because$Ticket number as a multiple of 3 and 5 = 15, 30, 45

$\therefore$ Number of tickets = 3

Price of one ticket = ₹50

$\therefore P(E) = \dfrac{3}{45} = \dfrac{1}{15}$

8. (d) Probability of getting A $= \dfrac{2}{7}$ [$\because$A repeated 2 times]

Probability of getting R $= \dfrac{2}{7}$

Probability of getting P $= \dfrac{1}{7}$

Probability of getting O $= \dfrac{1}{7}$

Probability of getting T $= \dfrac{1}{7}$

9. (b) $\because$ Number of days in a non-leap year = 365

$\therefore$Number of days in a leap year = 366

Now, in an year, there are 52 complete weeks, which constitutes $= 52 \times 7 = 364$ days.

$\therefore$ Number of days left = 2

$\therefore$ Required Probability $P(E) = \dfrac{2}{7}$

10. (b) Total number of outcomes = 12

P (drawing a black ball) $= \dfrac{x}{12}$

If 6 more black balls are added, then

total number of outcomes $= 12 + 6 = 18$ and number of black balls $= x + 6$

$\therefore P$(drawing a black ball)

$= \dfrac{x + 6}{18}$

According to the question,

$\dfrac{x + 6}{18} = 2 \times \dfrac{x}{12}$

$\Rightarrow x + 6 = 3x$

$\Rightarrow 2x = 6$

$\therefore x = 3$

11. (b) Total number of products = (1, 1), (1, 4), (1, 10), (2, 1), (2, 4), (2, 10), (4, 1), (4, 4), (4, 10)

E = Number of favourable outcomes

= (1, 1), (1, 4), (2, 1), (2, 4), (4, 1)

$\therefore P(E) = \dfrac{5}{9}$

12. (c) Probability of choosing discs with a combination of 4 concentric circles $= \frac{6}{15} = \frac{2}{5}$

And, the probability of choosing discs with a combination of 2 concentric circles $= \frac{6}{15} = \frac{2}{5}$

∴ Required probability

$$= \frac{2}{5} + \frac{2}{5} = \frac{4}{5}$$

13. (a) Total outcomes are

HHH, HHT, HTH, THH, HTT, THT, TTH, TTT

Favourable outcomes for losing game are

HHT, HTH, THH, HTT, THT, TTH

Therefore probability of losing the game is :

P (Losing the game) = 6/8 = 3/4

14. (d) Total number of outcomes $= 365 \times 365$

If both, have same birthday, then the number of favourable outcomes for their birthday = 365

$$= \frac{365}{365 \times 365} = \frac{1}{365}$$

15. (d) Now, number of dice in pack II = 2

∴ Probability of choosing a die from pack II $= \frac{2}{8}$

Now, the probability of choosing a ball from Ist pack.

$$= \frac{3}{8}$$

∴ Required probability

$$= \left(\frac{2}{8} + \frac{3}{8}\right) = \frac{5}{8}$$

16. (b) I. $\frac{\text{Number of favourable outcomes}}{\text{Total number of possible outcomes}}$

II. 0 III. 1

IV. ∵ Number of vowels = 5 {A, E, I, O, U}

and getting an $E = 1$; $P(E) = \frac{1}{5}$

V. Number of red cards

$= 13 + 13 = 26$

∴ Probability of getting a red card $= \frac{26}{52} = \frac{1}{2}$

VI. The favourable outcomes are (1, 1) (2, 2) (3, 3) (4, 4), (5, 5) (6, 6).

Number of favourable outcomes = 6

Probability of getting a doublet $= \frac{6}{36} = \frac{1}{6}$

17. (a) I. True; Prime number,

$E = 2, 3, 5$

$$\therefore \quad P(E) = \frac{3}{6} = \frac{1}{2}$$

II. False

Getting equal numbers

$E = (1, 1), (2, 2), (3, 3),$
$(4, 4), (5, 5), (6, 6)$

$$\therefore \quad P(E) = \frac{6}{36} = \frac{1}{6}$$

Now, P (not getting equal number) $= 1 - P(E)$

$$= 1 - \frac{6}{36}$$

$$= \frac{5}{36}$$

III. True

E = Number of face cards = 12

$$\therefore \quad P(E) = \frac{12}{52} = \frac{3}{13}$$

IV. True

Total outcomes = HH, TT, HT, TH

and E = Heads on both = HH

∴ $P(E) = 1/4$

18. (a) (A)

∵ E = Getting a number 3, 4 or 5 and total outcomes = 1, 2, 3, 4, 5, 6

$$\therefore \quad P(E) = \frac{3}{6} = \frac{1}{2}$$

(B) A number divisible by 3 and 5 = 15

Hence, 15 not occur on dice

$$\therefore \; P(E) = \frac{0}{6} = 0$$

(C) $E = (1, 5), (1, 6), (2, 5), (2, 6), (3, 5), (3, 6), (4, 5), (4, 6), (5, 5), (5, 6), (6, 5), (6, 6)$

$$\therefore \quad P(E) = \frac{12}{36} = \frac{1}{3}$$

19. (a) As a black jack, a red queen and two black kings fell off, i.e.

Number of cards left

$= 52 - 4 = 48$

I. Number of black cards left

$= 26 - 3 = 23$

$$\therefore \quad P(E) = \frac{23}{48} \text{ (correct)}$$

II. Number of kings left

$= 4 - 2 = 2$

Number of red queens left

$= 2 - 1 = 1$

$$\therefore \; P(E) = \frac{2+1}{\text{Total number of cards}}$$

$$= \frac{3}{48} = \frac{1}{16} \text{ (Not correct)}$$

Answers

Practice Set 1

1. (d)	2. (d)	3. (a)	4. (d)	5. (d)	6. (a)	7. (a)	8. (a)	9. (c)	10. (d)
11. (d)	12. (b)	13. (a)	14. (a)	15. (b)	16. (c)	17. (a)	18. (b)	19. (c)	20. (d)
21. (b)	22. (a)	23. (b)	24. (b)	25. (c)	26. (c)	27 (b)	28. (c)	29. (a)	30. (c)
31. (c)	32. (a)	33. (d)	34. (b)	35. (c)	36. (a)	37. (a)	38. (c)	39. (c)	40. (c)
41. (c)	42. (a)	43. (a)	44. (a)	45. (d)	46. (b)	47. (b)	48. (c)	49. (b)	50. (a)

Practice Set 2

1. (b)	2. (b)	3. (b)	4. (c)	5. (c)	6. (a)	7. (c)	8. (d)	9. (b)	10. (b)
11. (b)	12. (d)	13. (a)	14. (d)	15. (c)	16. (a)	17. (a)	18. (a)	19. (a)	20. (c)
21. (b)	22. (b)	23. (b)	24. (c)	25. (a)	26. (b)	27 (b)	28. (b)	29. (c)	30. (d)
31. (d)	32. (b)	33. (b)	34. (c)	35. (a)	36. (d)	37. (c)	38. (b)	39. (b)	40. (b)
41. (a)	42. (a)	43. (c)	44. (c)	45. (a)	46. (c)	47. (d)	48. (b)	49. (a)	50. (b)